the politics of RIGHT SEX

SUNY series in New Political Science

Bradley J. Macdonald, editor

and

SUNY series in Queer Politics and Cultures

Cynthia Burack and Jyl J. Josephson, editors

the politics of RIGHT SEX

transgressive bodies, governmentality, and the limits of trans rights

courtenay w. daum

Published by State University of New York Press, Albany

Printed in the United States of America

For information, contact State University of New York Press, Albany, NY
www.sunypress.edu

Library of Congress Cataloging-in-Publication Data

Names: Daum, Courtenay W., author.
Title: The politics of right sex : transgressive bodies, governmentality, and the limits of trans rights / Courtenay W. Daum.
Description: Albany : State University of New York Press, [2020] | Series: SUNY series in new political science | Series: SUNY series in queer politics and cultures | Includes bibliographical references and index.
Identifiers: LCCN 2019036159 | ISBN 9781438478876 (hardcover : alk. paper) | ISBN 9781438478869 (pbk. : alk. paper) | ISBN 9781438478883 (ebook)
Subjects: LCSH: Transgender people—Civil rights—United States. | Transgender people—Legal status, laws, etc.—United States. | Gender nonconformity—Political aspects—United States. | Pressure groups—United States. | United States—Politics and government—2009–2017. | United States—Politics and government—2017–
Classification: LCC HQ77.95.U6 D38 2020 | DDC 323.3/30973—dc23
LC record available at https://lccn.loc.gov/2019036159

10 9 8 7 6 5 4 3 2 1

Contents

Preface

On June 26, 2015, the U.S. Supreme Court decided *Obergefell v. Hodges* (576 U.S. ___) legalizing marriage equality in the United States. Despite the immense joy I felt at this expansion of liberties for gays and lesbians and the affirmation that rights-based social movements and their use of the courts are a powerful mechanism for advancing interests (given that a single Supreme Court decision had the effect of overturning state prohibitions on same-sex marriage and opening the institution of marriage and the associated economic, sociocultural and legal benefits to everyone), this victory also comes with costs. It privileges homonormativity and distributes benefits to those couples interested in and/or able to enter into marriages, it expands the disciplinary power of the state, and the fight for marriage equality drained extensive financial resources and social capital that could have been used to advance various other pressing priorities within LGBTQ communities including pursuing economic justice, validating alternative family and kinship relationships, pushing to disconnect the distribution of benefits from legally sanctioned marriages in the first place, combating homophobic and transphobic violence, and so on.

In the days and weeks that followed the *Obergefell* decision, I reflected on what this legal victory would mean for the future and looming battles surrounding LGBTQ interests as well as the potentially negative consequences of this decision for many individuals within the LGBTQ communities. In particular, like many others, I worried that *Obergefell* would become the pinnacle of the gay rights movement despite the significant work that remains to be done in pursuit of collective liberation for all LGBTQ individuals, and I watched to see if attention and resources would shift to other causes and movements now that a major battle for gay rights had been "won." As we now know, debates about trans rights have become more prevalent in the years following the marriage equality victory, and liberal gay rights groups and mainstream civil rights organizations have mobilized on behalf of trans individuals, suggesting that this is the next front in the battle for LGBTQ rights. As these events unfold, I find that I am increasingly pessimistic about the viability and efficacy of traditional rights-based movements for facilitating substantive change to include the growing push for a trans politics of rights. The election of Donald Trump as president in November 2016, and the confirmation of his two nominees to the U.S. Supreme Court, Associate Justices Neil Gorsuch and Brett Kavanaugh, further erode my faith in an imminent and successful politics of trans rights. While the motivations for pursuing equal rights and legal protections through legislation and litigation are logical, the reality is that any attempt to achieve recognition from the very institutions and people that benefit from your subjection is likely to be of limited utility.

As I pondered the *Obergefell* decision and the simultaneous pros and cons of the politics of rights, I was wrapping up final revisions on an article, "The War on Solicitation and Intersectional Subjection: Quality-of-life Policing as a Tool to Control Transgender Populations," that examines how the selective enforcement of solicitation laws on transgender women of color—a phenomenon referred to as "walking while trans"—operates as a force of governmentality that is intended to remove transgender women's bodies from public spaces.[1] This article moved beyond a critique of the state and individual law enforcement officers' transphobia to argue that privileged members of society are complicit in these exercises of governmentality on intersectionally subjected transgender women. At the time, I did not know it, but that research would provide the theoretical framework for this book, and an updated version of the original published article now functions as chapter 6 of this book.

Synthesizing my growing pessimism about rights movements and their inability to facilitate substantive change and my interest in forces of governmentality as tools of population management and social control, *The Politics of Right Sex* argues that the politics of rights are of limited utility for marginalized communities because they are unable to reach the myriad forces of governmentality that work as a type of infra law—the informal and implicit norms and regulations that operate below the surface—to mark and discipline transgressive individuals in order to maintain extant hierarchies. In light of the increased public, media, political, and legal attention focused on trans rights post-*Obergefell*, this book examines how a politics of trans rights will be limited by the institutional constraints of hegemonic power structures and unable to reach the forces of governmentality that operate on trans people in contemporary American society. Furthermore, these forces of governmentality are not happenstance, but actually work in tandem with the politics of rights to ensure that privileged populations maintain power even if and when rights movements are victorious and the contours of civil rights laws change and evolve. In these instances, successful rights movements may find that legal victories and rights recognition translate into limited substantive gains.

Throughout the process of writing this book, I kept returning to Jacob Hale's "Suggested Rules for Non-Transsexuals Writing about Transsexuals, Transsexuality, Transsexualism, or Trans ____," in which he states that researchers who are not trans need to "[i]nterrogate your own subject position: the ways in which you have power that we don't (including powers of access, juridicial power, institutional power, material power, power of intelligible subjectivity), the ways in which this affects what you see and what you say, what your interests and stakes are in forming your initial interest, and what your interests and stakes are in what you see and say as you continue your work."[2] As such, it is imperative to make clear that as a cisgender woman I am not an expert on the lived experiences of trans people; trans individuals are the experts on their own diverse and abundant experiences. The field of transgender studies continues to grow from what was arguably its genesis in 1991 with the publication of Sandy Stone's "The *Empire* Strikes Back: A Posttranssexual Manifesto," and trans scholars continue to make invaluable contributions to the academic and public discourses. These scholars are the authoritative experts on transgender identities and experiences. As such, I draw extensively on trans scholarship throughout the book, and I am indebted to the many trans, gender nonconforming, and queer individuals who shared their experiences with me.

As a political scientist and a legal scholar, my goal in *The Politics of Right Sex* is to draw attention to the limitations of the politics of rights and expose the systems of subjection and infra laws that operate in the shadows of contemporary American society in order to demonstrate how the dominant public utilizes forces of governmentality to maintain the ongoing marginalization of trans individuals in this country. The politics of rights and the associated legal reforms are not sufficient to improve the lives of many trans individuals, because these processes force marginalized communities and individuals to pursue their interests within the confines of hegemonic institutions that are designed to protect dominant players and their interests.[3] In fact, the focus on legal reform and the mythology of the politics of rights enables governmentality by diverting attention and resources to eradicating de jure discrimination while leaving de facto infrahumanization (the dominant population's perception that outgroup members are less than human), discrimination, and violence unchecked. In order to facilitate transformative change and the collective liberation of all trans individuals, we need to move beyond rights discourse, political mobilization, and legal strategies.

At the same time, intersectionally privileged individuals need to own our roles in sanctioning and perpetuating the marginalization of and violence against people of color, LGBQ individuals, the poor, the disabled, the intersectionally subjected, and transgender and gender nonconforming individuals. Recognizing my own power and privilege as a white cisgender woman, my personal interest in writing this book is to draw attention to and interrogate the myriad ways that dominant populations utilize our power to maintain white heterosexist supremacy in the contemporary United States. Specifically, I hope that the analyses that follow make clear that the "system" of white, heterosexist, transphobic, xenophobic supremacy is not an exogenous institution to be viewed from afar, but rather is constituted by the endogenous roles that many of us play in the creation and maintenance of said "system." As such, this book seeks to draw attention to intersectionally privileged populations' vested interest in and extensive deployment of myriad disciplinary tools to maintain systems of supremacy and hierarchy, and to make clear how these forces of governmentality limit the utility of legal reforms and the politics of rights precisely because those with power do not want to facilitate substantive transformative change. Ultimately, I hope this book will serve as an intervention for those who regularly benefit from their intersectionally privileged positions at the expense of trans lives.[4]

A brief note about terminology. The term *transgender* often is used as an "umbrella" term to describe those "individuals whose gender identity or expression does not conform to the social expectations for their assigned sex at birth."[5] This definition includes transgender men who are individuals assigned the female sex at birth and identify as men as well as transgender women who are assigned the male sex at birth but identify as women, but the term also is "more complex and variant than can be accounted for by the currently dominant binary sex/gender ideology."[6] Consequently, more recently, the term trans has been utilized to indicate the broad array of gender identities, expressions and experiences beyond the transgender men and transgender women described above. As such, the use of the term *trans* includes transgender men and transgender women, but expands to include those who are gender nonconforming and nonbinary, such as those who are agender, genderqueer, genderfluid, and pangender. Throughout this book, I utilize the term *trans* to describe transgender individuals as well as the broad array of gender nonconforming and nonbinary individuals. I use the term *transgender* to describe individuals assigned the male sex at birth who identify and/or transition to women and individuals assigned the female sex at birth who identity and/or transition to men.

Acknowledgments

I would like to acknowledge the many people in my professional and personal life that made this book possible including Michael Rinella, SUNY Press editor, for his help in facilitating this book to press. In addition, I would like to thank all of the participants at the CLAGS After Marriage Equality conference in October 2016 for their thoughtful comments, presentations, and inspiration as well as their generous responses to and helpful feedback on an early presentation of one of the chapters in this book. Similarly, a big thanks to the many co-panelists, roundtable participants and attendees at the 2015, 2016, and 2017 APSA meetings, the 2016 MPSA meeting, and the 2017 Caucus for a New Political Science fiftieth anniversary conference who generously contributed time and thought to the working pieces of this book. In particular, Erin Mayo-Adam, Susan Burgess, Jocelyn Boryczka, Logan Casey, Joseph DeFilippis, Jennifer Disney, Melissa Michelson, Zein Murib, and Jami Taylor deserve special thanks for their helpful comments.

I would like to thank my colleagues at Colorado State University for creating an environment where I can thrive and pursue my passions. A special thanks to Holly Boux, Matthew Hitt, and David McIvor for reading a draft of this book and providing constructive criticism and feedback. Also, a huge thanks to Brad Macdonald for suggesting that I submit my book proposal for consideration to SUNY Press's New Political Science series. I also would like to thank my students at Colorado State University for challenging me to always do and be better. In particular, a huge thanks to the students in my spring 2016 capstone (The Power of Law: From Civil Rights to Critical Race Theory) who undoubtedly made this a better book as a result of our intense class discussions about the relationships among power, the law, and society.

Special thanks to my incredible family and friends for their unlimited support and generosity of spirit including my mother Carol and my sister Megan. I owe a particular debt to my dear friend Erika Strote who always was willing to take my children for an afternoon, send a meal, or lend a hand, and who has spent more time asking and talking about my work than should be expected of any friend. Also, a huge thank you to Rachel Olsen and Shelly Peterson for your help and encouragement throughout this process. I would also like to thank the wonderful women of NoCo Spark who gave me refuge in the darkness following the November 2016 election and came through with food and love whenever my family was in need.

Finally, I would like to thank my husband Joseph and my children Zoe and Bodhi. They sacrificed a great deal so that I could have the time and energy to write this book. To Joe—thank you for being a true partner and co-parent; I am so blessed to have your love and support and without you this book would not have been possible. To Zoe and Bodhi—you are my greatest gifts and I hope that you are empowered to be whomever or whatever you want to be as you grow up. Each of you is perfect exactly the way you are, and do not let anyone ever tell you otherwise.

Chapter 5, "The War on Solicitation and Intersectional Subjection: How Quality of Life Policing Is Used as a Tool to Control Trans Populations," is a slightly modified version of my article "The War on Solicitation and Intersectional Subjection: Quality-of-life Policing as a Tool to Control Transgender Populations," published in *New Political Science* 37, no. 4, 562–81.

In closing, I would like to acknowledge Gwen Araujo, Vontashia Bell, Keyonna Blakeney, Nikki Enriquez, Lorena Escalera, Lateisha Green, Viccky Gutierrez, Tonya Harvey, Roxana Hernandez, Nireah Johnson, Ciara McElveen, Dee Dee Pearson, Kashmire Nazier Redd, Betty Skinner, Ally Steinfeld, Rae'Lynn Thomas, Sasha Wall, Victoria Carmen White, Jamie Lee Wounded Arrow, Angie Zapata and the numerous other trans individuals who have been murdered in recent years. You are not forgotten. This book is dedicated to each of you.

Introduction

In the mid-2010s, the media began reporting that the transgender "moment" is now.[1] Growing public attention to and interest in trans issues combined with political and legal developments in the push for gay rights—notably the Supreme Court's decision to validate marriage equality in *Obergefell v. Hodges* (576 U.S. ___ [2015])—to suggest that the sociolegal context has changed to create opportunities for political and legal mobilizations around trans rights. While the election of Donald Trump as president in November 2016 and his administration's transphobic policies and rules complicate the transgender "moment," these developments have fomented increased political and legal mobilization resulting in numerous court challenges to Trump administration policies. As such, the conditions may be right for a vibrant trans rights movement that wields the "politics of rights" to challenge discrimination on the basis of gender identity.[2] While there are numerous obstacles to successfully advancing trans rights via legislation and litigation—e.g., Republican opposition in Congress, the growing conservative ideological composition of the federal judiciary, and the replacement of U.S. Supreme Court Justice Kennedy who wrote every single U.S. Supreme Court pro–gay rights decision by Justice Kavanaugh who refused to even state that *Obergefell v. Hodges* was binding precedent at his confirmation hearings—political and legal mobilization around trans rights is likely to continue to accelerate in the years ahead.

In contrast to extant research that evaluates the efficacy of different strategies for advancing trans rights in the United States,[3] this book seeks to expose the limitations of the politics of rights for advancing trans interests broadly defined in the first place. While the advancement of trans rights is a desirable, and hopefully inevitable, goal, a successful trans rights movement in and of itself is not capable of reaching the multiple forces of oppression and discipline that operate on trans bodies and people in the United States, and collective liberation for all trans individuals requires more than the eradication of de jure discrimination and the simultaneous recognition and expansion of trans individuals' rights. While scholars generally agree that legal change alone cannot eradicate discrimination or prompt social change, limited attention has been focused on how and why this is the case.[4] As such, in this book I identify and examine some of the myriad disciplinary forces that will continue to subject trans individuals even if and when they achieve the legal recognition of their rights in order to elucidate how governmentality works in the shadow of the law to maintain hierarchical distributions of power and privilege in the United States. Absent the recognition of and a direct challenge to these complimentary forces of subjection, collective liberation for all trans individuals will remain elusive.

While antidiscrimination laws and the expansion of equal rights guarantees by the courts may produce some benefits and substantive changes, the beneficiaries of these laws and policies are not going to be equally distributed across affected populations. In particular, as this book endeavors to make clear, intersectionally subjected individuals—those located at the intersection of multiple marginalized identities—will continue to be subject to and uniquely vulnerable to the myriad forces of governmentality that work to mark certain bodies as transgressive and locate them outside of the legitimated public. As such, the benefits that derive from successful rights mobilization and litigation including increased humanization, growing public recognition and support, and the end of de jure discrimination are not sufficient to reach the ongoing infrahumanization—the perception by members of an in group that individuals in out groups are less than human—and forces of governmentality at work in contemporary American society that reify white patriarchal heteronormative values and power.

This chapter begins with a brief review of the development of the trans rights movement in the United States and then proceeds to discuss the limitations associated with a trans politics of rights including an introduction to how forces of governmentality—the myriad tactics, discursive strategies, and tools available for dominant populations to target, isolate, and subject trans people that go beyond the power of the state—work to hinder the advancement of marginalized populations' interests in spite of rights recognition and expansion. Finally, this chapter concludes with an outline of the book ahead.

The Development of a Trans Politics of Rights

Throughout modern U.S. history, social movements pursuing civil rights claims have found the manipulation of rights, political mobilization and litigation vital to the success of their identity-based movements. The "myth of rights" leads individuals and social movements to identify legal advocacy as one of the primary mechanisms for pursuing the recognition of rights.[5] As such, racial and ethnic minorities, women, the disabled, and more recently gays and lesbians have wielded the symbolic power of the "myth of rights" to leverage a "politics of rights" that "politicize[s] needs by changing the way people think about their discontents,"[6] and mobilizes constituent groups.

Successful civil rights movements have utilized multiple strategies to build political momentum to pressure legislatures to take action and to leverage the power of the courts to protect their interests including the Black, women's, gay, and disability rights movements.[7] In addition, conservative interests now utilize similar strategies to pursue their interests, as exemplified by the gun rights and religious rights movements.[8] As such, it is not surprising that trans individuals and their allies would emulate prior rights movements and their strategies in pursuit of their own goals.

Notably, the history of trans rights mobilization and advocacy is inextricably linked with gay rights mobilization and advocacy. In the years following World War II, gay neighborhoods began to develop in major urban centers such as San Francisco, Washington, D.C., and New York, and trans individuals often lived in these communities and shared social spaces with gays and lesbians. Similarly, the criminalization of sexual "deviants"—via criminal prohibitions on same-sex sodomy and cross-dressing—and the prevalence of police stings and entrapment techniques during this period instilled fear in trans individuals as well as gays and lesbians.[9] Yet, in spite of their shared vulnerabilities, mid-twentieth century gay and lesbian interest groups such as the Mattachine Society (1950) and Daughters of Bilitis (1955) practiced exclusionary policies that privileged gender conformity and assimilation as exemplified by the latter's focus on recruiting female members who complied with gendered norms of femininity and discouraging more masculine (or butch) lesbians, trans individuals or cross-dressers from joining the group.[10]

At the same time, however, the fight for liberation was not limited to gays and lesbians, as exemplified by the Compton's Cafeteria riot in

San Francisco in 1966—when transgender sex workers and drag queens raged against police profiling and brutality—and the Stonewall Rebellion in 1969—with queer and trans people of color in the front lines of the revolt.[11] The active resistance of transgender and gender nonconforming individuals in places such as Compton's Cafeteria and the Stonewall Inn was facilitated by the strong sense of community and early social movement formation among trans individuals in these locations.[12] Thus, trans individuals have been active players in the fight for LGBTQ liberation since the earliest days of the modern U.S. gay liberation movement even as they were excluded from many interest groups and later cis-washed and whitewashed out of history.

In the aftermath of the Stonewall Rebellion, the formation of organized interest groups focused on advancing gay rights—at that time an umbrella term for the interests of all LGBTQ individuals—accelerated, but the relationships between trans communities and these new gay rights organizations continued to be fraught with difficulties as gays and lesbians and their allies disagreed about the utility of including transgender individuals and interests in their organizations. For example, oftentimes, gay rights groups would capitalize on the energy and participation of trans individuals within their organizations, but then marginalize their interests in legislative and legal battles, as exemplified by the Gay Activists Alliance's (GAA) push for a broad antidiscrimination bill in New York City in the early 1970s only to later drop its demand for protections for transgender individuals and drag queens because gay male leaders feared that this went too far and jeopardized the likelihood that the bill would pass.[13] This practice of prioritizing gay rights with the promise of getting to trans rights later continues to the present day as exemplified by the Human Rights Campaign's (HRC) decision to advocate for a national Employment Non-Discrimination Act (ENDA) that did not include protections for trans workers as recently as 2007.

Despite this mistreatment, trans individuals continued to be active in the fight for gay rights. While some trans individuals and activists emphasized the collective struggle shared by gays, lesbians, and trans people and fought for recognition in gay civil rights groups, other trans individuals created their own organizations, and still others participated in both spaces by challenging the former to be more inclusive and working to advance a trans-specific agenda within the latter.[14] For example, Sylvia Rivera, a transwoman and self-identified drag queen, actively participated in the founding of the Gay Liberation Front (GLF) and the GAA in the period following Stonewall, but dropped out of these organizations after members worked "to really silence us."[15] Shortly thereafter, she and Marsha P. Johnson founded Street Transvestite Action Revolutionaries (STAR), an organization focused on assisting homeless queer and trans youth. While STAR did not receive the same national attention as GLF and GAA, its existence is demonstrative of the type of local trans community building and mobilization that developed in the shadow of mainstream gay rights groups at this time, including the Transvestite-Transsexual Action Organization in Los Angeles, the Cockettes in San Francisco, and Queens (later the Queens Liberation Front) in New York City.[16]

Throughout the 1970s and into the early 1980s, gay rights organizations proliferated and focused on legal advocacy (e.g., Gay and Lesbian Advocates and Defenders, Lambda Legal Defense and Education Fund, National Center for Lesbian Rights), political advocacy (e.g., Human Rights Campaign), and grassroots mobilization (e.g., the National Gay Taskforce). Similar to prior civil rights movements located in the politics of rights, these groups utilized political and legal mobilization to combat prohibitions on same-sex sodomy, discrimination in education and employment, and fought to expand legal protections for gay and lesbian parents, marriage equality, and so on. As their names indicate, these groups identified the advancement of gay and/or lesbian rights as their organizational priorities and often marginalized transgender individuals and their interests. Yet, regional transgender gatherings such as the Texas "T" Party beginning in the 1980s and the Southern Comfort Conference initiated in the 1990s served as important locations for trans community and movement building.

A number of significant developments during the 1990s raised the saliency of trans interests. The devastating effects of the AIDS crisis forced many gay and lesbian activists to reframe their relationships with the trans community as they recognized that an efficacious response required "a new kind of alliance politics in which specific communities came together across the dividing lines of race and gender, class and nationality, citizenship and sexual orientation. . . . [This] required gay liberation politics and feminist public health activism to take transgender issues far more seriously than they had in the past."[17] New "queer" alliances that encompassed gay, lesbian, bisexual, and trans individuals and interests began to proliferate as evidenced by the growth of Queer Nation chapters across the United States between 1990 and 1992.[18] As the interests of trans individuals began to (re)enter the gay rights discourse, trans activists engaged in new and concerted efforts to bring attention to the discrimination experienced by trans people including their marginalization within the gay rights movement. Trans activists challenged their exclusion from the title of the 1993 National March on Washington for Lesbian, Gay and Bi Equal Rights and Liberation, and while they were not successful in changing the march's branding, transgender interests were included in the march's platform alongside those of gays, lesbians, and bisexuals (notably, the 1993 march marked the first time that bisexuals were recognized in the title and a bisexual speaker was invited to address the crowd).[19]

In addition, the 1990s witnessed the growth of new independent forms of trans mobilization. In 1992, Phyllis Randolph Frye organized the first International Conference on Transgender Law and Employment Policy in Houston, Texas, in order to bring attention to the various legal issues and obstacles confronting trans people that were not being discussed or addressed in lesbian and gay rights legal organizations. The conference was such a success that it was held regularly until 1997, at which point the legal concerns of trans individuals were being integrated into mainstream gay and lesbian rights groups.[20] Also in 1992, Trans Nation was created as a spinoff of the San Francisco Queer Nation chapter, and its members engaged in a number of political protests including explicitly challenging gay and lesbian rights groups to be inclusive of trans interests.[21]

The mobilization within the trans community and the demands for recognition by gay rights groups began to produce results around the turn of the twenty-first century as a number of national organizations committed to advancing the equal rights of specifically transgender and gender nonconforming individuals began to develop heralding the arrival of an organized and institutionalized transgender rights movement.[22] The National Transgender Advocacy Coalition was founded in 1999, the Transgender Law Center in 2002, and the National Center for Transgender Equality in 2003. In addition, in 2002, Dean Spade created the Sylvia Rivera Law Project in New York City, which provides legal services to trans individuals "to guarantee that all people are free to self-determine gender identity and expression, regardless of income or race, and without facing harassment, discrimination or violence."[23] More recently, in 2011, the Intersex Campaign for Equality was founded in order to advance the rights of intersex individuals.

In addition, throughout the twenty-first century many gay rights groups expanded to include trans and queer interests in their platforms. In 2001, HRC responded to intensive lobbying and added transgender interests to its mission statement, and other organizations have even changed their names to reflect their new inclusivity (e.g., the National Gay Task Force—renamed the National Gay and Lesbian Task Force in 1985—became the National LGBTQ Task Force in 2014, and Gay and Lesbian Advocates and Defenders changed its name to GLBTQ Legal Advocates and Defenders in 2016).[24] While previously the trans community was not able to capitalize on its inclusion in the politics of LGBT rights and legal mobilization around trans rights within LGBT groups had been largely symbolic, post-*Obergefell* the calculus within liberal gay rights groups appeared to shift and the advancement of trans rights was identified as the next battle in the fight for LGBTQ rights. As such, many of the interest groups and legal advocacy organizations working to advance trans rights in the current context are longstanding civil rights entities including the American Civil Liberties Union (ACLU), GLAAD, Lambda Legal, HRC, and the National LGBTQ Task Force. While there is a long history of antagonisms between liberal gay rights groups and trans communities, the fact that many of the former are now advocating for the rights of the latter reflects the mainstreaming of trans interests in the pursuit of contemporary LGBTQ civil rights. In 2014, the President of HRC publicly apologized to the transgender community for the organization's failure to represent its interests.[25]

As such, the question of whether or not trans interests should be subsumed under the LGBTQ umbrella or exist as an independent social movement may no longer be as relevant today given both the proliferation of trans-specific advocacy organizations and the fact that, in practice, mainstream civil and gay rights groups are advocating on behalf of trans rights alongside trans-specific organizations. Litigation on behalf of individuals alleging discrimination on the basis of one's gender identity is on the rise, and this litigation is being supported by well-established civil rights groups such as Lambda Legal and the ACLU. For example, in 2018, the Sixth Circuit Court of Appeals ruled that the 1964 Civil Rights Act's Title VII protections against workplace discrimination on the basis of sex protected individuals from discrimination on the basis of their gender identity (*EEOC v. R.G. & G.R. Harris Funeral Homes, Inc.*, 884 F.3d 560 [6th Cir. 2018]), and in 2017, the Seventh Circuit Court of Appeals ruled that Title IX's prohibition on sex discrimination in education and the Fourteenth Amendment's guarantees of equal protection of the laws protected trans students as well (*Whitaker v. Kenosha Unified School District*, 858 F.3d 1034 [7th Cir. May 30, 2017]).

While the election of Donald Trump as president and his administration's transphobic policies are creating legal uncertainty, civil rights groups are instigating litigation challenging the Trump administration's policies including, for example, numerous lawsuits contesting the exclusion of transgender individuals from the military. The fact that the national executive and legislative branches are proving to be inhospitable to trans interests may facilitate increased rights mobilization and litigation as advocates for trans interests seek outlets for positive change in the federal courts and across the states.

While it seems likely that the pursuit of trans rights recognition will continue to follow the well-trod paths of prior civil rights movements and deploy a multipronged strategy that emphasizes social movement support of litigation and legislative reforms, even under the best circumstances in which the conditions may be right for a viable trans politics of rights cannot guarantee that agitating for legal and legislative changes will translate into efficacious change in trans people's lives. While Scheingold explained that "[t]he myth of rights may work in behalf of change, but its dominant tendency is surely to reinforce the status quo," the politics of rights is similarly constrained.[26]

The Limitations of a Trans Politics of Rights

While the deployment of rights in the political and legal realms may coalesce individuals to mobilize and enable them to work to change and remove existing discriminatory laws and policies, the politics of rights alone cannot transform "the space of public life itself."[27] As this book endeavors to make clear, trans bodies and lives are not only regulated by the state, but by various disciplinary tools within the public as well. The combined effects of de jure discrimination and de facto infrahumanization constitute forces of governmentality that deny, constrain, and erase trans bodies, and many of these instruments are located outside of and beyond the realm of rights.[28] As such, the recognition of rights for trans people will not only fail to reach these disciplinary tools, but may actually enhance their operation as dominant populations within the public work to maintain the marginalized and subjected position of trans people in order to substantiate their own power and privilege within the public.

In Foucault's work on disciplines, he explains how disciplinary mechanisms developed in tandem with representative regimes predicated on egalitarian juridical frameworks:

> The general juridical form that guaranteed a system of rights that were egalitarian in principle was supported by these tiny, everyday, physical mechanisms, by all those systems of micro-power that are essentially non-egalitarian and asymmetrical that we call the disciplines. And although, in a formal way, the representative regime makes it possible, directly or indirectly, with or without relays, for the will of all to form the fundamental authority of sovereignty, the disciplines provide, at the base, a guarantee of the submission of forces and bodies. The real, corporal disciplines constituted the foundation of the formal, juridical liberties. The contract may have been regarded as the ideal foundation of law and political power; panopticism constituted the technique, universally widespread, of coercion. It continued to work in depth on the juridical structures of society, in order to make the effective mechanisms of power function in opposition to the formal framework that it had acquired. The "Enlightenment," which discovered the liberties, also invented the disciplines.[29]

Understood as "counter-law," these minute disciplines are the "political counterpart of the juridical norms according to which power was redistributed."[30]

As such, while "the universal juridicism of modern society seems to fix limits on the exercise of power, its universally widespread panopticism enables it to operate, on the underside of the law, a machinery that is both immense and minute, which supports, reinforces, multiplies the asymmetry of power and undermines the limits that are traced around the law."[31] While political mobilization, litigation and legislative reforms predicated on the recognition of rights reflect the universal juridicism of modern society, they cannot reach the widespread panopticism; the subtly coercive disciplinary mechanisms that operate on the underside of the law to maintain the asymmetry of power that benefits some and marginalizes others. In this way, the politics of rights may enable political and legal reforms, but fail to redistribute power, end coercion, or initiate substantive sociocultural reforms within the public. Consequently, it is likely to be of limited utility for trans individuals seeking transformative change and collective liberation because absent a redistribution of power within the public a trans politics of rights risks becoming a transnormative politics of right (or "right") sex with significant costs for those who are not easily located in the existing sex binary as well as intersectionally subjected individuals across trans communities.

As Thomas explains, it is necessary to go beyond legal reform in order to advance trans interests, because

> politics involves more than the effort to influence the content of public policy through arguments about the requirements of public reason or appeals to the rule of public law. Political is both a cultural form and a cultural force. To put the point another way modern politics is "a matter of *fantasies*, in which the way people 'imagine' themselves [and others] occupies a crucial place." Accordingly, effective struggle on behalf of the transgendered will entail . . . a kind of "cultural work" *at the level of collective political fantasy*. From this perspective, a successful transgender human rights strategy must find ways to enlarge the public imagination regarding the lives and aspirations of trans people.[32]

In this book, I argue that a successful trans civil rights movement cannot in and of itself do the "cultural work" that is required to reconstitute the public's collective imagination and discourse about its own position of power and privilege, because "[d]ominant publics are by definition those that can take their discourse pragmatics and their lifeworlds for granted, misrecognizing the indefinite scope of their expansive address as universality or normalcy."[33] In this way, dominant individuals within the public consciously and unconsciously capitalize on their power to establish universal norms against which all populations and individuals are measured. Those who are found lacking or deviate from these norms are marked as illegible and located at the margins of the public.

For trans people this means that as "society violently demarcates the territory of gender," those who do not conform with the public's expectations are subject to "social, economic, judicial, political, and interpersonal exclusion" thereby undermining their ability to "enlarge the public imagination regarding the lives and aspirations of trans people."[34] As such, opportunities for trans people to substantively contribute to and shape the dominant discourse are severely constrained in the public. As Fraser explains, "Where social inequality persists, deliberative processes in public spheres will tend to operate to the advantage of dominant groups and to the disadvantage of subordinates . . . these effects will be exacerbated when there is only a single, comprehensive public sphere. In that case, members of subordinated groups would have no arena for deliberation among themselves about their needs, objectives and strategies."[35] In response to their ongoing marginalization within the public, trans individuals have worked to create alternative spaces and counterpublics where they have the freedom and room to articulate their "needs, objectives and strategies" free from the constraints of the public. Due to the counterpositioning of trans and queer counterpublics, they have the potential to be transformative loci for challenging the dominant discourse and distribution of power within the public.

As the forthcoming analyses in this book make clear, one of the biggest obstacles to collective liberation for trans individuals is that the dominant public polices and censors illegible subjects in order to relegate them to the margins of public life, thereby maintaining a sense of decorum and normalcy in the public that mitigates against any attempts at substantive transformations and redistributions of power.[36] The public recognizes marginalized populations' appeals for rights if and when they agree to pursue their grievances through the hegemonic institutions of power using sanctioned tools and discourses. As such, a trans politics of rights risks becoming a strategically logical but substantively problematic transnormative pursuit of the recognition of rights for transgender individuals to transition to their "right" or "true" sex after being assigned the "wrong" sex at birth. The pursuit of legibility via the politics of rights implicates appeals to normativity and subsequently excludes those who do not fit in the existing sex and gender binaries. Yet, "[i]f we want a truly inclusive social project, we have to imagine that not all its citizens will be good or conform to the expectations for social participation (be educated, interested, rational, not frivolous). A project that strives for social transformation must embrace and negotiate both complexity and frustrating political subjects."[37]

The viability of a truly inclusive social project, however, is unlikely because the public requirements of "uniformity within political and cultural spheres" are "dependent upon an internally complex social and political economy of racial [and gender] stratification and colonial violence" that is not acknowledged or discussed in the context of the politics of rights.[38] In this way, the universal juridicism of rights allows for the recognition of marginalized individuals to the extent that they are willing to conform with expectations for good behavior, uniformity, and normalcy as defined by the public while simultaneously eliding the ongoing racialized and gendered "labor, social practices, and cultural representations" that continue to work on these individuals.[39] Absent a transformation of "the space of public life itself," forces of governmentality will continue to operate on trans people and subject them to extensive social control in the public even if and when the state recognizes their rights.[40]

In spite of these limitations, the pursuit of rights via the courts and legislatures continues to be one of the most prominent forms of recourse for aggrieved and marginalized populations. "The contemporary proliferation of efforts to pursue legal redress for injuries related to social subordination by marked attributes or behaviors: race, sexuality, and so forth . . . delimits a specific site of blame for suffering by constituting sovereign subjects and events as responsible for the 'injury' of social subordination," and then "casts the law in particular and the state more generally as neutral arbiters of injury rather than as themselves invested with the power to injure."[41] In this way, laws and the state are constituted as the legitimate, and perhaps the only viable, mechanisms of redress. Yet, this is highly problematic in light of the state's role in the maintenance of hierarchies and population management regimes, and may explain why even so-called successful civil rights movements fail to eradicate the ongoing marginalization of some populations and the privileging of others.

While Black individuals, women, and most recently the gay rights movements have utilized rights discourse and the politics of rights to secure important legal victories that expand the rights recognized and granted by the state, these victories often are limited because they do not change the hegemonic power structure.[42] To be clear, the recognition and expansion of civil rights comes with tangible benefits, but successful rights-based claims operate within state institutions and impose obligations on the state to protect and facilitate the rights of marginalized groups, and this remains problematic in a system where the institutions of power continue to be controlled by the privileged and powerful. Furthermore, "[t]he civil rights approach fails to address a variety of forms of inequality rooted in the economy, other institutions and power relations in a variety of social settings that are impervious to civil rights remedies."[43] As such, the politics of rights itself operates as a privileging mechanism for dominant populations that obfuscates the need for ongoing social, political, and economic reforms in favor of ongoing political mobilization, litigation, and rights recognition, and effectively enables the continued marginalization and subjugation of civil rights "victors" in the public. It is these limitations on the politics of rights for facilitating substantive and transformative change, and the synergies among formal and informal sources of power that are located beyond the reach of the politics of rights but that work to mark trans individuals as transgressive bodies subject to the disciplinary power of the public that are the focus of this book.

Governmentality as a Tool of Social Control and Population Management

In his later work, Foucault introduced the idea of governmentality and diffuse power as an alternative to sovereign conceptions of unilateral power.[44] In *Security, Territory, Population*, Foucault asked: "What if the state were nothing more than a type of governmentality? What if all these relations of power that gradually take shape on the basis of multiple and very diverse processes which gradually coagulate and form an effect, what if these practices of government were precisely the basis of which the state was constituted?"[45] Foucault's articulation of governmentality as simultaneously internal and external to the state draws attention to the ways in which individuals, groups, knowledge, and objects are governed or managed by various entities within society including, but not limited to, the state.[46] More recently, Judith Butler described governmentality as "a mode of power concerned with the maintenance and control of bodies and persons, the production and regulation of persons and populations, and the circulation of goods insofar as they maintain and restrict the life of the population."[47]

The goals of governmentality may vary, but when there is "a 'problem population' that frustrates the routine practices of governmentality through which the subjects best suited for rule by that regime's internal operative logics are produced," then mechanisms "for variously segregating, eradicating, or (re)integrating can operate at the level of 'problem bodies' as well as problem populations."[48] As the discussion that follows in this book demonstrates, governmentality works to maintain extant legal, political, economic, and social hierarchies in order to preserve the privileged position and power of those located in the dominant public. Here it is useful to distinguish between the public sphere (as articulated by, e.g., Habermas in *The Structural Transformation of the Public Sphere*) and public space.[49]

"The public sphere should not be considered as a universally accessible public space; rather, it should be regarded as 'the *structured* setting where cultural and ideological contest among a variety of publics take place,' "[50] whereas "public space must be taken literally as a material space precisely because this dimension provides visibility to political action."[51]

Within the structured setting of the public, the maintenance of the status quo is facilitated via the forces of governmentality that socially construct and designate certain bodies as transgressive or "problem bodies," and then work to deny, constrain, and remove those bodies from public spaces in order to mitigate the challenge that transgressive bodies pose to the hegemonic power structure and discourse. Transgressive bodies have regularly been removed from public spaces because they constitute a public nuisance.[52] In a review of San Francisco legislation in the nineteenth century, Sears demonstrates how the city deployed policies that sought to exclude, confine, conceal, and remove problem bodies from public spaces in order to create and maintain heteronormative public spaces.[53] This practice continues into the present day as demonstrated by the extensive policing of gay men in public spaces for alleged cruising and the practice of profiling trans women as sex workers which will be discussed in detail in chapter 5.

To achieve these goals, governmentality implicates various entities—ranging from state to social actors—utilizing diverse tactics—including laws, norms, and stereotypes—in the pursuit of governing. While elite and state actors play an important role in governmentality as demonstrated by the evaluations of legislators, bureaucrats, law enforcement officers, and others in the chapters ahead, it is important to understand that nonelites and ordinary people are implicated and invested in the maintenance of hierarchies and extant power arrangements. For example, the de facto policing of bathrooms by ordinary citizens operates as a powerful disciplinary constraint on trans people. Furthermore, this is not purely a conservative exercise of power. Liberals are implicated in forces of governmentality as well. While they may disagree about tools and practices, the combined effects of conservative and liberal discourses and strategies often work in powerful ways to privilege dominant populations and marginalize others. As Naomi Murakawa explains when discussing crime policies and race, while conservatives and liberals advocated for different types of criminal justice policies the mutually constitutive effects of their different interests worked to the detriment of racial and ethnic minorities in their interactions with the criminal justice system:

> Postwar crime policy was not only about race conservatives pushing for more aggressive policing, more prisons, and longer sentences. It was also about race liberals who aimed to build the bias out of the criminal justice system with more procedural rights, more guidelines, more formal protocols in everything from arrest to sentencing calculations. These political "sides" appeared to be in opposition to each other, as they were divided on partisan lines, but they actually worked together to build a criminal justice system that is larger, more punitive, more rule-based, more procedurally grounded, and more "procedurally just." These two forces tend to work together in mutual escalation, authorizing an even grander scale of racial brutality. This history is important because we keep cycling back to the same set of proposals even though they have done nothing to curtail racial brutality, indeed, they have helped to legitimate it.[54]

In this way, liberals interested in the expansion of procedural rights actually contributed to the creation of a criminal justice system that not only enables, but actually legitimates racial brutality. This cognizance is essential in order to elucidate the myriad ways in which governmentality operates on transgressive bodies as competing discourses manifest in mutually constitutive state policies that maintain social stratifications.

For example, debates about gender markers on identity documents implicate distinctive but mutually constitutive ideologies as both liberals and conservatives deploy the discourse of "true" and "real" gender when discussing why trans individuals should be allowed to change these documents. While liberals and conservatives may seek different ends regarding whether or not trans people should be able to change their gender markers on identity documents, the fact that they both regularly talk about individuals' "right" sex reifies the sex and gender binaries that are powerful tools for distributing costs and benefits across the public.

Furthermore, recognizing that an essential facet of governmentality is social control and population management, the tools utilized for controlling and managing targeted populations are varied and include formal laws, norms, and stereotypes. While governmentality is "understood as an extra-legal field of policy, discourse," it often makes law into a tactic.[55] Thus, laws may be passed that specifically target some populations for differential treatment, and when de jure discrimination is prohibited neutral laws are powerful and integral tools for managing particular populations and not others via the selective enforcement of criminal prohibitions.[56] In this way, certain populations are criminalized, which is an essential facet of governmentality. As Kelley explains when talking about the criminalization of the Black population in the United States:

> The point here is not just to punish Black communities but to mark them, to create a record of "criminal behavior," to transform them from citizens to thugs. . . . Criminalization is to be subjected to regulation, containment, surveillance, and punishment, but deemed unworthy of protection. Those targeted by the state are not rights-bearing individuals to be protected but criminals poised to violate the law who thus require vigilant watch—not unlike prisoners.[57]

Similarly, the criminalization of trans populations occurs through laws that target trans people for differential treatment such as bathroom bills, but also through the selective enforcement of facially neutral laws such as prohibitions on solicitation.

In addition, forces of governmentality evolve in tandem with rights in order to continue to enact supremacist and hierarchical regimes and socially construct illegible populations and institutionally locate them at the margins of the public. For example, one consequence of the recognition of rights for Black Americans was that the dominant public had to reimagine how to control and manage Black bodies in light of advances in Black civil rights. As Gilmore and Gilmore explain:

> The shift from state-sanctioned mob violence [via the KKK] to arrest and incarceration is one mark of the transition from American apartheid. While the rural and urban Black freedom struggle created the crises that compelled the transition, the movement's interdependent ideologies and tactics ran up against counterrevolutionary forces that regrouped behind a blue line they could move at will. Eventually massive expansion and capitalization of local law enforcement, community policing, and accelerated criminalization produced a temporary stasis. The legitimacy of the badge replaced the discredited Klan hood.[58]

These processes make it difficult if not impossible for rights-based strategies to provide and produce holistic substantive change. Instead, the recognition of rights alleviates inequities on paper and removes laws that explicitly target certain identity groups for differential treatment while simultaneously allowing the forces of governmentality to continue to operate and maintain the marginalized status of designated populations.

A powerful way that the law operates as a force of governmentality and renders people illegible is the legal system's use of and emphasis on binary identities. As Foucault wrote in *Discipline and Punish: The Birth of the Prison*, "Generally speaking, all the authorities exercising individual control function according to a double mode; that of binary division and branding. . . . The constant division between the normal and the abnormal, to which every individual is subjected, brings us back to our own time, by applying the binary branding."[59] To that end, legal actors have emphasized binary identities in the context of the politics of rights that assign costs and benefits depending upon where individuals are located in the binary, and subsequently render intersectionally subjected individuals invisible before the law. When individuals are required to identify one facet of their identity in order to advance rights claims because the courts of law and the politics of identity resist the recognition and validation of the complexity of identities, this deprives individuals of the ability to self-identify and obfuscates and erases the reality of people's lives and experiences.[60] This is an exercise of governmentality because "[t]hese blind spots are not spaces in which social power is absent, but rather spaces in which social power's first and foremost defining quality is the reproduction of distinct social practices of domination and exploitation that profit from the shadow of disposability cast by the liberal edifice of universality."[61]

At the same time, however, rights movements are successful when they operate within the constraints of hegemonic power structures and cast their appeals for rights in the discourses of normalcy, universality, and immutable binary characteristics. Yet, a trans politics of rights that seeks to eradicate discrimination in these ways risks promulgating the sex and gender binaries and forcing trans people to locate themselves in the "right" binary categories. This transnormative politics of right sex fails to get at discrimination against nonbinary and gender fluid individuals, trans people of color and intersectionally subjected populations.[62] As such, gender alone is not sufficient for "understanding transgender issues today, as evidenced, for example, by the growing body of scholarship on the importance of gender-variant and transgender identities in contemporary queer communities of color."[63]

While governmentality operates on all trans bodies because of their perceived deviance from governing norms, "dominant notions of what constitutes proper feminine or masculine behavior are grounded in ideals of whiteness, class privilege and compulsory heterosexuality, and individuals might be read as non-conforming depending on particular racial, cultural, economic or religious expressions of gender, without ever being classified as transgender."[64] Using an intersectional lens it is possible to elucidate and avoid the potential pitfalls of social movement building and a politics of trans rights predicated on "transgender whiteness" and transnormativity in favor of a broader and more varied articulation of trans identities.[65] An acknowledgment of the complexity and fluidity of gender identities will be an essential precursor for the collective liberation of all trans people and may avoid the limitations of a politics of right sex, but it also is imperative to evaluate the ways that race, ethnicity, citizenship, gender, and socioeconomic status intersect and inform interactions among social and institutional actors and trans people via the processes of governmentality. For example, systemic racism and existing stereotypes about racial and ethnic minorities' criminality—e.g., the "blackmancriminal," "illegal" immigrants—intersect with assumptions about sexual deviance to exacerbate social and governing institutions' negative treatment of trans people of color.[66]

Stereotypes work in myriad ways to locate individuals and groups at the margins of the public. For example, stereotypes of Black women—the mammy, the Sapphire, the welfare queen, hypersexual—work as powerful forces of governmentality. The myth of hypersexuality simultaneously places Black women inside of society—as bodies readily available for sexual conquest—and outside of the state—these bodies are rendered unrapeable and hence Black women are deprived of legal recourse for sexual assaults:

> Hypersexuality was more than a demeaning and false stereotype, this inaccurate portrayal was intentional. Myth advances specific economic, social and political motives. In this case, sexual lasciviousness was a deliberate characterization that excused both profit-driven and casual sexual exploitation of black women. Emancipation did not end the social and political usefulness of this sexual stereotype. White men's right of access to black women's bodies was an assumption supported both by their history as legal property and by the myth of their sexual promiscuity. This myth meant that neither the law nor social convention allowed that black women might be victims in this arrangement. The rape of black women, like the lynching of black men, was both a deep personal violence and a form of community terrorism that reinforced their vulnerability and lack of self-ownership.[67]

These stereotypes shape the way that the public perceives Black women, but also contours how Black women see themselves and informs where the Black community locates Black women. Similarly, the stereotypes of trans individuals as frauds and sexual deviants enable the public to pathologize trans people in order to locate them at the margins of the public, but simultaneously affect the way that trans people perceive their own abilities to function in contemporary American society. In addition, these stereotypes inform where others within LGB communities locate trans individuals. Furthermore, stereotypes of trans individuals and the mythology of sexual deviance inform discussions and legal debates around bathroom laws and other sex-segregated facilities, sanction the selective enforcement of solicitation laws, and limit trans individuals' abilities to move freely across public spaces.

The failure to acknowledge and mitigate these forces of governmentality is one of the biggest shortcomings of the politics of rights. In part, this is because once rights have been conferred it is difficult for subjected populations to articulate their ongoing discontents in the public discourse because the dominant vernacular conveys legitimacy on rights discourse, individual equality of opportunity, and democratic participation as opposed to collective liberation, equality of results/outcomes, and redistributions of power. This distinction between the right to equality and the right to difference validates and upholds the hegemonic discourse and power structure. As Ochoa explains:

> The right to equality corresponds to the liberal definition of citizenship, while the right to differences corresponds to what [Dagnino] calls the "new citizenship." The new citizenship is defined outside the relationship between the state and the individual. This implies not only "access, inclusion, membership and belonging in a political system," but also "the right to participate in the definition of that system." In the redefinition of citizenship, it is seen as both a political strategy and a cultural politics.[68]

Yet, the hegemonic power structure and discourse are constructed to mitigate against the "new citizenship" and a cultural politics that would allow those who are marked as transgressive or illegible to articulate their needs or demands and seek to contest the distribution of power within the public in favor of sanctioned rights discourses that define the relationship between the state and the individual. Furthermore, the politics of rights works in conjunction with other sources of power and forces of governmentality precisely because the former presents the illusion of change and progress via political strategy without challenging the latter or changing the culture. If anything, rights recognition provides cover to the ongoing deprivation of power and the continuation of governmentality as a means to control historically subjected populations.

For trans people, forces of governmentality regularly work to mark them as illegible, substantiate their marginalization, and sanction the removal of trans bodies from public spaces in order to locate them at the margins of the public. In the discussion that follows, I argue that this illegibility is not an unfortunate side effect of discriminatory policies, but rather reflects a concerted effort to mark

> those whose gender identities and gender expression do not conform to their assigned birth sex are not even seen to count as human; they are not deemed, in other words, to be human in the sense that "ordinary" humans are. The belief that the bodies and lives of transgendered people "cannot be humanized" has rendered them vulnerable to the terrorisms of structural and physical violence.[69]

Thus, "trans activists must contend with a social order and a legal regime of 'infrahumanity' under which transgendered people are viewed as 'non-persons, with no right to marry, to work, to use a public bathroom, or even to walk down the street in safety.'"[70] In order to advance trans interests, it is essential to challenge the infrahumanization that is facilitated via processes of governmentality in addition to combating discrimination via the recognition of trans rights. Absent an organized resistance to the broader hegemonic and systemic forces of governmentality that continue to decenter and marginalize targeted populations, rights recognition will continue to be of limited utility for many within the trans community.

Outline of the Book

This book proceeds as follows. Part One investigates the prevalence of binary identity categories and their role in the designation and construction of transgressive bodies in contemporary rights jurisprudence. Chapter 1 examines the role that the courts have played in facilitating and maintaining the sociolegal construction of the race, sexual orientation, and sex binaries in order to demonstrate how the binary construction of identity works as a powerful tool for distributing costs and benefits across society. Then, chapter 2 explores the complexity of gender identity in order to evaluate the pros and cons of advancing trans rights via existing prohibitions on sex discrimination or the recognition and addition of a new protected gender identity category.

Recognizing the intransigence of binary categories of identity, Part Two of the book proceeds to an analysis of how trans individuals are targeted and controlled by myriad forces of governmentality that work to deny, constrain, and remove trans individuals from public spaces in order to police and maintain the sex binary and associated gender norms. Chapter 3 argues that state requirements for including gender markers on identity documents work in tandem with public and private actors' policing of gender to deny the existence of trans individuals in order to render them illegible or mark them as abnormal. Then, chapter 4 investigates how the maintenance of sex-segregated bathrooms and the de jure and de facto gender policing that occurs in and around these spaces constrain the ability of trans individuals to enter and move freely through public spaces. Finally, chapter 5 interrogates how the selective enforcement of solicitation laws on trans individuals, in particular transgender women of color, works to remove these individuals from public spaces. An earlier version of this chapter was previously published in 2015 in the journal *New Political Science* (37, no. 4) as "The War on Solicitation and Intersectional Subjection: Quality-of-life Policing as a Tool to Control Transgender Populations."

Next, Part Three explores the possibilities and limitations of a trans politics of rights including what types of social, political, and legal strategies are necessary and likely to be successful in eradicating the forces of governmentality that mark trans people as transgressive and abnormal in order to facilitate ongoing discrimination and marginalization against these individuals. Chapter 6 examines the efficacy of pursuing a politics of trans rights and explores the different options for political mobilization—working within existing liberal gay rights groups or nurturing independent trans rights groups—as well as the viability of litigation strategies and legislatives strategies in the current political and legal climates. Chapter 7 offers counterpublics as an alternative mechanism for trans and queer mobilization and suggests that their counterpositioning may enable these entities to challenge the dominant discourse and distribution of power within the public in order to reach the forces of governmentality that operate on trans bodies in pursuit of collective liberation for all trans people, and concludes with a brief discussion of the need to demythologize the politics of rights in order to create space for a broader array of organizational entities and discourses in the pursuit of change. While there is much to be gained from rights recognition, there are major forces of social control and population management that operate on trans people that are beyond the reach of rights. As such, while a successful trans politics of rights will come with benefits, these legal recognitions and protections are likely to be of limited utility for many within trans communities. Absent the redistribution of power that is necessary in order to transform the public, governmentality will continue to locate trans people at the margins of the public with significant costs. Collective liberation for all trans people requires creating space for alternative voices, embodiments, perspectives, organizations, and disruptions in order to challenge the space of public life and the infrahumanization that occurs there.

Part One

Transgressive Bodies

Chapter 1

Binary Identities and the Construction of Privileged versus Transgressive Bodies

Introduction

Power and privilege are allocated to those "bodies that matter" based on various physical traits including race, sex, sexual orientation, and the intersectional dynamics of these attributes.[1] As such, one of the biggest obstacles for trans rights activists and allies is persuading the public, legislators, and the courts that *all* trans bodies—as opposed to promulgating a transnormative politics of rights that privileges white transgender bodies—matter and are worthy of legal protection. Yet, as this chapter endeavors to make clear, U.S. Supreme Court justices historically have preferred the parsimony of binary categories of identity and regularly issue decisions that create and/or reify dichotomous groups of people. More often than not, differences are operationalized as binaries that work in effect to privilege one group at the expense of another (e.g., male/female, white/not white, gay/heterosexual). While these dichotomies are social constructs, they have been politically and legally operationalized as immutable characteristics that effectively reify power differentials in American society. Yet, this either/or approach to American civil rights jurisprudence is distinctly anti-intersectional and forces individuals to locate themselves in socially constructed diametrically opposed categories of identity—one is either Black or white, heterosexual or gay, male or female—which is not only an inaccurate description of many individuals' identities but works as a powerful privileging mechanism for some bodies as well.

At the same time, however, the Black, women's, and gay rights movements often have seen their greatest successes when they are able to cast questions about civil rights as debates about the legitimacy of state and/or state-sanctioned discrimination between two groups of individuals where one group is targeted for differential treatment on the basis of a single and shared immutable characteristic. Most recently, the gay rights movement's arguments that gays and lesbians have a same-sex sexual orientation not a sexual preference, and that consequently states cannot deny same-sex couples access to the civil institution of marriage that is open to opposite-sex couples, proved to be a persuasive political and legal argument culminating in the U.S. Supreme Court's decision in *Obergefell v. Hodges* (576 U.S. ___ [2015]) declaring state prohibitions on same-sex marriages unconstitutional. The majority opinion, however, validated the binary operationalization of sexual orientation that consistently has informed the justices' gay rights jurisprudence. In this instance, a majority of the justices determined that it is unconstitutional to deny same-sex couples access to the social, legal and economic benefits that accrue to married heterosexual couples, thereby following a pattern in which major civil rights victories validate and perpetuate the binary construction of identities.

This chapter explores the role that the courts play in the sociolegal construction of binary identities, and how the white/not-white, heterosexual/gay, and male/female binaries effectively create and perpetuate hierarchical categories of identity in relation to one another. This oversimplification of the complexities and nuances of individuals' identities works to privilege, marginalize, and erase different individuals based on whether or not they can be located within these binaries and, if so, where they are situated. These norms prove to be especially problematic for individuals located at the intersection of various categories of identity such as genderqueer and trans people of color as well as those with fluid sexual and gender identities.

As such, the analysis in this chapter begins with a discussion of how traditional rights jurisprudence is commensurate with the sociolegal construction of binary identities as a privileging mechanism in the contemporary United States. Then, specific attention is focused on the U.S. Supreme Court's role in the social construction of whiteness and the myriad ways in which the white/not-white dichotomy works to empower white individuals by designating nonwhite individuals as transgressive Others. Next, a review of the Supreme Court's validation of sexual orientation as both a binary and an immutable characteristic (e.g., gays and lesbians are "born that way") demonstrates how this jurisprudence limits the legibility of those bodies that are not easily located in the gay/heterosexual binary. Finally, the sociolegal construction of the male/female binary is examined in depth because this dichotomy works in myriad ways to restrict the legibility of trans bodies. Notably, the current trans rights litigation strategy, which is premised on situating discrimination against trans individuals in employment and education in the existing prohibitions on sex discrimination in Title VII of the 1964 Civil Rights Act and Title IX, risks reifying the sex binary in problematic ways by privileging those who can "pass" versus those who are marked as gender nonconforming members of their sex as assigned at birth. Recognizing the binary operationalization of immutable categories of identity as a successful and viable tactic in civil rights litigation suggests that a trans politics of rights is likely to be predicated on the sociolegal construction of a gender binary (cisgender/transgender) and the demand that an individual's right to transition to their right sex be legally validated. Yet, as the analyses below demonstrate, binary categories of identity are highly problematic because they are inaccurate and simultaneously work to mark some bodies as legible and privileged and other as illegible and transgressive.

The Sociolegal Construction of Binary Identities in the United States

Social and legal constructions of binary identities operate as tools of social control that privilege those "bodies that matter."[2] The creation and reification of binary identities may lend parsimony to legal proceedings, but simultaneously they work to maintain the power of privileged bodies in myriad ways because dichotomous identities help to "divide and rule" and mitigate the threat that a unified populace poses to the oppressors' hegemony.[3] Furthermore, the binary construction of identities distinguishes among those who are unmarked and have their identities universalized and those who are marked and find that their identities are particularized:

> The difference between self-abstraction and a body's positivity is more than a difference in what has officially been made available to men and to women, for example. It is a difference in the cultural/symbolic definitions of masculinity and femininity. Self-abstraction from male bodies confirms masculinity. Self-abstraction from female bodies denies femininity. The bourgeois public sphere is a frame of reference in which it is supposed that all particularities have the same status as mere

> particularity. But the ability to establish that frame of reference is a feature of some particularities. Neither in gender nor in race nor in class nor in sexualities is it possible to treat different particulars as having merely paratactic, or serial, difference. Differences in such realms already come coded as the difference between the unmarked and the marked, the universalizable and the particular. . . . The bourgeois public sphere has been structured from the outset by a logic of abstraction that provides a privilege for unmarked identities: the male, the white, the middle class, the normal.[4]

In this way, the privileges that accrue to unmarked identities are not correlated with identity whereas the costs that are imposed on marked bodies are understood to reflect their particularities and abnormalities. These distinctions insulate the beneficiaries of the binary construction of identity from interrogation within and by the public as "[t]he powerful are in this way discursively normalized, naturalized, while the dominated appear as mutants, disabled."[5]

Similarly, consistent with the idea that "the master's tools will never dismantle the master's house," a review of landmark litigation in the areas of Black, gay, and women's civil rights demonstrates how the legacies of racism, homophobia, and sexism are reproduced when those bodies that matter are the same individuals tasked with managing challenges to the dominant norms that validate their own power and privileges.[6] When courts validate social constructs as immutable characteristics, these innate physical markers sanction the perpetuation of stereotypes that are then used to further substantiate the intractable differences between identity groups. The mutually constitutive relationship among legal meaning and individual and social identities facilitates processes of governmentality and makes it exceedingly difficult for transgressive bodies to challenge governing norms.[7]

Successful civil rights litigation strategies historically have been predicated on socially constructed binaries—whites and Blacks, whites and nonwhites, men and women, gays and heterosexuals, etc.—that are then validated as real constructs via legal decisions and legislation. In this way, binaries that are themselves social constructs are validated as legal categories that work to privilege some at the expense of others. As such, it seems evident that those with power are invested in the maintenance of binary identities predicated on immutable characteristics and the legal validation of these binaries, and this is enhanced when "the dominators try to present themselves as saviors of the women and men they dehumanize and divide."[8]

Yet, it is precisely because these legal victories are significant, end de jure discrimination, and mandate the expansion of rights under the law—e.g., ending segregation in education in *Brown v. Board of Education* (347 U.S. 483 [1954]), declaring prohibitions on same-sex sodomy unconstitutional in *Lawrence v. Texas* (539 U.S. 558 [2003]), and recognizing marriage equality in *Obergefell v. Hodges* (576 U.S. ___ [2015])—that it is difficult to criticize these cases. These legal victories are exalted as validation that the state is capable of eradicating past wrongs and/or expanding the realm of rights to include new identities and groups while simultaneously eliding the myriad forces of governmentality that continue to operate on marginalized and intersectionally subjected populations after these landmark cases are decided. Furthermore, these binary categorical distinctions are understood as efficacious in legal decisions because the law is often operationalized as a mechanism for neatly distinguishing between right and wrong, criminals and victims, and so on. Yet, the courts' emphases on immutable characteristics and dependence on binary categories are not innate to the legal system or happenstance. These norms are instrumental in maintaining a system that identifies some as "beings for others."[9] An alternative approach would seek to validate individuals as "beings for themselves," but this requires challenging the system itself because

> the oppressed are not "marginals," are not people living "outside" society. They have always been "inside"—inside the structure which made them "beings for others." The solution is not to "integrate" them into the structure of oppression, but to transform that structure so that they can become "beings for themselves." Such transformation, of course, would undermine the oppressors' purposes.[10]

As such, any attempt to dismantle the governing binaries is likely to meet with systemic resistance.

Before one can entertain how making the case for the fluidity of gender and a spectrum of gender identities challenges the structures of oppression and has the potential to enable oppressed individuals the freedom to be "beings for themselves," it is first necessary to examine the structures that must be transformed in pursuit of change. In particular, the courts' reliance on immutable characteristics and binary categories of identity has had significant ramifications that work in effect to erase the identities of individuals who do not fit into binary categories, and creates a politics of division that reifies the power and privilege of those in the dominant binary identity categories at the expense of others. In this way, these legal tools produce and regulate persons and populations.[11] As such, the success of political and legal arguments predicated on binary identities reflects the challenges and limitations of advancing civil rights claims in the American political and legal systems. While the Black, gay, and women's rights movements have achieved great success in the courts, the legal constructions of race, sexual orientation, and sex come with costs, and the same will be true if civil rights advancements for trans individuals are predicated on a binary construction of gender identity.

Race: The Construction of Whiteness

Throughout U.S. history it has been "critical to define who was 'white' and on what grounds."[12] In Ian Haney López's *White by Law* (2006), he examines the role that the courts have played in the construction of race throughout U.S. history. López explains:

> First, the courts constructed the bounds of Whiteness by deciding on a case-by-case basis who was *not* White. Though the prerequisite courts were charged with defining the term "white person," they did not do so by referring to a freestanding notion of Whiteness. No court offered a complete typology listing the characteristics of Whiteness against which to compare the petitioner. Instead, the courts defined "white" through a process of negation, systematically identifying who was non-White. . . . In this relational system, the prerequisite cases show that Whites are those not constructed as non-White.[13]

López proceeds to identify the courts' assignment of value to these two categories—whites are superior and nonwhites are inferior—as their second major contribution to the construction of race through law.[14] The legal construction of race validates and perpetuates the social construction of a binary racial identity whereby whites are privileged and recognized as legitimate bodies and nonwhites are designated as inferior marginalized transgressive bodies.

This two-step process by which courts (1) decide who is *not* white, and (2) assign value to the categories of white and nonwhite is evidenced in the following quote from the U.S. Supreme Court's decision in *Plessy v. Ferguson* (163 U.S. 537 [1896]):

> Plessy, being a passenger between two stations within the State of Louisiana, was assigned by officers of the company to the coach used for the race to which he belonged, but he insisted upon going into a coach used by the race to which he did not belong. Neither in the information nor plea was his particular race or color averred. The petition for the writ of prohibition averred that petitioner was seven-eighths Caucasian and one eighth African blood; that the mixture of colored blood was not discernible in him, and that he was entitled to every right, privilege and immunity secured to citizens of the United States of the white race; and that, upon such theory, he took possession of a vacant seat in a coach where passengers of the white race were accommodated, and was ordered by the conductor to vacate said coach and take a seat in another assigned to persons of the colored race.[15]

First, the Court clearly identities Homer Plessy as nonwhite despite the fact that he identifies himself as seven-eighths white and one-eighth Black. The Court's decision makes clear that Plessy does not have the power to articulate his racial identity because that authority rests with the state to determine "the race to which he belonged."[16] Second, the Court legitimates that individuals who are not white may be forced to utilize separate accommodations thereby marking them as inferior. Despite protestations to the contrary, there is little doubt that the separation of whites from nonwhites was intended to maintain the power and privileges of the former relative to the latter. The Court's confirmation of the "one drop rule" plays a significant role in the creation of the racial binary by ensuring that multi- and biracial individuals will be located in the category of nonwhite thereby restricting who is allowed to identify as white. Justice Brown's majority opinion in *Plessy v. Ferguson* (163 U.S. 537 [1896]) demonstrates the extent to which the racial binary is understood as a given: "A statute which implies merely a legal distinction between the white and colored races" is legitimate because this distinction "is founded in the color of the two races and which must always exist so long as white men are distinguished from the other race by color."[17] In addition, this holding confirms that those with power and authority—law enforcement officers, lawmakers, judges—will determine who is white and who is not white.

Throughout the twentieth century, the Black civil rights movement utilized various means of political and legal mobilization and protest to advance the interests of Black communities and challenge de jure segregation and discrimination on the basis of race. Notably, the Black civil rights movement successfully challenged de jure segregation when the U.S. Supreme Court pronounced that "in the field of public education, the doctrine of 'separate but equal' has no place."[18] Yet, even the landmark civil rights decision *Brown v. Board of Education* (347 U.S. 483 [1954]) long celebrated as *the* breakthrough in the battle for Black civil rights is predicated on and validates the binary operationalization of race, and the legal and political developments that followed did not challenge the sociolegal construction of race as a binary identity. Instead, the U.S. Supreme Court's *Brown* opinion depended on and revalidated the race-binary that had been crafted and codified into law in earlier cases—e.g., in *Plessy v. Ferguson* (163 U.S. 537 [1896]), the Court wrote that "[w]e consider the underlying fallacy of the plaintiff's argument to consist in the assumption that the enforced separation of *the two races* stamps the colored race with a badge of inferiority. If this be so, it is not by reason of anything found in the act, but solely because the colored race chooses to put that construction upon it"[19]—by explaining that "[s]egregation of *white and colored children* in public schools has a detrimental effect upon the colored children. The impact is greater when it has the sanction of the law, for the policy of separating the races is usually interpreted as denoting the inferiority of the negro group."[20]

The creation of two races—"whites" and "coloreds"—is more than simply an oversimplification that ignores the abundance of racial and ethnic identities. It is also a social construct parading as biological fact. "The insistence that 'white persons' constitute a natural grouping prohibits at the level of basic assumptions any exploration of the social origins and functions of Whiteness, rendering its socially mediated parameters invisible and impossible to discern correctly."[21] By identifying individuals as either "white" or "colored," the hegemonic power of law works to privilege those who fit in the category of "white" while continuing to designate any and all individuals who do not fit into that category as "colored" and inferior. In this way, "Ontology does not allow us to understand the being of the black man, since it ignores the lived experience. For not only must the black man be black; he must be black in relation to the white man."[22]

Furthermore, the practice of defining those who are nonwhite in relation to those who are white works in effect to locate multiracial individuals in the category of nonwhite.[23] The law's inability to recognize the complexity of racial identities denies recognition to those individuals who are multiracial and/or intersectionally identified and perpetuates a mechanism for assigning privilege and power. Courts have long resisted the recognition of complex and dynamic identities forcing, for example, Black women to litigate employment discrimination cases as sex *or* racial discrimination but not both. This practice is grounded in the binary assumptions that work in effect to systematically erase Black women and their unique experiences as Black women from the legal lexicon and deny them access to legal remedies.[24] The same is true for other intersectionally identified individuals including trans people of color, as the analyses in forthcoming chapters will make clear.

As such, the sociolegal construction of a race binary privileges those who are identified as white while systematically marginalizing and stigmatizing nonwhite individuals. It does this by creating a fictitious racial category and giving those with power and privilege the authority to act as gatekeepers and determine who will be identified as white in practice and in law. In this way, the racial binary is both fluid—the categories of white and nonwhite change throughout U.S. history—and fixed—the authority to determine who is white and nonwhite rests in the hands of the few. As such, race becomes a mechanism for distributing benefits and costs across society in ways that work to maintain the power and privilege that accrues to those bodies and persons that matter while simultaneously stereotyping and ostracizing those who fail to conform with privileged norms and values even after civil rights victories in the courts and legislatures.

While de jure racial discrimination is outlawed, it is the process of marking certain bodies as permanently transgressive via forces of governmentality that aids in the maintenance of the racial binary today. Socioeconomic, cultural, and legal factors interact as tools of oppression and perpetuate systemic racism, but blame and a failure of responsibility are projected onto those individuals who are unable to overcome the powerful forces of governmentality working against and on their bodies. In this way, for example, Black bodies are marked as transgressive bodies—it is their failure to comply with the established rules and norms that locates them outside of the system as opposed to a systemic failure—rendering them vulnerable to economic exploitation, police harassment, violence, and execution. This gross mischaracterization and stereotyping of Black individuals (as well as other individuals and populations designated as "not white") works to maintain the racial binary and the power and privileges that accrue to white individuals while simultaneously absolving those with power of their complicity in the maintenance of ongoing racial hierarchies. Thus, it is essential to understand that the race binary is not merely an antiquated legal holdover, but rather a contemporary privileging mechanism that is utilized to manage populations, distribute power, and enable violence.

Sexual Orientation: Born This Way

The mainstream gay rights movement successfully co-opted the legal strategies utilized by the Black civil rights movement. Liberal gay rights groups emphasized litigation as a valuable form of legal mobilization and argued that discrimination on the basis of sexual orientation should be recognized as a violation of constitutional guarantees because sexual orientation is a fixed identity and not a preference.[25] Notably, the liberal gay civil rights movement's argument that gays and lesbians have an immutable same-sex sexual orientation as opposed to a sexual preference has proved to be a persuasive political and legal argument in favor of extending civil rights protections and marriage equality to gays and lesbians. By analogizing sexual orientation to other "immutable" characteristics such as race and sex, gay rights groups utilized a legal strategy modeled on the successful tactics of prior civil rights movements. This argument aided in the construction of a heterosexual/gay binary and proved to be a persuasive tool for changing public perceptions thereby creating opportunities for legal change and confirming the efficacy of the politics of rights.

In fact, the Court's rapidly evolving gay rights jurisprudence can largely be attributed to the justices' growing recognition and acceptance of an immutable binary sexual orientation. In 1986, in *Bowers v. Hardwick* (478 U.S. 186), a majority of the justices dismissed that Georgia's antisodomy statute violated the privacy guarantees of the U.S. Constitution finding that the legislative authority of the state to regulate immoral conduct trumps one's personal sexual preferences.[26] Yet, just a few years later in *Romer v. Evans* (517 U.S. 620 [1996]), the justices concluded that Amendment 2 to the Colorado Constitution, which denied "protected status" to individuals on the basis of their "homosexual, lesbian or bisexual orientation,"[27] violated the Constitution's guarantees of equal protection because it "identifies persons by a single trait and then denies them protection across the board. The resulting disqualification of a class of persons from the right to seek specific protection from the law is unprecedented in our jurisprudence."[28] Writing for the majority, Justice Kennedy explained that animus toward a class of people on the basis of a "single trait" does not constitute a legitimate government interest thereby indicating both a move away from the moral justifications accepted in *Bowers* and a simultaneous step toward recognizing sexual orientation as an individual characteristic instead of a preference.[29] In addition, while Amendment 2 was added to the Colorado Constitution via popular referendum in response to various municipal codes that attempted to protect individuals from discrimination on the basis of their sexual orientation broadly defined (e.g., the city of Boulder, Colorado, ordinance stated "the choice of sexual partners, i.e., bisexual, homosexual or heterosexual"),[30] Justice Kennedy reduced sexual orientation to a binary and explicitly excluded bisexual orientation from his analysis when he wrote: "Amendment 2 . . . prohibits all legislative, executive or judicial action at any level of state or local government designed to protect the named class, a class we shall refer to as *homosexual persons or gays and lesbians*."[31]

The justices further validated the binary construction of sexual orientation in *Lawrence v. Texas* (539 U.S. 558 [2003]) when they determined that a Texas law prohibiting sodomy between "same-sex" participants but not "different-sex" participants violated the Constitution by depriving "homosexuals" of the same liberty protections extended to "heterosexuals." Finally, in the U.S Supreme Court's decision in *Obergefell v. Hodges* (576 U.S. ___ [2015]), Justice Kennedy stated that "sexual orientation is both a normal expression of human sexuality and immutable," and in doing so provided definitive legal support for the idea that sexual orientation is an innate and fixed characteristic.[32] Furthermore, throughout the majority opinion, Kennedy repeatedly refers to same-sex couples in relation to opposite-sex couples as follows: "Under the Constitution, same-sex couples seek in marriage the same legal treatment as opposite-sex couples, and it would disparage their choices and diminish their personhood to deny them this right."[33] This holding is firmly grounded in the gay/heterosexual binary and validates the pursuit of homonormativity as a viable political and legal mechanism for advancing gay rights.[34] In this way, dominant groups and elite actors (in this case Supreme Court justices) are able to signal that a gay politics of rights "that does not contest dominant heteronormative assumptions and institutions, but upholds and sustains them, while promising the possibility of a demobilized gay constituency and a privatized, depoliticized gay culture anchored in domesticity and consumption" has the greatest likelihood of success in the American legal system.[35]

While these gay rights cases are substantive victories, they are not without costs. Operationalizing sexual orientation as a heterosexual/gay binary excludes bisexuals and individuals who reject this type of classification in favor of more dynamic and fluid sexual orientations and preferences. Much like the sociolegal construction of race, the sociolegal construction of sexual orientation ignores the complexity and fluidity of identities. In this way, the sexual orientation binary posits "gays" as a cohesive group of individuals when in fact the LGBQ community is comprised of complex and diverse individuals with varying sexual identities, orientations, and preferences. In particular, this essentialism and the practice of analogizing race and sexual orientation "erases the ways that legal and social structures work together and against the people who live at those intersections—queer people of color."[36] While this legal strategy may have been successful, it comes with significant costs for those who are gender fluid, bisexual, and or intersectionally identified as well as individuals who are not interested in or able to enter into a homonormative lifestyle.[37] In practice, many individuals are located outside of the sociolegally constructed heterosexual/gay binary.

For example, while marriage equality is often celebrated as the pinnacle achievement of the gay rights movement, in practice it sanctions that those gay and lesbian couples willing to enter into same-sex marriages predicated on heterosexual norms may under the best circumstances be deemed legitimate citizens with the associated socioeconomic and legal benefits whereas those who aspire to alternative lifestyles, domestic partnerships, or are unable to wed will continue to be excluded from the privileges that accrue to those who are married.[38] Yet, in spite of this legal victory, privileged elites and government actors are still able to act as gatekeepers and police access to and the distribution of benefits via formal laws and practices of governmentality. For example, gays and lesbians who are able to marry remain economically, legally, and physically vulnerable given that many states still lack laws prohibiting discrimination on the basis of sexual orientation, resulting in an entire class of "fragmented citizens."[39] Furthermore, human resource directors, state legislators, local bureaucrats, and so on continue to exercise outsized influence on the lives of many gays and lesbians in spite of the aforementioned rights victories,[40] and the implementation of marriage equality has been accompanied by unintended consequences including the elimination of recognition for domestic partnerships in some states and private workplaces.[41] As such, the practice of marking certain gay and lesbian bodies as transgressive continues in spite of rights recognition for "homosexuals," and those bodies that cannot be located squarely in a hetero or homonormative lifestyle continue to be rendered illegible.

Sex: The Immutability and Exclusivity of Male and Female

Much like the sociolegal constructions of race and sexual orientation, the male/female dichotomy is a sociolegal creation.[42] At the same time, however, the categories of male and female are among the most powerful privileging and organizing mechanisms in contemporary American society and law. Sex, understood as an unambiguous characteristic assigned at birth, informs society's and the legal system's operationalization of gender—the masculine versus feminine binary are "expressive attributes of 'male' and 'female' "[43]—and sexual orientation—the homosexual/heterosexual binary is created in relation to one's sex: " '[H]omosexuals' are oriented or attracted to individuals of the same sex, while 'heterosexuals' prefer to have sexual relationships with members of the 'opposite' sex."[44] Similarly, the male/female dichotomy informs transgender identity as well. Transgender individuals are defined as those individuals who seek to identify as the opposite gender of the sex they were assigned at birth. Thus, transgender individuals regularly are referred to as male-to-female or female-to-male reflecting how they have now transitioned into their right gender.

Furthermore, even individuals operating outside of the confines of the sex binary are still defined in relation to it. For example, " 'bisexuals' are those relatively unusual individuals who are attracted, or could be, to persons of 'either' gender. . . . Even 'intersexual' persons—individuals who do not conform to 'either' sex because they demonstrate physical characteristics of 'both'—are defined with reference to this binary scheme."[45] As such, it is clear that the sex binary is one of the most powerful tools for assigning and regulating identity, as indicated by the fact that numerous other identities often are the derivatives of sex. As Butler explains, "The notion that there might be a 'truth' of sex, as Foucault ironically terms it, is produced precisely through the regulatory practices that generate coherent identities through the matrix of coherent gender norms."[46]

In addition to being erroneously understood as an immutable and unambiguous characteristic, sex has been operationalized by the courts as a distinguishing characteristic that allows and, in some instances, requires differential treatment of males and females consistent with the law. While laws that classify and/or treat individuals differently on the basis of race are subject to the most exacting judicial review because there are nearly no compelling reasons for treating individuals differently on the basis of their race, laws that treat individuals differently because of their sex are not subject to the same rigorous review. Throughout history, the courts have upheld laws that treat individuals differently on the basis of sex for a variety of reasons including "woman's physical structure" and the fact that "healthy mothers are essential to vigorous offspring,"[47] women's central role in "home and family life,"[48] and the belief that women's presence in certain domains may lead to "moral and social problems,"[49] or sexual assaults.[50] While the courts have largely abandoned many of these stereotypical and antiquated assumptions about women's roles in the private versus public spheres, differential treatment of men and women continues to be legal in those instances in which the courts find that men and women are not "similarly situated."[51] This standard continues to operate as a tool for distinguishing between men and women based on both physiological differences as well as stereotypical assumptions about caregiving and parenting. For example, as recently as 2001, in *Nguyen v. INS* (533 U.S. 53), the U.S. Supreme Court upheld more onerous citizenship requirements for illegitimate children born on foreign soil to American male citizens than illegitimate children born on foreign soil to American female citizens, a precedent that was finally overturned in 2017 in *Sessions v. Morales-Santana* (582 U.S. ___) when the Supreme Court determined that this differential treatment is based on outdated gender stereotypes thereby violating the Constitution's equal protection guarantees.

Thus, while protectionist legislation has been subject to greater legal scrutiny in recent decades as women integrated the workforce, politics, and public spaces, stereotypical and essentialist assumptions about males and females continue to inform the courts and U.S. law and policy. Despite significant advancements in women's rights, the belief that there are two sexes and that they are fundamentally and physiologically different, and hence may under certain circumstances be treated as such under the law (e.g., sex-specific statutory rape laws, accommodations for maternity leave as opposed to parental leave, the military draft, regulation of women's reproductive rights as well as fetal protection laws) distinguishes sex from race (and possibly sexual orientation moving forward). The continued affirmation by the courts that there are innate differences between the two sexes reifies the immutable sex binary on a regular basis.

Much like the sociolegal construction of race and the continued policing of the boundaries of whiteness, the sociolegal construction of sex and the emphasis on its immutability and the innate differences between males and females work to police the boundaries of Man and Woman beyond the law. As Butler reminds us, "The foundational reasoning of identity politics tends to assume that an identity must first be in place in order for political interests to be elaborated and, subsequently, political action to be taken. My argument is that there need not be a 'doer behind the deed,' but that the 'doer' is variably constructed in and through the deed."[52] Just as white individuals are invested in maintaining the power and privileges that accrue to them as a result of the race binary, men and women are invested in the sex binary. Notably, men benefit from protecting the boundaries of "male" so that they may continue to benefit from the de jure and de facto privileges that accrue to men despite the advances of the women's movement.[53] In addition, men are invested in having a clearly marked class of women who are sexually available to men and prepared to bear children and act as mothers.[54]

At the same time, women are invested in the maintenance of the category of "female" as well. Throughout U.S. history, the "logic of essentialism" has informed discussions and analyses of sex and gender including the various women's rights movements.[55] The essentialist tendencies of the mainstream white women's movements have been well documented by Black, Latina, and lesbian feminist theorists who draw attention to the diversity of women's experiences based on one's race, ethnicity, immigrant status, sexual orientation, intersectional identities, and so on.[56] In practice, however, many women continue to be the beneficiaries of essentialist assumptions that are mapped onto the a priori sex binary. As Fuss explains, "For the essentialist, the natural provides the raw material and determinative starting point for the practices and laws of the social. For example, sexual difference (the division into 'male' and 'female') is taken as prior to social differences which are presumed to be mapped onto, *a posteriori*, the biological subject."[57] As such, for better or for worse, some women continue to benefit from certain privileges and concessions that accrue to women based on stereotypes about their physical differences from males as well as those that derive from the mythology of the cult of true womanhood and the accompanying stereotypes about femininity and domesticity.[58] In this way, the policing of the boundaries of "woman" works to maintain those accommodations.

At the same time, the policing of the boundaries of "woman" distinguishes those female "bodies that matter" from those that are outside of the bounds of womanhood, and implicates the racial, heteronormative, and class dimensions of the "logic of essentialism" that privilege some women and not others. This process regularly reifies femininity as the measure of a real woman in order to ostracize women who deviate from these expectations. For example, women who are perceived as being too masculine historically have been excluded from the category of "real woman," including women of color and lesbians.[59] Similarly, trans exclusionary radical feminists (TERFs) have worked to exclude transwomen from "women's" spaces, organizations, and events based on the belief that "real women" are born with vaginas.

Questions and stereotypes about the intersections of race, femininity, and sexuality are especially pervasive in contemporary athletics as demonstrated by the ongoing fervor over South African runner and 2016 Olympic 800-meter gold medalist Caster Semenya and whether or not she is a "real woman." Semenya, like many Olympic athletes before her, has been subject to extensive sex testing since her breakout performance at the 2009 world track and field championships because she is perceived as " 'being too fast and supposedly too masculine' by Western standards."[60] The policing of masculine women competing in the Olympics has evolved from visual inspection of one's genitalia to chromosomal testing to the current procedures that utilize measures of testosterone to determine one's eligibility to compete as a woman.[61] The ongoing criticism of Semenya's participation in the women's 800-meter track and field event cannot be disaggregated from sexism, racism, or homophobia, and exemplifies the ways in which race, sexuality, and sex intersect to privilege some women and certain conceptions of womanhood over others. This policing of the boundaries of "woman" works to privilege those women deemed to be appropriately feminine and attractive and often favors white heterosexual women. The Polish runner Joanna Jozwik, who placed fifth in the 800-meter event at the 2016 Olympics, stated that she "feels like a silver medalist" suggesting that the second and third place finishers—Black women from Burundi and Kenya respectively—also are not "women," and then went on to say "I'm glad I'm the first European, the second white" to finish the race.[62] The policing of female masculinity works to reify "the versions of masculinity we enjoy and trust; many of these 'heroic masculinities' depend absolutely on the subordination of alternative masculinities."[63] In this way, masculinity continues to be associated with maleness and female masculinity is obfuscated and erased.[64]

Similarly, the privileging of feminine women works to the detriment of those masculine women located at the intersection of gender stereotypes and sexual orientation. The history of the women's liberation movements and the "lavender menace" is well documented, but these antagonisms remain today in both similar and different manifestations. The stereotype that all lesbians are dykes, and are therefore too masculine to be included in the category of woman, works to marginalize these individuals[65] and has perpetuated a myth that masculine lesbians are not feminists or are not women.[66] At the same time, Halberstam writes, "female masculinity is generally received by hetero- and homo-normative cultures as a pathological sign of misidentification and maladjustment."[67] When heteronormative forces of governmentality are utilized to police the category of woman, those women who are lesbians, bisexuals, masculine, or women of color are removed and intersectional subjection is left unacknowledged.

The reality remains that as long as certain men and women benefit from the artificial categorical distinctions between male and female there will be resistance to acknowledging the complexities of sex and gender. As such, the courts' facilitation of the "logic of essentialism" aids in the maintenance of the sex and gender binaries by reifying the belief that women are unified by a shared biology, characteristics, and experiences that are distinct from and/or defined in opposition to men. This approach and positioning inevitably informs the current discourse surrounding trans rights, and raises questions about how a trans politics of rights is similar or dissimilar to prior civil rights movements. While many trans activists reject the suggestion that gender should be understood as a fixed and immutable characteristic, as evidenced by the analysis to follow, extant legal doctrines and constitutional jurisprudence validate the efficacy of litigation strategies predicated on binary and immutable categories of identity.

Conclusion

Throughout U.S. history, the courts have played an important role in the creation and implementation of binary categories of identity. By linking the viability of rights claims under the law to the immutability of binary characteristics, judge have empowered both state and social actors to police the boundaries of identities in order to allocate costs and benefits. As long as these sociolegal constructs are treated as biological or natural facts, it is difficult to challenge and dismantle the hierarchies that are created on the scaffolding of the politics of identity. Recognizing that these dyads are fictions and work to the detriment of many individuals, the social and legal opposition to the deconstruction of binary categories of identity is not about biology, but rather reflects the power struggles between bodies that matter and transgressive bodies that have been systematically marginalized in order to reify the regulatory norms of race, sex, and sexual orientation.

Those with power are likely to resist efforts to challenge the existing identity binaries because they benefit from the systemic enforcement of sexed, raced, and intersectionally subjective body politics. In particular, the sex binary operates as a powerful privileging and organizing binary because it is understood as being based on immutable characteristics, and it is the foundation by which other identities are constructed including gender, sexual orientation, and transgender identity. The maintenance of the sex binary privileges some at the expense of others, informs the construction of other privileging binaries, and works as a powerful force of governmentality via de jure regulations and de facto policing of sex. Yet, an accurate understanding of gender undermines the governing sex binary and offers an explicit challenge to sociolegally constructed binaries that could work to expose these dichotomies as fictitious constructs that empower the few to determine the identities and destinies of the many, and work to maintain the privileged position of those bodies that matter. In order to truly eradicate discrimination on the basis of race, sex, sexual orientation, and gender identity, it is necessary to validate the complexities of these identity categories. This requires recognizing how and why categories of identity are socially constructed, multiple, and/or fluid as opposed to binary and immutable, and overlap and intersect in significant ways with one another as well as formal and informal mechanisms of power.

Recognizing the challenges that confront trans individuals seeking to litigate cases and/or pursue legislative change by advocating for the application of prohibitions on sex discrimination to trans individuals and the limitations of advocating for prohibitions on discrimination on the basis of a gender binary, the chapter that follows makes the case that understanding gender identity as a complex fluid characteristic is a more desirable alternative than working within the conventions of binary rights claims because the former opens the door for a more complex and nuanced understanding of identity including intersectional analyses. An accurate understanding of gender identities and how they interact with other facets of identity is an essential first step in facilitating transformative change because complex and fluid conceptions of gender liberate individuals from the binary politics of right sex and challenge a fundamental hegemonic organizing and privileging mechanism.

Chapter 2

The Complexity of Gender Identities and the Dangers of the Politics of Right Sex

Introduction

Proponents of trans rights must navigate a variety of complex decisions regarding the best and most efficacious strategies for advancing their goals. As noted in the previous chapter, the strategies of successful prior civil rights movements often serve as a template for later movements. In the context of the push for trans rights, this has manifested in two ways. First, litigants have worked to situate discrimination on the basis of gender identity within the existing constitutional sex discrimination jurisprudence predicated on the sex binary. Arguing that discrimination against trans individuals is sex discrimination because it penalizes people for failing to comply with gender norms has proven to be a successful litigation tactic in recent years. At the same time, however, these legal victories often inadvertently validate the myth of immutable and "real" sex in problematic ways, as will be discussed below. Another option for a politics of trans rights modeled on successful prior civil rights movements entails operationalizing gender identity as a binary (cisgender/transgender) in the pursuit of legal prohibitions on gender discrimination. This strategy, however, risks becoming a transnormative politics of right sex that privileges those trans individuals who are able and/or willing to locate themselves in the sex binary while excluding those who reject these categories and/or fail to "pass" or comply with gendered and sexed norms of presentation and behavior. As such, this chapter endeavors to make clear that sex and gender are significantly more complicated than the legal operationalization of the binary categories of male/female and cisgender/transgender would suggest.

This chapter begins with an examination of the complexities of gender and sex and how these identities intersect with others to render some trans individuals more vulnerable to discrimination and infrahumanization than others. Then, it interrogates the pros and cons of advancing trans rights via existing prohibitions on sex discrimination. While trans individuals have been, and likely will continue to be, able to gain some legal protections by pursuing trans rights via the parameters of existing sex discrimination jurisprudence, these strategies are limited by both the confines of existing sex discrimination legislation—which tends to focus on issues related to employment and education while locating many other spaces beyond the reach of the law—and the formal and informal institutional constraints associated with the courts, including the discretion and biases of individual judges. This chapter concludes by making the case that in order to circumnavigate the exclusionary tendencies of binary rights recognition described in the prior chapter it is necessary to agitate for the full recognition of the nuances and fluidities of gender identities. It is only by assiduously avoiding the politics of "real" sex and right sex in favor of recognizing and advancing an accurate definition of gender identity as a nuanced and fluid characteristic that trans activists will be capable of opening the door to intersectional analyses and challenging the hegemonic power structures that substantiate both de jure discrimination and de facto infrahumanization against trans people.

Identity Politics as Privileging Mechanisms

The ways in which identities are constructed and embedded with meanings matters because, as Valentine explains, "[p]eople everywhere categorize themselves and others; this is one of the most fundamental aspects of human language and meaning making. But the ways in which these categorizations are made, and which categories come to have effects in the world are never neutral."[1] The categories of sex and gender become effective tools for validating and enforcing homonormativity,[2] heteronormativity and the heterosexual matrix,[3] and cissexist culture.[4] The sex and gender binaries are integral to the maintenance of homo- and heteronormativities because the object of one's sexual desire is defined in reference to his or her sex, as well as cissexual privilege as exemplified by the pressure that is placed on transgender individuals to "pass" as males or females.[5]

The emphasis on "passing" in public reifies the sex binary by requiring that representations of gender correlate with the expectations assigned to male and female presentation, and excludes any and all other potential presentations of gender. This constrains the actions and movements of trans individuals who must choose to comply with expectations—oftentimes by misrepresenting their actual gender identities in order to avoid detection—but also affects the public's understanding and expectations about gender diversity. The policing of gender through de jure and de facto public exclusion "reinforce[s] the very notion of 'difference' as anomalous by exaggerating the prevalence of the 'norm.' "[6] Furthermore, the emphasis on "passing" validates and reifies sexual stereotypes and suggests that "all trans women are on a quest to make ourselves as pretty, pink and passive as possible."[7] In this way, "the feminization of trans women is a by-product of [the] sexualization of all women," while simultaneously trans men are more or less ignored in the media "because they are unable to sensationalize them the way they do trans women without bringing masculinity itself into question."[8] The bar for passing also implicates intersectionality as well, because in order to be accepted one needs "the exact right combination of *visible* 'difference' passability *and* nonvisibility (a combination assisted by whiteness, abledness, legal citizenship, employment and noncriminal status) to hope to be granted authenticity, transparency, and belonging within a chosen gender."[9] Finally, even when trans individuals are able to "pass" as males and females, their very existence "upset[s] the master signifiers of sexual differences that heteronormative and non-trans people often depend upon" because they challenge the "essential fixity of the sexed body, revealing it to be something that can be altered and brought into alignment with a psychically invested gender identity."[10]

The dominant public's fixation on identifying and categorizing individuals as male or female—based on sex assigned at birth or one's ability to "pass"—is evidence of the power that the sex and gender binaries exercise via the politics of identity in the contemporary United States. As described in chapter 1, the politics of identity have become powerful tools for distinguishing among populations in order to privilege some and marginalize others, because "[d]efinition, naming, confers a certain kind of visibility while obscuring that-which-will-not-be-named."[11]

As such, public antipathy toward trans people exists because they are trans—that-which-will-not-be-named—and not because they are not successfully "passing" as male or female. Even those individuals who are able to "pass" are still marked as abnormal and located at the margins of the public. For example, one individual reported the following about a friend who is a trans woman:

> She's recognizable as a trans woman, she definitely does not look like a man. Long hair, very feminine, dresses, skirts, everything. . . . And . . . [a patron looked at my friend] . . . and looked at the sign on the door, and then looked at her again. . . . [People like this patron] . . . would say, "Oh, I was afraid because I thought it was a man." But it's actually, like, no, you thought it was a trans woman. She didn't look like a man. Men don't wear . . . long skirts and wear make-up. The girl dresses in high heels. She looks like a trans woman, right? And that's where it's not about danger. It's about, like, who is normal.[12]

The processes of defining, categorizing, and policing the gender of individuals work to make trans people illegible and sanction violence, discrimination, marginalization, and erasure via de jure and de facto maintenance of the sex and gender binaries.

The policing of the sex and gender binaries has always been a tool of population management. As Stryker and Aizura explain:

> "Gender" is not merely the representation in language and culture of a biological sex; it is also an administrative or bureaucratic structure for the management of sexual difference and reproductive capacity (the ticking off of M's and F's on state-issued or state-sanctioned forms). In this sense, and to the extent that "gender identity" is understood as the psychical internalization and somaticization of historically contingent modes of embodied personhood, *transgender* is intimately bound up with questions of nation, territory, and citizenship, with categories of belonging and exclusion, of excess and incorporation, and with all the processes through which individual corporealities become aggregated as bodies politic.[13]

As such, for some trans scholars, "the term *transgender* is a political rather than a social identity, or better, a political *strategy* that tries 'to get *beyond* identity politics by invoking a term so broad and inclusive as to make room for multiple identities and expressions, and still refer to the specific oppressions that transpeople faced.' "[14] The goal here then becomes " 'an identity politics movement that seeks the *dissolution of the very category under which it is organized*.' "[15] As the discussion that follows makes clear, such a strategy will require moving beyond the binary operationalization of identities typically associated with the politics of rights recognition in the courts, and concerted and strategic efforts to not privilege the politics of right sex—recognizing the rights of transgender individuals to transition from male to female and female to male—over self-determination and collective liberation for all trans individuals.

Intersectional Subjection of Trans Individuals

Gender intersects with various other facets of identity to further complicate the relationships among individuals and institutions, and suggests that a politics of right sex will not reach the multiple and intersecting forces that subject many trans people. It is imperative to recognize that many trans individuals are intersectionally identified and have different sexual orientations, racial and ethnic identities, and come from a variety of socioeconomic backgrounds, geographic areas, and so on. For some trans individuals, gender and sexuality are connected and for others they are not, and it is important that individuals be allowed to articulate these relationships or the lack thereof for themselves.[16] As such, for many trans individuals the discrimination and infrahumanization they experience cannot be wholly eradicated by recognizing the right to change one's sex as assigned at birth from male-to-female or female-to-male. Thus, there are costs associated with talking about the trans community as a monolithic entity when in fact it is a very diverse community, and these facts caution against a transnormative politics of rights that operates within the constraints of binary operationalizations of sex and gender. In the analyses that follow, particular attention will be dedicated to the ways in which different identities within the trans community intersect with forces of governmentality to enhance the intersectional subjections enacted on some trans individuals.

The trans community is one of the most marginalized populations in the United States, and the effects of the ongoing discrimination against trans people are readily evident. Yet, the costs of de jure and de facto discrimination and the forces of governmentality are not evenly distributed.

In 2015, the National Center for Transgender Equality surveyed 27,715 trans people across the United States and reported that survey respondents experienced verbal harassment (46 percent), physical assaults (9 percent), and sexual assaults (10 percent) in the preceding year, and 40 percent of survey respondents reported that they had attempted suicide at some point in their lives, including 54 percent of disabled respondents in comparison to 4.6 percent of the general population.[17] Trans individuals also reported higher rates of poverty than the average American (29 versus 14 percent), and higher rates of unemployment as well (15 versus 5 percent).[18] These numbers were exacerbated for trans people of color with poverty rates of 43 percent for Latinx, 41 percent for American Indian, 40 percent for multiracial, and 38 percent for Black respondents, and trans people of color had an unemployment rate of 20 percent.[19] Undocumented trans individuals also experienced high rates of violence as well as extreme economic hardship; 24 percent reported that they had been physically attacked in the prior year.[20]

The law's inability to accommodate intersectional identities and evaluate allegations of discrimination against intersectionally subjected populations has particularly nefarious results for intersectionally subjected trans individuals who are targeted on the basis of their race, ethnicity, socioeconomic status, sexual orientation, and gender identity.[21] As Minter explains, "[G]iven how persistently the devaluation of cross-gendered expression has been tied to the devaluation of working-class, African American, and immigrant people within queer history, it seems dangerous to assume that gender is necessarily the only or even the most important frame of reference for understanding transgender issues."[22]

As such, attempts to advance trans interests must endeavor to improve the lives of all trans individuals, not merely the most privileged or normalized within the community. Given the extent to which socially constructed binary identities are utilized by the courts to privilege some and marginalize others, as discussed in the prior chapter, this problematizes the strategies available to trans communities seeking to advance their interests within the confines of the politics of rights. While some trans individuals may find utility in capitalizing on the opportunities afforded by analogizing discrimination on the basis of transgender identity with sex discrimination, in the hands of individual judges this approach may inadvertently validate the sex binary and leave those who cannot fit into the stereotypes of male and female out of the legal lexicon. In this way, a politics of trans rights may be misappropriated as a politics of right sex that is exclusionary and transnormative. Similarly, attempts to agitate for gender identity to be added to the litany of identity categories protected under federal and state civil rights legislation as distinct and separate from sex comes with similar problems given the likelihood that gender identity will be operationalized as a binary—transgender versus cisgender—consistent with the "Rainbow Theory" approach to identity politics.[23] The increasing prevalence of the term *cis* in the popular vernacular suggests that this dichotomy is already gaining traction as a mechanism for distinguishing transgender and cisgender individuals.

Much like the binary operationalization of sex, the binary operationalization of gender identity will effectively distribute costs and benefits across trans communities based on one's ability to fit within this binary, with significant detriments for nonbinary individuals, and similarly, risks perpetuating transnormativity and the politics of right sex. As mentioned before, the recognition of rights and legal protections based on binary identities leaves many individuals outside of the protections of the law, including intersectionally subjected individuals, because legal recognition often results in the expansion of individual liberties and rights, rather than collective liberation.[24] In addition, within the gender binary the term *cisgender* may become normalized as the "correct" gender identity whereas transgender becomes problematized as the "incorrect" gender identity. Or, as Currah and Minter explain, "identifying gender identity as a distinct classification may reinforce the perception, which is already so pervasive and damaging in the case law, that transgender people are somehow fundamentally distinct from—and by implication, inferior to—non-transgender people, i.e. that transgender people are not men or women, but something other or in-between."[25] Thus, a truly liberationist framework for all trans people must move beyond the binary categories of sex and gender created and perpetuated by the hegemonic powers in order to include intersectional identities and subjections as well. Collective liberation, however, is not likely to be achieved via a trans politics of rights focused on legal reforms and litigation strategies that seek to expand prohibitions on sex discrimination, to include gender discrimination.

The Limits of Prohibitions on Sex Discrimination for Trans Individuals

As described in the prior chapter, throughout the history of modern civil rights movements, the courts have identified and focused on the immutability of binary identities, and then utilized these socially constructed categories to extend heightened equal protection standards and liberty guarantees to people of color, women, and gays and lesbians. Early attempts by trans litigants to work within the confines of extant laws and the courts' privileging of the binary construction of identity were problematic, as governing norms about immutable characteristics initially proved insurmountable for transgender individuals bringing legal claims in the courts. Notably, in 1999, the Fourth Court of Appeals for Texas rejected a transgender woman's female identity "because she was declared a male at birth and presumably had XY chromosomes, Christie Lee Littleton would always be male. [The Judge] wrote that gender is 'immutably fixed by our Creator at birth.'"[26] The judge in this case issued this ruling despite the fact that Littleton had undergone three genital reassignment surgeries twenty years prior and had legally married a male in 1989.[27] According to Chief Justice Hardberger, sex is an immutable characteristic that could not be changed under any circumstances. While this is a particularly egregious example, it is demonstrative of the challenges associated with seeking legal recognition via the courts, where individual judges exercise enormous authority.

Similarly, early attempts by transgender individuals to litigate workplace discrimination as sex discrimination under Title VII of the 1964 Civil Rights Act initially were not successful. "With few exceptions, courts dismissed claims by transgender people on the grounds that (1) sex discrimination laws were not intended to protect transgender people; and (2) the 'plain' or 'traditional' meaning of the term *sex* refers only to a person's biological identity as male or female, not to change of sex."[28] For example, in 1977, an employee who transitioned from male to female during their tenure at the accounting firm Arthur Andersen, and was subsequently terminated after requesting that employment records reflect her new first name, sued the company for sex discrimination in violation of Title VII (*Holloway v. Arthur Andersen*, 566 F.2d 659 [9th Circuit 1977]). The Ninth Circuit ruled that Congress did not intend the definition of the word *sex* to include "sexual preference" or encompass claims of gender discrimination, and then explained that Holloway was not discriminated against because of her sex (e.g., she was not targeted for differential treatment because she is a woman) but rather "because she is a transsexual who chose to change her sex."[29] Similarly, in *Ulane v. Eastern Airlines, Inc.* (742 F.2d.1081 [7th Circuit 1984]), the Seventh Circuit Court rejected Karen Ulane's claim that she had been the victim of sex discrimination under Title VII when Eastern Airlines terminated her job as a pilot. Ulane, a transgender woman, did not have grounds to file a sex discrimination claim against the airline because the court found that Eastern Airlines did not discriminate against Ulane "because she is female, but because Ulane is a transsexual—a biological male who takes female hormones, cross-dresses, and has surgically altered parts of her body to make it appear to be female."[30]

These holdings demonstrate the challenges that transgender individuals have confronted when attempting to challenge discrimination on the basis of sex in the courts. As such, fighting for legal protections for transgender individuals via existing sex discrimination jurisprudence has proven complicated, given that some judges are committed to the construction of sex as an immutable characteristic, and in other instances, "because of the extreme discomfort that transgender people often evoke, courts have also relied on the dehumanizing argument that transsexual people cannot be classified as either male or female and, therefore, do not fall into a protected category under sex discrimination laws."[31] In both of these ways, the courts maintain the status quo and the privileges that accrue to those on the basis of the sex binary.

More recently, however, transgender litigants have had greater success in the courts under Title VII as they have sought to challenge the sex and gender stereotypes that disadvantage many trans individuals utilizing the U.S. Supreme Court's decision in *Price Waterhouse v. Hopkins* (490 U.S. 228 [1989]), which prohibited discrimination in the workplace based on sex stereotypes. The *Price Waterhouse* case is notable because the justices determined that prohibitions on "sex" discrimination include differential treatment on the basis of one's gendered behavior and/or appearance, thereby expanding "sex" beyond male and female anatomy to include gender discrimination based on one's masculine and feminine traits.

While the courts initially resisted applying *Price Waterhouse*'s prohibitions on gender discrimination in cases involving transgender individuals' allegations of workplace discrimination on the basis of their gender identities, by the twenty-first century the tide was changing. In cases such as *Smith v. City of Salem* (378 F.3d 566 [6th Circuit 2004]), federal judges recognized that terminating an individual for transitioning from male to female (in this case the firefighter Smith was in the midst of a multiyear transition when they were terminated) violated Title VII's prohibitions on sex discrimination because Smith was fired for their failure to comply with expectations about male presentation of self and masculinity. The Court explained:

> [D]iscrimination against a plaintiff who is a transsexual—and therefore fails to act and/or identify with his or her gender—is no different from the discrimination directed against Ann Hopkins in *Price Waterhouse*, who, in sex-stereotypical terms, did not act like a woman. Sex stereotyping based on a person's gender non-conforming behavior is impermissible discrimination, irrespective of the cause of that behavior; a label, such as "transsexual," is not fatal to a sex discrimination claim where the victim has suffered discrimination because of his or her gender non-conformity.[32]

Similarly, in 2011, the Eleventh Circuit Court of Appeals ruled in favor of a transgender woman who had been terminated from her job in *Glenn v. Brumby* (663 F.3d 1312 [11th Cir. 2011]). The court determined that the plaintiff had been terminated because she was transitioning from male to female, and that this was tantamount to sex discrimination because she had been fired for her failure to conform to sex stereotypes consistent with the *Price Waterhouse* precedent. "The court further concluded that discrimination based on sex stereotypes is subject to heightened scrutiny under the Equal Protection Clause, and government termination of a transgender person for his or her gender nonconformity is unconstitutional sex discrimination."[33]

In both *Smith* and *Glenn v. Brumby*, the courts held that discriminating against an individual because of his or her "gender nonconformity" constitutes a Title VII violation, and in doing so determined that Smith and Glenn could not be penalized for being gender nonconforming *males*. In each case, the transitioning individual is understood to be a member of their sex as assigned at birth as opposed to a transgender woman, thereby suggesting that they are men who are being penalized for presenting as feminine. While these court victories are significant, this legal reasoning fundamentally misrepresents the identities of Smith and Glenn. As Diane Schroer, a transgender woman who won a Title VII employment discrimination case *Schroer v. Billington* (577 F. Supp. 2d 293, District Court, District of Columbia 2008) explains, "I haven't gone through all this only to have a court vindicate my rights as a gender non-conforming man."[34] Instead, Schroer wants to be legally recognized as a woman consistent with how she identifies herself, but this requires judges to move beyond an immutable sex binary—e.g., if an individual is assigned the male sex at birth he is always a male—toward more complicated understandings of sex and gender.[35]

In Schroer's case, the court ruled that Title VII prohibitions on workplace discrimination "because of sex" are analogous to those "because of religion," and as long as employers cannot rescind a job offer if someone converts from one religion they also cannot do so if one changes their sex. In doing so, the court recognized that individuals may change their gender identities and determined that Title VII prohibitions on "sex" discrimination include gender identity, which is a more expansive interpretation than prior courts' reliance on *Price Waterhouse*'s prohibitions on sex stereotypes. This holding is a significant landmark in the fight for trans rights, and the combined effect of the aforementioned victories for trans plaintiffs suggests that a legal strategy predicated on *Price Waterhouse* and its progeny may be a viable way for trans individuals to challenge employment discrimination via litigation.

At the same time, however, while attempts to challenge discrimination against trans individuals on the grounds that such differential treatment is akin to sex discrimination have been more successful in recent years, there are both practical and theoretical limitations to this approach. For example, litigation strategies predicated on prohibitions on sex discrimination are limited to those areas where laws explicitly prohibit discrimination on the basis of sex (e.g., employment and education), and cannot reach the broad array of locations and spaces where such protections do not exist and many trans individuals are particularly vulnerable to violence and exploitation. In addition, the success of this litigation strategy remains dependent on the discretion of elite judicial actors and their willingness to recognize discrimination against trans individuals as sex discrimination. Given that the U.S. Supreme Court has yet to issue a single opinion in a trans rights case, this means that there is variation across the district and circuit courts as well as state and local laws, and many trans individuals remain vulnerable to discrimination in spite of these circuit court victories.

Furthermore, there is uncertainty about the viability of utilizing prohibitions on sex discrimination to protect trans individuals in the current changing political and legal climates. While trans litigants making sex discrimination claims have had some successes in the lower federal courts, the election of Donald J. Trump and his subsequent ability to reshape the courts and the federal bureaucracy complicate this strategy going forward. To date, President Trump's judicial nominations have shifted the ideological composition of the U.S. Supreme Court to the right, and he has nominated, and the U.S. Senate has confirmed, a record number of appellate court judges.[36] While a nominating president's party identification is no guarantee of a judge's ideological predisposition, President Trump has worked closely with the conservative Federalist Society to generate his nominees to the federal courts, resulting in the confirmation of individuals who are overwhelmingly young and conservative thereby suggesting that the federal courts may actually become less hospitable to the rights claims of trans litigants in the years ahead.

In addition, President Trump has taken concrete steps to reduce protections for trans individuals during his time in office, including rescinding the Obama administration's executive orders that sought to treat discrimination against trans individuals as sex discrimination under Title VII and Title IX and ordering a halt to transgender military service. Under the Obama administration, the Equal Employment Opportunity Commission (EEOC) issued guidance and supported employee litigation prohibiting discrimination on the basis of gender identity consistent with the Title VII's prohibitions on sex discrimination,[37] and the Obama Justice Department supported transgender students in their attempts to gain access to public facilities in schools via Title IX as exemplified by its support of Gavin Grimm, a transgender male, in his litigation against the Gloucester County School Board for its refusal to allow him to use the boys' restroom at his high school.[38] The Obama Justice Department's brief filed in the District Court on behalf of Gavin Grimm stated: "Under Title IX, discrimination based on a person's gender identity, a person's transgender status, or a person's nonconformity to sex stereotypes constitutes discrimination based on sex. As such, prohibiting a student from accessing the restrooms that match his gender identity is prohibited sex discrimination under Title IX."[39] Shortly after taking office, however, President Trump rescinded the Obama administration's Title IX guidance, and this decision led the U.S. Supreme Court to return *Gloucester County School Board v. GG* to the Fourth Circuit Court of Appeals to be reconsidered in light of the Trump administration's Title IX interpretation. In May 2018, the federal district court relied on *Price Waterhouse* to rule that Title IX's prohibitions on "sex" discrimination include sex stereotyping and gender nonconformity, and determined that the school district violated Title IX when it refused to allow Grimm to use the boys' restroom. Unfortunately, by the time the district court reached this conclusion Grimm had graduated from high school, and this litigation remains ongoing.

These machinations demonstrate the precarious nature of the current processes for protecting transgender youth via Title IX because enforcement is too easily contingent upon the political predispositions of the governing party. In fact, in October 2018, the Department of Health and Human Services (HHS) initiated efforts to define "sex" as "a person's status as male or female based on immutable biological traits identifiable by or before birth" for purposes of Title IX.[40] Furthermore, HHS proposes that "[t]he sex listed on a person's birth certificate, as originally issued, shall constitute definitive proof of a person's sex unless rebutted by reliable genetic evidence."[41] While the EEOC has not changed course on Title VII at this time, the Trump Justice Department (DOJ) has argued that Title VII's prohibitions on sex discrimination do not extend to transgender individuals, creating a rift between the EEOC and the DOJ on this issue that may need to be resolved by the U.S. Supreme Court.

All of that being said, while it may be possible to pursue and achieve the extension of legal rights to trans communities under the auspices of sex discrimination law, as demonstrated by the successful use of the *Price Waterhouse* precedent, this approach depends on judicial discretion and risks inadvertently reifying the sex binary. As the prior chapter demonstrates, the courts have a history of creating and validating binary categories of identity even when litigants argue for more complicated and nuanced identities, as exemplified by Justice Kennedy's erasure of bisexuals in *Romer v. Evans* (517 U.S. 620 [1996]) in favor of a gay/heterosexual binary, despite the fact that cities in Colorado specifically included protections for bisexuals in their laws. If the courts situate transgender individuals in the sex binary this is not only an inaccurate description of many trans individuals' sex and gender identities, but also fails to recognize the members of the population that are intersex or have sexually ambiguous or noncongruent sex features.[42] For example, intersex individuals are excluded from the sex binary and located outside of the legally and socially acceptable and recognized categories of male and female. The perpetuation of the binary myth ostracizes and erases intersex individuals thereby precluding the need for legal considerations and accommodations of this population's needs and interests.

According to the National Center for Transgender Equality's 2015 survey, 35 percent of the 27,715 respondents identified as nonbinary in comparison to 29 percent who identified as trans men and 33 percent as trans women, and privileging the sex binary over the complexity of gender identity works to erase these individuals from the legal discourse and policies.[43] In addition, some individuals do not want to be located in the male-female sex binary, and instead prefer to be identified as trans. "Such participants are resentful or upset by gender misreadings that nullify their cross-gender, trans, or genderqueer identities. While some transsexual interviewees want their gender identifications to be rendered intelligible *as* male *or* female, masculine *or* feminine, other trans interviewees—particularly those who identify as genderqueer—do not want to have any one single gender identity imposed upon their person."[44] These individuals are likely to remain located outside of the protections of sex discrimination laws if the courts maintain the rigidity of the sex binary. Thus, "[t]hose who seek to modify sex-classification policies to include transgender people wrongly presume that the discriminatory impact of sex classification policies on transgender-appearing people is exclusion from sex-classificatory schemes, when in fact the sex-classification schemes are the harm."[45]

Furthermore, the evolving medical research on sex, coupled with the growing understanding that sexual identity is more complex than the male-female binary, demonstrates that there are "[a] variety of factors [that] could contribute to determining whether an individual should be considered male or female for legal purposes. These factors include chromosomal sex, gonadal sex, external morphologic sex, internal morphologic sex, hormonal patterns, phenotype, assigned sex, and self-identified sex. . . . For the millions of individuals with incongruent or ambiguous sex features, however, legal institutions must establish which factor(s) will determine a person's legal sex."[46] The question, however, remains whether the best interests of intersex and trans individuals are furthered by legal actors and judges deciding which factors discussed above dictate male or female identity. Empowering judges to police the boundaries of identity is problematic, as discussed in chapter 1, and validates the existence of these socially constructed categories. As Cavanagh explains, cissexist cultures "are predicated on the idea that transsexual identities are inauthentic or inferior copies of those gender identities had by non-trans folk," and the expectation that legal professionals are able to accurately and objectively make these determinations is inaccurate.[47]

Finally, utilizing sex discrimination law as the means to legal protection has significant consequences for trans communities given that many individuals argue that sex is a social construct and not an immutable characteristic.[48] As Currah explains, many "transgender rights activists . . . reverse the traditional idea that gender is an expression of sexed bodies and instead identify gender identity as the prosocial fixed category."[49] In this way, "biological sex characteristics are cast as aspects of genders, and largely mutable ones at that."[50] When trans activists argue that sex is "assigned" at birth and is not an immutable characteristic, they are positing sex as a malleable identity that challenges the hierarchical dichotomy of male-female that government and society use as an organizational and privileging mechanism.

While the medical community has come to understand that sex is much more complex than the binary categories of male and female, efforts to maintain sex as an unambiguous dichotomy are prevalent across myriad formal and informal institutions in the United States, including the courts. Recognizing "as political the very terms through which identity is articulated," there will be concerted opposition to deconstructing the sex binary from those who derive its benefits and it will be difficult for a marginalized community to overcome this resistance.[51] At the same time, if successful, such strategies must take care to avoid replacing the immutable sex binary with an immutable gender binary thereby replicating the constraints associated with traditional identity politics. The recognition of gender as an independent category of identity would enhance legal protections for trans individuals, but those benefits would be limited in distribution and application if it is operationalized by the courts as a binary.

For example, the argument that individuals should be able to utilize their gender identities to dictate their sex identities may still work in effect to validate the sex binary, with costs for those who do not identify as "male" or "female" as well as those who embrace a more fluid conception of gender identity.[52] The cis-trans binary misrepresents gender as a stable binary identity that is both inaccurate and discriminatory because it erases the identities and experiences of those who do not easily fit into one of the two categories.[53] In addition, the increased use of the term *cisgender* problematizes analyses of gender because it suggests that "one *is* 'born a woman' after all," and thereby privileges cisgender status with significant consequences.[54] As Enke explains, "It is hard to overstate how dramatically sex/gender congruence, legibility, and consistency within a binary gender system buy a privileged pass to social existence, particularly when accompanied by the appearance of normative race, class, ability, and nationality. The term 'cisgender' was to name that privileged pass."[55] Similarly, cissexual privilege works to mark trans women and trans men as trans, as opposed to allowing them to simply identify themselves as women and men, or locate themselves outside of the sex and gender binaries.[56] Furthermore, the cis-trans binary facilitates the use of language that identifies some individuals as biologically male or biologically female while marking trans individuals as unnatural.[57]

Consequently, attempts to advance trans rights by working within the parameters of existing sex discrimination laws and precedents are constrained by the collective imaginations and socioeconomic and sociocultural interests and prejudices of governing elites. Based on prior civil rights jurisprudence, the evidence suggests that judges are likely to reify the sex binary and promulgate a politics of right sex. Similarly, lobbying to have prohibitions on discrimination on the basis of gender added to the "alliance politics" of race, sex, and sexual orientation runs the risk of inadvertently expanding the problematic reach of binary identities in ways that will be disadvantageous for certain facets of the trans community.[58] For example, this approach inadvertently may validate "the orthodoxy of 'sex-as-genitalia,'" and exclude trans individuals who do not want to or cannot change their genitalia to match their preferred gender identity as well as gender nonconforming individuals who may not wish to identify as either female or male or be forced to choose one sex as their permanent identity.[59]

The Complexity and Fluidity of Gender

In contrast, a movement that emphasizes the fluidity of both sex and gender and prioritizes a strategy of self-determination as opposed to elite recognition may be better positioned to problematize the binary as a starting point for a trans politics of rights, thereby avoiding the transnormative pitfalls that derive from a politics of right sex and distinguishing it from prior rights-based social movements via the move away from binary immutable characteristics. Yet, any attempts to advance the understanding and recognition of sex and gender in all of their complexities must first draw attention to the myriad ways those with power are implicated in the sociolegal construction of sex and the enforcement of a sex binary that is advantageous to their interests, including the role that the courts play in this process. It is only then that we can truly understand how the efforts of trans activists to craft creative ways to pursue their interests within the confines of existing sex discrimination jurisprudence or a new jurisprudence of gender are limited by the strategic interests of political and legal elites who are deeply invested in the maintenance of the status quo and its associated binary categories of identity.

As Butler explains, "Inasmuch as 'identity' is assured through the stabilizing concepts of sex, gender, and sexuality, the very notion of 'the person' is called into question by the cultural emergence of those 'incoherent' or 'discontinuous' gendered beings who appear to be persons but who fail to conform to the gendered norms of cultural intelligibility by which persons are defined."[60] The sex and gender binaries become regulatory mechanisms for identifying and excluding those individuals who fail to conform to "gendered norms" from the realm of "persons." These binary methods of categorization are invaluable tools for dominant groups because they are the means by which certain bodies become marked as transgressive bodies, and suggest that dominant populations may be more receptive to a politics of right sex than attempts to recognize and protect the spectrum of gender identities. As Ward explains, "Numerous critical and race theorists have pointed to the ways in which identities themselves function as sites of discipline, or systems of categorization that neatly package similarities and differences in ways that enable dominant groups and institutions to control what counts as legitimate claims of knowledge or claims of rights."[61]

As such, individuals' abilities to self-determine their gender identities are constrained by myriad neoliberal forces, and the ability to freely exercise individual choice is restricted by laws and regulations and by market forces as well.[62] Thus, those with power are not interested in "confounding the very binarism of sex, and exposing its fundamental unnaturalness."[63] To the contrary, they are invested in the maintenance of binary identities because they simultaneously maintain the status quo and obfuscate the recognition of the dynamism of identities. This is because "heteronormativity is dependent upon a means of sorting bodies into two divergent and mutually exclusive gender locales. Male is to masculinity as female is to femininity, and the normative concord underpins the institution of heterosexuality."[64] As such, any attempt to empower individuals to engage in gender self-determination is likely to be met with profound resistance.

Thus, advocating for a trans politics of rights that extends legal protections to trans individuals on the basis of sex or gender identity will likely confront the same limitations encountered by prior civil rights movements due to the inherent constraints associated with seeking the recognition and expansion of rights via the hegemonic powers. Instead, it is necessary to first draw attention to the myriad forces of governmentality that operate on transgressive bodies in order to assign costs and benefits and effectively work as tools of social control and population management, as will be demonstrated in chapters 3, 4, and 5 to follow. It is only when the constraints of the hegemonic system are made clear and understood as reaching beyond the formal mechanisms of the state and law that there will be discursive space to challenge the regulatory norms of "sex" in favor of empowering individuals to exercise self-determination. As Angela Davis reminds us, "We are interested not in race and gender (and class and sexuality and disability) per se, by themselves, but primarily as they have been acknowledged as conditions for hierarchies of power, so that we can transform them into intertwined vectors of freedom."[65] Absent discussion, recognition, and challenges to governmentality, law will continue to change in response to rights claims but only to the extent allowed by those with power and privilege, and the disciplinary power of binary identities is likely to remain. Thus, when push comes to shove, the hegemonic powers may sanction a transgender politics of right sex that preserves the sex and gender binaries as privileging mechanisms and limits the expansion of rights to some trans individuals but not others.

Yet, as Butler explains:

> If identities were no longer fixed as the premises of a political syllogism, and politics no longer understood as a set of practices derived from the alleged interests that belong to a set of ready-made subjects, a new configuration of politics would surely emerge from the ruins of the old. Cultural configurations of sex and gender might then proliferate or, rather, their present proliferation might then become articulable within the discourses that establish intelligible cultural life, confounding the very binarism of sex, and exposing its fundamental unnaturalness.[66]

Explicitly challenging the fixity of gender identity would undermine the transnormative tendencies of a politics of right sex. Understanding that governing binaries are instrumental to identity politics, Currah explains that many transgender "activists are working to 'dis-establish' gender from the state by ending the state's authority to police the relation between one's legal sex assigned at birth, one's gender identity, and one's gender expression; by attempting to stop the state's use of 'sex' as a marker of identity on identification documents; and by ending the state's reliance on sex as a legal category to distribute resources."[67] While approaches such as this are likely to meet with resistance because they pose an explicit threat to the status quo, they also have the greatest transformative potential because they limit the reach of the state *and* forces of governmentality.

Conclusion

Gender and sex are very complicated, and while the medical community increasingly has come to understand that sex and gender cannot easily be defined by biological factors alone, the law and courts continue to lag behind. One reason that the courts are slow to recognize and substantiate the complexities of sex and gender is that they operate under myriad institutional and political constraints. At the same time, however, it is important to recognize that the maintenance of the sex and gender binaries is an important facet of social control that works in tandem with other aspects of identity politics and neoliberalism in order to manage populations and assign costs and benefits, and the courts play an integral role in the maintenance of these systems by validating the status quo and fixating on the business of deducing one's "real" sex.[68] This fixation on "authenticity" of sex remains a powerful disciplinary force that acts as both a constraint on legal actors and a powerful resource for justifying the maintenance of the sex binary in legal proceedings. As such, within the legal system, future discussions and litigation are likely to result in judicial decisions that reify the sex binary via a politics of right sex that continues to focus on which "traditional criteria such as chromosomes, genitalia, and gonads [will be used] to define a person's legal sex."[69] Regardless of the best efforts of trans litigants to challenge these binary constructions in the courts, as long as these criteria remain the focus of judges' legal reasoning and analyses the sex binary will be maintained and rendered a viable legal framework, with particularly dire consequences for agender and gender-fluid individuals, intersex peoples, and intersectionally oppressed populations.

As trans scholars have demonstrated, the maintenance of the sex and gender binaries are important organizational mechanisms in contemporary American society and they play an integral role in the privileging of those who are easily located in the categories of male and female while simultaneously sanctioning the marginalization and othering of those who are not. Rather than creating and reifying new categories of identity, the trans critique encourages us to revisit the categories of male and female, man and woman to understand that "those terms are no less constructed than *transgender* itself, and they circulate transnationally in discourse and analysis with no less risk of being conceptually colonizing. What new understandings of vitality and diversity of bodily being, we ask, might emerge from putting as much pressure on the categories of *man, woman,* and *homosexuality* as *transgender*?"[70]

As demonstrated in the foregoing analysis, situating discrimination against trans individuals within the confines of sex discrimination comes with pros—transgender individuals may win their individual cases—and cons—this strategy risks reifying the sex binary and excluding those who do not fit or identify as male or female. Similarly, attempts to get gender recognized as a distinct category of identity may expand the legal protections available to trans individuals, but they risk operationalizing gender as a binary identity—cisgender versus transgender—and creating a new problematic and exclusionary category in identity politics. Thus, pursuing rights recognition based on sex or gender is challenging because these strategies are unlikely to result in accurate and encompassing recognitions of sex and/or gender as complex and fluid categories, and risk reifying extant and/or new identity politics. In fact, "[a] transgender rights framework demanding inclusion and recognition within the institutions, norms, and arrangements structured around gender could be described, if it has not already, as 'trans-normative.'"[71] Throughout U.S. history, the pursuit of rights and social respectability have required normalizing populations via the "purging of social undesirables," as demonstrated by the gay rights movement's homonormativity and subsequent purging of "genderqueer, transgender, transsexual, gender non-conforming, people of color and those who live and work on the street."[72] A trans politics of rights that intentionally or inadvertently privileges binary identities and enables a politics of right sex risks transnormativity and the purge of those who do not meet norms of social respectability.

In order to craft ways to make all trans people legible, as opposed to only those who fit within the categories of male and female, it is necessary to shift the analysis away from an exclusive focus on the legal realm and the courts in order to examine how the forces of governmentality described in the introduction work as tools that socially construct exclusive and restrictive categories of identity as mechanisms of social control and population management. Furthermore, it is necessary to elucidate how the recognition and conferral of rights works in tandem with forces of governmentality to maintain the subjection of transgressive bodies. "The urge to juridify identity in rights discourse and, moreover, to specify the contours of that identity with some precision means that rights discourse becomes not the neutral mechanism for achieving liberation for oppressed social groups, but rather the occasion for constituting those groups and subjecting them to modes of surveillance and control."[73] As the analyses in the following three chapters will make clear, attempts to maintain the sex binary and police the boundaries of gender implicate myriad forces of social control and population management ranging from the state to social actors and formal regulations to informal disciplinary mechanisms. Chapter 3 examines how government regulations regarding gender markers on identity documents enable both the state and social actors to enforce the sex binary and mark individuals who deviate from sexed and gendered norms as transgressive at best and deny their existence at worst. Chapter 4 investigates how de jure and de facto policing of the sex binary in public restrooms further locates and constrains transgressive bodies' access to public spaces. Finally, chapter 5 explores how the selective enforcement of solicitation laws on transgressive bodies effectively removes those that dare to enter into public spaces. The combined effects of these formal and informal disciplinary measures are forces of governmentality that act in concert with and in the shadow of the law to privilege some and marginalize others.

Part Two

Governmentality

Chapter 3

The Illegibility of Trans Bodies

How the Mandatory Reporting of Gender Markers on Identity Documents Facilitates Governmentality

Introduction

This chapter examines state and national laws governing gender markers on official government identification documents and the implications of these policies for trans individuals. There is great variation among the states regarding one's ability to change gender markers on state-issued identity documents, including birth certificates and driver's licenses, and some states require that sex reassignment surgery has been performed, which is not only cost prohibitive and especially burdensome for the poor and intersectionally subjected, but also unwanted by many trans individuals. These costly and burdensome requirements are not merely bureaucratic obstacles to be remedied, but rather reflect institutionalized processes for denying and delegitimating the existence of trans bodies. First, the state denies trans individuals recognition, and then it facilitates increased public scrutiny of those trans individuals who enter and/or attempt to navigate the public sphere. Gender-incongruent documentation exposes trans individuals to violence and discrimination across different venues including the workplace, schools, housing, places of public accommodation, the banking and credit industries, and so on. In this way, forces of governmentality work to force trans individuals to conform to conventional sex norms by denying their identities or in some instances by mandating permanent relocation in the male-female binary consistent with a politics of right sex. Those who fail to comply are then marked as illegible and located outside of the legally recognized domain of the state and/or subject to increased public scrutiny that simultaneously renders trans people as "administratively impossible"[1] and/or a "queer security threat."[2]

This chapter begins with a brief introduction to the idea that the sex and gender binaries have becoming powerful regulatory norms before proceeding to a discussion of how individuals are assigned a sex at birth based on their external genitalia and the challenges associated with trying to change this designation. Then, attention shifts to how the regulation of sex and gender markers on identity documents works to empower a broad array of individuals to police gender and facilitate governmentality. Incongruence between one's gendered presentation and gender markers enables administrators to make trans individuals administratively impossible and/or mark them as queer security threats. This chapter concludes with a discussion of how government-issued identity documents facilitate and privilege gender normativity and render trans individuals, particularly intersectionally subjected trans individuals, as illegible and vulnerable to social, political, and economic mistreatment.

The Regulatory Norms of the Sex and Gender Binaries

One of the most powerful mechanisms for maintaining the sex and gender binaries is via state regulation and control of identity documents. Both the national and state governments surveil the population and control access to a broad array of resources via the issuance of birth certificates, passports, driver's licenses, and Social Security records. In addition, individuals are regularly asked or required to locate themselves in the male-female binary when completing a broad array of administrative forms, including banking and loan documents, medical intake forms, applications for housing, education, and so on.[3] Furthermore, one's sex as recorded and reported on the aforementioned documents determines one's access to a variety of public places that are sex segregated and resources that are predicated on one's sex.

While Butler has argued that the gendered subject is a "regulatory fiction," the bureaucratic regulation and reification of the gender binary remains a powerful means of disciplinary power that facilitates governmentality.[4] Via "hierarchical surveillance, continuous registration, perpetual assessment and classification," the universal widespread panopticisms of disciplinary power are able to "substitute for a power that is manifested through the brilliance of those who exercise it, a power that insidiously objectifies those on whom it is applied; to form a body of knowledge about these individuals, rather than to deploy the ostentatious signs of sovereignty."[5] In this way, the disciplinary force of gender radiates far beyond one's sex as recorded on identity documents to empower a broad array of formal and informal actors to insidiously objectify those onto whom it is applied.

Recognizing that "[g]ender has been so deeply naturalized—as immutable, as easily apprehended, and as existing before and outside of political arrangements—for so long that its installation in identity verification practices is taken for granted,"[6] the administrative codification of sex disciplines those who seek to deviate from the categories as prescribed by law and society in the interest of maintaining the hegemonic power structure while simultaneously furthering no legitimate policy goals that could not be advanced through other means.[7] Opposition to allowing individuals to change their sex as assigned at birth reflects the state's and society's investments in the maintenance of the sex binary as discussed in the prior two chapters. At the same, time, however, it is important to interrogate why the state needs to record individuals' gender markers on identity documents in the first place. As Davis argues:

> Not only can legitimate goals such as fraud prevention, safety, security, and privacy be met by alternative means, but also, and even more damning, there is no objective, socially agreed upon test for determining who is male and who is female. Hence, there is no way of ever enforcing sex-classification policies in a "rational," i.e., consistent way. And because gender perception is never race or class neutral, the subjective administration of sex-classification policies always raises the specter of intersectional gender judgments that are also irrelevant to legitimate policy goals, no matter their content or moral valence. I do not presume that every, or even most administrative agents wield their power to inspect and evaluate gender in discriminatory ways. The problem is that sex-classification policies prompt and permit such invidious treatment. If we cannot come up with good reasons for subjecting people to such caprice where something as personal as their sex identity and as crucial as their civil rights are concerned, then we have no business inspecting anyone's gender in the first place.[8]

As long as the state and society continue to insist that individuals' genders must be reported on their identity documents, some bodies will be normalized and others will be marked as transgressive or problem bodies, making them more vulnerable to myriad forces of governmentality. "Nothing short of the elimination of this communicative relation will alter the deep social mechanism that prohibits transpeople from existing within dominant mainstream with any authenticity at all."[9]

As the following analysis will make clear, the correlation between one's documents and one's gender identity designates an individual as a legible subject of the state entitled to the benefits that accrue to those bodies that matter. In contrast, incongruences between one's documents and one's identity mark an individual as illegible and substantiate the denial of both recognition as a subject and the associated benefits, services, and obligations to which legible bodies are entitled. While allowing transgender people to change their sex/gender marker on identity documents may work to make them more legible, the maintenance of the sex and gender binaries and the associated sanctioning of the government's and society's surveillance of sex means that trans individuals who do not identify as male or female or who identify as gender fluid will continue to be rendered illegible. Furthermore, trans individuals who fail to conform with gendered expectations about femininity and masculinity, presentation of self, and voice may continue to be read as incongruent and illegible by a broad array of actors even after the former have successfully changed their sex/gender markers on their identity documents.

The Assignment of Sex

In the United States, the sex recorded on one's birth certificate at the time of birth becomes one's official sex designation. This categorization is based on the external genitalia of newborn babies and marks the first instance in which "the orthodoxy of 'sex-as-genitalia'" is imposed on our bodies.[10] Despite the fact that some individuals' gender identities may not match their unambiguous genitalia, an additional issue is that some individuals are born with ambiguous genitalia. Oftentimes, parents of newborns with ambiguous genitalia follow the lead of medical professionals and make sex assignment decisions according to sex-role stereotypes.[11]

> The presence of an "adequate" penis in an XY infant leads to the label *male*, while the absence of an "adequate" penis leads

> to the label *female*. A genetic (XY) male with an "inadequate" penis (one that physicians believe will be incapable of penetrating a female's vagina when the child reaches adulthood) is "turned into" a female even if it means destroying his reproductive capacity. A genetic (XX) female who may be capable of reproducing, however, is generally assigned the female sex to preserve her reproductive capability, regardless of the appearance of her external genitalia. If her phallus is considered to be too large to meet the guidelines for a typical clitoris, it is surgically reduced, even if it means that her capacity for satisfactory sex may be reduced or destroyed. In other words, men are defined based on their ability to penetrate females, and females are defined based on their ability to procreate.[12]

As disturbing as this discussion may be, Greenberg concludes with a powerful recognition that "[s]ex, therefore, can be viewed as a social construct rather than a biological fact."[13] In this sense, even those individuals born with unambiguous genitalia are still being assigned a "sex" based on a socially constructed male-female binary sex identity. As discussed in the prior chapter, many trans activists and scholars similarly argue that sex is a social construct and that biological sex characteristics are mutable.[14]

Yet, despite this recognition, the state and society continue to police the sex binary and require that individuals be legally and socially situated in the categories of male and female. Approximately 0.6 percent of American adults, or 1.4 million people, are estimated to identify as trans.[15] While this is not a large portion of the population, both state and national governments have resisted attempts to allows trans individuals to easily change the gender markers on their identity documents, and there is little movement to remove these markers altogether. Today, the national government allows individuals to change their gender on Social Security records, U.S. passports, and immigration documents subject to certain verifications, but there is great variation among the states.[16] For example, in 2019, the National Center for Transgender Equality issued ten different grades ranging from A-plus to F to the U.S. states and territories for their different policies on changing gender markers on driver's licenses demonstrating the broad array of policies or their absence; four states and four territories have no written or clear policy directive.[17] Notably, while a handful of states included a gender-neutral option, nearly all of the states still require individuals to situate themselves in the male-female binary. Furthermore, ten states still require that individuals provide proof of gender reassignment surgery, a court order, or an amended birth certificate in order to change their gender identity marker on their driver's licenses. While modest progress has been made in recent years, the fact that states issue many citizens' primary identity documents—birth certificates and driver's licenses—allows for fifty different approaches to requests for changes to these documents, including varying restrictions on both name and gender marker changes.

Furthermore, extant research suggests that when birth certificate amendment laws were perceived as remedies to technical bureaucratic problems they were able to pass in both liberal and conservative states, but the growing political salience of trans rights and their affiliation with lesbian and gay rights movements may lead conservatives to coalesce against birth certificate amendment laws at the state level consistent with their mobilization against gay rights.[18] In this way, the growth of a trans rights movement may make some states less hospitable to legislative and statutory changes that make it easier for individuals to change their names and sex/gender markers on their identity documents.

In order to legally change one's name, a court order is often required, but the rules regarding who may get court orders and under what conditions vary from state to state,[19] and "[u]pdating the gender marker on any ID or record is typically a distinct process from updating the name, and may require documentation regarding gender transition from a healthcare provider, a court order of gender change, an updated birth certificate, or other documentation."[20] To date, some of the greatest resistance has accompanied individuals' attempts to change gender markers on birth certificates, and the majority of states still require that an individual have gender reassignment surgery in order to make this change.[21] Furthermore, many states mark the new birth certificates as amended and specifically note that the gender marker was changed; a practice that outs many transgender individuals.[22] In addition, according to the NCTE survey, individuals face the greatest resistance when they seek to change their name on their birth certificate in comparison to doing so on other identity documents; 6 percent of respondents who sought a name change on their birth certificates reported that they were denied the ability to do so.[23]

The National Center for Transgender Equality survey in 2015 reports that "[o]nly 11% of respondents reported that all of their IDs had the name and gender they preferred, while more than two-thirds (68%) reported that none of their IDs had the name and gender they preferred."[24] Of those who possessed identification and wanted to update their identities, respondents reported that they had greater success updating their names than their gender markers across all forms of identity: 44 percent changed their names on their driver's licenses, whereas only 29 percent were able to change their gender markers on these documents; 43 percent changed their names on their Social Security records, in comparison to 23 percent who changed their gender markers on these documents; 28 percent changed their names on their passports, in comparison to 18 percent who changed their gender markers; and 18 percent changed their names on their birth certificates, in comparison to 9 percent who changed their gender markers.[25] The discrepancy between the number of individuals who would like to change their names and gender markers and the number of individuals who are actually able to do so reflects a broad array of factors. Obstacles that individuals confront include the costs associated with transitioning and/or pursuing document changes, and the fact that some individuals have no interest in medically transitioning and hence are unable to meet the legal requirements for changing one's documents. The elimination of mandatory sex reporting on identity documents would alleviate these obstacles and enable people to self-identify sex and gender (or not) free from government surveillance and control.[26]

Prohibitive Costs: The Financial and Personal Burdens Associated with Changing Identity Documents

The costs for changing one's identity documents are prohibitive for many individuals. According to the NCTE survey, "35% of those who have not changed their legal name and 32% of those who have not updated the gender on their IDs reporting that it was because they could not afford it."[27] While it is easier to meet the legal requirements necessary to change one's name, this process entails a variety of different fees, including the costs associated with hiring legal counsel/assistance, court fees, and the money one must spend announcing their name change in the newspaper, sometimes multiple times, as is required by many state laws.[28] Twenty-seven percent of those who responded to the NCTE survey that they had successfully changed their names reported that it cost less than $100, 55 percent reported that it cost $100–$499, and 10 percent reported that it cost $500–$2,000.[29]

Understanding that many states require that individuals transition into the "right" sex—requirements vary from state to state with many mandating sex reassignment surgery, whereas others require that individuals undergo hormone conversion—in order to legally change their gender markers on identity documents, the costs are even greater for these individuals than for those that pursue a name change alone. These costs help to explain why only one-quarter of respondents to the NCTE survey had undergone some form of transition-related surgery.[30] Among these respondents, 42 percent of transgender men had some kind of surgery, in comparison to 28 percent of transgender women and 9 percent of nonbinary individuals.[31] Similarly, with respect to hormone therapy related to gender transition, 78 percent of NCTE respondents wanted hormone therapy but only 49 percent had ever received it.[32]

While there are different explanations for these variations, one thing that is clear is that financial means plays a role in determining whether or not one has access to and/or pursues surgery. Those NCTE respondents "living in poverty (17%) were less likely to have had any surgery as were those who had low incomes. Respondents who were uninsured (18%) were also less likely to have any surgery, while those who were insured through Medicare only were most likely (44%)."[33] Many trans individuals do not have access to adequate health care and/or insurance coverage to begin with, thereby making it extremely difficult to pursue transition-related medical support, and many states prohibit trans individuals from using Medicaid funds to pay for care related to trans health issues.[34] "Among people of color, Black (20%), American Indian (18%), and Latino/a (17%) respondents were more likely to be uninsured. Respondents who were not U.S. citizens were more likely to be uninsured, including nearly one-quarter (24%) of documented non-citizens and a majority (58%) of undocumented residents" in comparison to 12% of white respondents.[35]

Among those who have health insurance, 25 percent of NCTE survey respondents reported a problem with their insurance in the past year related to being transgender, including 55 percent of those who sought transition-related surgery coverage, who were denied, and 25 percent of those who requested that hormone treatments be covered, who also were denied.[36] One individual explained, "My state Medicaid does not cover hormones or surgeries. With my very limited income, it is difficult to afford the treatment I need and I will most likely never be able to have surgeries."[37] These financial obstacles are significant because the inability to transition often makes it impossible to legally change one's sex/gender marker on identity documents.

All of these factors are noteworthy because transitioning increases the likelihood that one will be able to change their gender on their identity documents. "For example, 29% of the overall sample have updated the gender on their driver's license, while 42% of those who have transitioned updated the gender marker on their driver's license. Transgender men and women who had transitioned (52%) were much more likely to have updated the gender on their driver's license, in contrast to non-binary respondents who had transitioned (9%)."[38]

At the same time, many people do not want to undergo sex reassignment surgery. Given that many states necessitate sex reassignment surgery in order to change one's sex marker on their birth certificate, this requirement acts as an obstacle for many individuals. "Eighty-eight percent (88%) of non-binary individuals who indicated that none of their IDs or records had the gender they preferred reported that it was because the available gender options (male or female) did not fit their gender identity, in contrast to 4% of transgender men and women."[39] Mandating vaginoplasties for transwomen and phalloplasties for transmen is not only cost prohibitive as described above, but enables these states to use the law as a tool for forcing people into unwanted surgeries and body modifications and additionally prevents individuals from being able to select or exercise their self-affirmed identities. Furthermore, 25 percent of respondents who had not tried to change their gender identity said it was because they were worried that they might lose access to resources and services, and these needs interfered with their ability to transition.[40]

Thus, the state has imposed numerous obstacles that foreclose an individual's ability to legally change one's name and/or gender marker, and it is clear that the state is invested in the maintenance and regulation of the sex binary and continuing the mandatory reporting of sex as an essential identity marker. Yet, it would be inaccurate to conclude that the legal requirements and obstacles to changing one's name and gender marker are the extent of the harm that is imposed on trans people. Recognizing that these institutional barriers impose great costs is not sufficient for understanding how onerous and nefarious the mandatory reporting of gender is for trans individuals. In order to get the full measure, it is essential to examine how these formal institutional constraints enable and facilitate a broad array of state and social actors to target trans individuals for discrimination and infrahumanization. It is the synergies among state and social actors and actions that constitute the full force of governmentality that operates on trans people to deny their recognition and sanction their removal from the public.

The Regulation of Identity on Documents Is a Tool of Governmentality

As one transgender woman put it, "I do not suffer from gender dysphoria. I suffer from bureaucratic dysphoria."[41] This statement effectively summarizes the experiences of many trans individuals who are completely aware of and secure in their gender, but are prevented from accessing identity documents that reflect their gender identity. While denying individuals the ability to possess identity documents that reflect their accurate names and identities is a facet of state control, this works in tandem with myriad forms of public scrutiny to subject trans people to forces of governmentality.

At the most basic level, incongruent identity documents subject individuals to public scrutiny, which has a chilling effect that limits the actions and movements of trans people who may be fearful of the discrimination and harassment that accompanies public scrutiny and go to great lengths to avoid situations and locales that subject them to said scrutiny.[42] At the same time, however, individuals cannot avoid all types of scrutiny. Via the social construction of administrative impossibilities and gender securitization, trans individuals are rendered illegible. These processes for denying the existence of trans people render them vulnerable to infrahumanization by interfering with their ability to secure employment and housing, access public services and benefits, and move freely in the public realm. For example, compliance with gender norms interacts in powerful ways with the U.S. capitalist economy to control access to the workforce.[43] Trans individuals confront numerous obstacles when seeking employment if and when their sex as reported by the Social Security Administration fails to match the sex on their driver's licenses thereby complicating their lives at best and jeopardizing their employment at worst.[44]

When trans people are unemployed and in need of services, public scrutiny often excludes them from much needed assistance. As Spade reports:

> When I met Bianca, she was homeless and unemployed and was trying to escape from an abusive relationship. She was afraid to go to the police both because of the retaliation of her

> boyfriend and because she rightly feared that the police would react badly to her because of her transgender status. Her IDs all said her male name and gender, and there would be no way for her to seek police protection without being identified as transgender. As we searched for places for Bianca to live, we ran up against the fact that all the homeless shelters would only place her according to birth gender, so she would be a woman in an all-men's facility, which she rightly feared would be unsafe and uncomfortable. Women's shelters for domestic violence were unwilling to take her because they did not recognize her as a woman.[45]

As a transgender woman with a male name and an M on her identity documents, Bianca was unable to report her abuse to law enforcement and could not secure temporary shelter without fear of mistreatment. By virtue of being rendered illegible, she was denied access to the public services available to others in her situation.

Fear of harassment or mistreatment by a broad array of actors constrains trans individuals. According to the NCTE survey, "Nearly one-third (32%) of respondents who have shown an ID with a name or gender that did not match their gender presentation were verbally harassed, denied benefits or service, asked to leave, or assaulted," but certain individuals within trans communities are more vulnerable than others to the de facto policing of gender that accompanies incongruent identification documents.[46] Those individuals that are intersectionally subjected are more vulnerable to mistreatment, as exemplified by the fact that Middle Eastern individuals (44%) and Native Americans (39%) were more likely to report these negative experiences.[47] Similarly, while 2 percent of respondents reported being assaulted or attacked after showing an identification document that did not match their gender, 9 percent of Middle Eastern, 6 percent of Native American, and 4 percent of Black respondents reported being assaulted or attacked.[48] These statistics demonstrate how people of color who are already marked as transgressive bodies find that their "otherness" and abnormalities are compounded when they also identify as trans. Similarly, 15 percent of undocumented residents reported being assaulted or attacked in comparison to 3 percent of documented residents and 2 percent of U.S. citizens.[49] These statistics reflect the extreme vulnerabilities of trans immigrants who often are unable to pursue recourse through the criminal justice or legal systems due to fears about their status within the

United States. Both documented and undocumented trans immigrants are vulnerable to incarceration and deportation when they interact with the legal system.

Finally, transwomen appear to be especially vulnerable to the risks associated with incongruent identification documents. According to the NCTE survey, 13 percent of transgender women reported being asked to leave a location after their identities were found to not match their documents in comparison to 9 percent of transgender men and 6 percent of nonbinary individuals.[50] Trans individuals' fears that they will be vulnerable to verbal or physical assaults work as forces of governmentality and infra law that regulate their movements and actions, and these fears and forces are exacerbated for intersectionally subjected trans individuals. For those individuals who dare to navigate public space, other disciplinary measures work to govern their movements and security.

Administrative Impossibilities and Queer Security Threats

In *Normal Life: Administrative Violence, Critical Trans Politics, and the Limits of Law*, Dean Spade examines the power that administrative classifications—including the rules that govern gender identification documents—have on trans people's lives, and identifies "laws and policies that produce systemic norms and regularities that make trans people's lives administratively impossible."[51] This administrative impossibility is exemplified by Heath Fogg Davis's analysis of the experiences of Charlene Arcila, a Black transwoman, who was denied service by the Southeastern Pennsylvania Transportation Authority (SEPTA) because individual bus operators concluded that her gender presentation did not conform with her gender marker on her city-issued bus pass.[52] Arcila was denied service when she attempted to utilize a bus pass that identified her as female and again when she attempted to utilize a bus pass that identified her as male.[53] Thus, Arcila was told that she is simultaneously not female and not male, with significant consequences:

> SEPTA's gender-sticker policy transfigured Arcila into a criminal suspect, someone who was summarily suspected, tried, and punished for trying to filch a bus trip. But that is subterfuge for what really happened in those moments, which is that

> bus operators used the gender-sticker policy as a pretext for conveying their personal disdain for Arcila's gender expression. Her "wrong" gender expression could not be corrected by using a male transit pass, as that, too, was rejected. To use Dean Spade's apt wording, Arcila became "administratively impossible," which made it administratively possible to take away her civil right to use the public transportation that she had paid for.[54]

Arcila's experience demonstrates how forces of governmentality work on trans people via the discretionary power of various social actors to control the access of individuals to public services and, subsequently, public spaces. In this instance, the power to determine who is and is not "administratively impossible" is not confined to the state in the issuing of government documents, but rather is simultaneously exercised across a broad array of informal and formal actors.

Similar factors are at work when a transwoman reports how she was unable to obtain a driver's license as follows: "I was intentionally misgendered and continually verbally harassed by DMV employees. Even after paying for proper identification to be issued, they refused to send the identification because my female photo didn't match my 'M' gender marker."[55] In this instance, this transwoman was not denied a driver's license that reflected her identity as a woman, but rather was denied a driver's license at all because her presentation of self did not correlate with the gender marker on her record. In a period of growing gender securitization in which identity documents are required to move freely across public spaces, as described below, the fact that this woman is "administratively impossible" greatly affects her ability to exist as a legible subject of the state, and renders her vulnerable to myriad forms of mistreatment.

The "War on Terror" instigated a variety of policies, ranging from the Transportation Security Administration's (TSA) Secure Flight program to Congress's Real ID legislation, that have increased government surveillance of the population. A central facet of these programs is the increased "securitization of identity" and the associated securitization of gender, which have myriad consequences for trans people.[56] For example, "Secure Flight" requires passengers to report their sex when purchasing airline tickets and the airlines must then convey this information to the TSA in order for it to compare passenger manifests to terrorist watch lists.[57] This government surveillance of gender subjects trans individuals whose gender presentations do not correlate to the gender reported on one's identity documents to increased scrutiny at airport security.[58] The use of 3-D X-ray body scanners in recent years has only exacerbated the scrutiny of trans bodies, and subsequently increased the anxiety experienced by trans people when traveling.[59] Statistics verify that airport security is a huge source of stress for trans people because of high rates of harassment, ridicule, and detention, and 43 percent of respondents to the National Center for Transgender Equality survey reported some form of mistreatment in the prior year.[60] These numbers were exacerbated for individuals who reported that none of their identity documents had their preferred name or gender, with 51 percent of these individuals reporting negative interactions with airport security.[61] This form of government surveillance exacts significant costs on trans people.

The state's failure to acknowledge and accommodate trans people sends a clear signal that these transgressive bodies are not worthy of state recognition. This is exemplified by the TSA's use of full body scanners that are operated by pink and blue buttons that the machine operator presses in order to initiate the appropriate body scanning protocol: pink for female and blue for male. "If a TSA officer presses the wrong button or if a passenger has body characteristics of more than one gender, unexpected body shapes may register as anomalies. These are considered potential threats and prompt an additional screening in the form of a pat-down."[62] In this way, trans bodies are operationalized as anomalous and as security threats. The discretion that is granted to TSA employees enables them to publicly identify these bodies as abnormal, thereby signaling to both trans individuals and the public that these bodies are problem bodies and that they constitute a threat because they do not conform to public expectations about gender congruence. The public flagging of individuals for additional scrutiny and possible interrogation in the context of airline security cannot be disentangled from questions of safety and the creation of a "queer security threat."[63] Ultimately, this public harassment and humiliation mitigates the ability of trans people to move and travel freely in the public. In this way, when states deny trans individuals the ability to be accurately recognized on their identity documents, it facilitates various forces of governmentality including, but not limited to, gender securitization.

Similarly, trans immigrants increasingly find themselves subject to state control as a result of increased surveillance of all immigrant populations. Post-9/11, state and national governments passed legislation intended to increase border security and identify undocumented immigrants within the United States in the interest of public safety.[64] One facet of these administrative policies was to utilize gender classification as a tool of population surveillance and management in order to flush out individuals with illegitimate identities.[65] While the national government has removed the surgical reassignment requirement for passports and Social Security documents, the federal Real ID Act (Pub.L. 109–13, 119 Stat. 302, 2005) requires gender markers on all state-issued identity documents and utilizes "batch checking" to ensure that one's identity is consistent across all government databases. This practice draws attention to any variation in one's gender marker across identity documents with significant consequences for trans individuals, in addition to raising privacy considerations. Furthermore, legislation such as the Real ID Act established federal minimum standards for all state-issued identification in the interest of guaranteeing that each individual has a single legal identity.[66] Yet, "Non-citizens, including undocumented residents (68%), were more likely to say that none of their IDs or records reflected the name they preferred. Respondents with lower incomes were also more likely to say that none of their IDs or records had the name they preferred."[67] As explained above, state laws governing gender markers on identity documents are idiosyncratic, resulting in confusion about one's gender identity for Real ID purposes as well as the outing of trans individuals.[68]

In this way, "the 'security' in securitization reflects forms of control associated with sovereign power—barriers, bans, prohibitions, punishments, searches by uniformed personnel, interrogations. But identity in general and gender in particular are also securitized in another sense—as a form of risk management, as techniques for 'governing the future,' " which is "a central mechanism of governmentality."[69] The securitization of gender works to pressure trans individuals to permanently relocate themselves in the sex binary and subsequently reifies gender as a fixed binary characteristic. In this way, gender securitization privileges those individuals who are able to demonstrate that their gender is a "unitary component of their identity" because their genitalia conform with their gendered presentation of self, or those who have documentation that can "attest to the permanence of the new gender in the future," will find it easier to navigate this space.[70] This surveillance interacts with one's gender identity, socioeconomic status, and immigrant status to make some trans bodies more vulnerable to governmentality than others.

The combined effect of these security laws is to expand the surveillance state, thereby increasing the likelihood that trans individuals will be subject to increased policing with significant costs for those who are unable to present congruent documents. In particular, the application of immigration laws to trans individuals can proactively exclude and/or retroactively remove trans immigrants from the United States because their presence poses a "queer security threat."[71] Notably, trans people of color are likely to be subject to racial profiling under new immigration laws because race is often used as a proxy for immigrant status.

Sex Reporting on Identity Documents Increases Intersectional Subjection of Trans Individuals

As the foregoing analysis makes clear, the costs associated with transitioning and/or changing one's documents make it difficult if not impossible for many individuals to change their bodies and/or their documents. These economic considerations interact with one's class, race, and immigrant status to make some trans individuals more vulnerable to forces of governmentality than others. In states where transition surgery is a requirement for changing one's sex/gender markers on identity documents, "[t]he surgery requirement would make legal sex—for transgender people, at least—a privileged category legally mediated by one's class status . . . [and] would mean, in effect, that one's legal sex would be dependent on one's location in the social structure. Bluntly put, only by purchasing the anatomical markers ($30,000–$50,000) meant to guarantee permanence could a transgender person meet the metric for legal sex reclassification"[72]

The socioeconomic marginalization and poverty that is a consequence of one's inability to conform with gendered norms then intersects with the fact that most social welfare programs and services are heavily gendered to further exacerbate the forces of governmentality that operate on trans people. Those who are intersectionally subjected because of the ways that class, race, and gender intersect will be more vulnerable to gender surveillance than others.[73]

> Employed people with stable housing are subjected to far fewer gender-segregated facilities on a daily basis than poor or homeless people. While we all must contend with bathrooms or locker rooms that are gender segregated, those of us with homes and jobs may even be able to avoid those a good deal of the time, as opposed to homeless people who must always use public facilities that are likely to be segregated and highly

> policed. Additionally, all of the essential services and coercive control institutions (jails, homeless shelters, group homes, drug treatment facilities, foster care facilities, domestic violence shelters, juvenile justice facilities, housing for the mentally ill) that increasingly dominate the lives of poor people and disproportionately people of color use gender segregation as a part of the gendered social control they maintain.[74]

As reported by the NCTE survey, "Sixteen percent (16%) of people who showed IDs with a name or gender that did not match the gender they present in were denied services or benefits. Transgender men and women were more likely to have been denied services or benefits (20%) compared to non-binary respondents (10%)."[75]

Identity Control and the Enforcement of Gender Normativity

Despite the fact that there are no objective criteria for determining who is male or female, social and state actors continue to insist on the construction and implementation of subjective measures in order to locate individuals in these two categories. This is because the public is invested in the maintenance and preservation of gender normativity, and utilizes forces of governmentality to enforce the sex and gender binaries. The requirement that individuals locate themselves in the categories of male and female based on the sex assigned at birth or relocate themselves in the sex binary based on a permanent transition serves two purposes. First, it denies the existence of individuals who are agender, gender fluid, and/or in transition by excluding them from access to legitimate identification and subsequent recognition as legible subjects of the state. In this way, those individuals who are "administratively impossible" or a "queer security threat" are rendered more vulnerable to containment and removal from public spaces if they dare to subject themselves to public scrutiny, as will be discussed in the next two chapters. Second, it does so in order to preserve the hierarchy of male-female and sustain a patriarchal and neoliberal system that is classed, raced, and gendered.

As demonstrated above, "[t]he political harm of sex-classification policies is that they transfer the crucial and deeply personal matter of sexual identity to administrative agents who then have the power to use their normative ideas about gender to deprive people of their civil right to use the public accommodations under their watch."[76] The power exercised by administrative agents in these instances, and other actors under similar circumstances, is an exercise of governmentality and requires that "[w]e should direct our researches on the nature of power not towards the juridical edifice of sovereignty, the State apparatuses and the ideologies which accompany them, but towards domination and the material operators of power, towards forms of subjection and the inflections and utilizations of their localized systems, and towards strategic apparatuses."[77] The subjective and discretionary power that is located in localized systems and strategic apparatuses allows for the ongoing subjection of trans individuals regardless of the role of the state. As previously described, when Charlene Arcila's city-issued bus pass identified her as female she was refused entrance to the bus because the bus operator identified her as "not female," but she was also denied admission when her bus pass identified her as male.[78] In this way, governmentality facilitates the maintenance of the sex binary by ostracizing and criminalizing those who do not conform. "Because of the systematic representational alignment between gender presentation and sexed body, transpeople are never allowed to be ourselves in the first place insofar as we are fundamentally constructed as deceivers/pretenders."[79]

Government actors offer various arguments for why one's gender must be reported on documents, but all explanations work to defend the maintenance of the sex binary. One of the most common explanations is that one's gender must be recorded in order to prevent fraud.[80] This argument privileges gender as a fixed and immutable characteristic, and pathologizes trans individuals by identifying them as deceptive and possibly criminal. The social construction of stereotypes and the associated criminalization of populations is a powerful tool of social control and governmentality as illustrated by the construction of Black criminality.[81] These social constructs sanction and legitimate increased public scrutiny of transgressive bodies and facilitate the normalization of those bodies deemed to matter. In these ways, "governmentality exceeds formal politics and is embedded in the social and cultural structures that become our collective and individual everyday habits."[82]

While official opposition to allowing individuals to change their sex markers has morphed over time—"the shift from viewing transsexuals as 'frauds' in 1965 to basing official recognition of gender transition around the notion of 'permanence' in 2005"—the latter privileges the sex and gender binaries as well.[83] These arguments validate the gender binary but sanction the one-time mutability of gender for those willing to transition in order to live permanently as one's "true" self. As such, one of the challenges associated with fighting to enable trans individuals to change their gender identity on official government documents is that this discourse often reifies the sex binary. As Currah and Moore explain in a discussion of the debates surrounding sex designations on birth certificates in New York City, transgender individuals "deployed arguments that seemed to re-naturalize gender as a legal category—albeit one based on gender identity rather than the body: 'I was assigned male at birth but I am now a woman. Get it right.' Or, 'I was born female but now I am a man. Fix that on my ID, please.' "[84] This strategy fulfills both personal and strategic goals: "The attempt by trans advocates to amend the criteria for legal sex designations resonates with the inescapably liberal quest to be recognized as possessors of the personal attributes we deem central to our selves. For transgender women, recognition means being 'Ma'amed' instead of 'Sir'ed,' having an 'F' rather than an 'M' on identity papers, and being housed in women's wings in hospitals, residential homes, and prisons."[85] In this way, transgender individuals are seeking both the power of recognition and the associated benefits of fitting within sanctioned identity categories.

At the same time, however, the requirement that individuals undergo sex reassignment surgery or submit to a permanent transition in order to change their sex markers on their birth certificates effectively maintains the sex binary and simultaneously excludes those who do not fit within these fixed categories of male and female moving forward.[86] "Instead of changing the criteria for markers on identity documents, officials insist that individuals change their bodies to align with the 'natural attitude.' In so doing, officials can retain the integrity of the ideological and discursive system. The sex/gender binary, which is in perpetual crisis, is actually preserved—not by the physiological requirements guaranteeing permanence and irreversibility, because they can't—but by the legal machinations the state requires of its people."[87]

Regardless of the arguments, the notion that sex is an immutable or permanent binary identity is a social construct designed to exercise control over the population. "The anxiety about the possible inability of an identity document to secure a constant, socially legible correspondence with an individual is summed up by a lead bureaucrat on the issue fretting, 'But we won't know who you are.' "[88] State and social actors need to "know who we are" in order to situate each and every one of us in the categories of male and female to facilitate social control. Institutions and individuals are invested in the maintenance of the sex binary because they derive power and privilege from this hierarchical binary identity as well as others. "If the words 'men' and 'women' no longer appear on the doors of public restrooms or locker rooms, then the formal mechanism for making a 'citizen's arrest' of someone who appears too masculine or too feminine to be sharing a bathroom or locker room with us evaporates into thin air."[89] Individuals would no longer be empowered to police gender in public spaces, and this would be especially costly for those who benefit from these practices. In particular, the bureaucratic regulation of sex " 'serves' male dominant interests through its disciplinary function: state agencies of every variety create disciplined, obedient, rule-abiding subjects."[90] As Brown explains:

> Bureaucracy's regulatory and disciplining capacities enable and mask male dominant interests external to bureaucracy, much as Foucault casts the disciplinary organizations of schools and hospitals as auxiliaries of a generalized aim of social control. The fact that bureaucracy as discipline is both an *end* and an *instrument*, and thereby operates *as power* as well as *in the service of other powers*, all the while presenting itself as extrinsic to or neutral with regard to power, makes it especially potent in shaping the lives of female clients of the state.[91]

Thus, it is essential to understand how these bureaucratic regulations are not only exercises of state power, but also work "in the service of other powers" as well. In this way, those with power are able to utilize tools of the state as substantiated via other disciplinary mechanisms and infra laws to subject trans bodies to governmentality. Thus, policing the categories of male and female is an essential facet of maintaining male dominance and, consequently, attempts to allow individuals to freely select or reject sex/gender markers on identity documents is resisted by the proponents of patriarchy.

Conclusion

As government increases it surveillance of the U.S. population in tandem with advances in technology and heightened concerns about national security, trans individuals are regularly forced to account for themselves.[92]

Incongruent identity documents come with great costs for trans individuals. They are exposed to increased risks of mistreatment, made socioeconomically vulnerable, and denied the ability to define themselves as they see fit. When trans people are allowed to change their identity documents they often are required to transition into the "right" sex, and those individuals who are unable to meet the prohibitive personal and financial costs associated with transitioning or who do not want to do so are rendered illegible. As one individual explained, "As a non-binary person, not being able to change my gender on any of my identification documents is really disheartening, dysphoria inducing, and kind of dehumanizing. I'm not allowed to be me."[93] When the state assigns individuals a sex at birth and then mandates that they continue to adhere to that categorization, it makes people legible and subjects of the state on the terms defined by the state. The corollary is that the state denies the existence of individuals outside of the definitions articulated by the state.

At the same time, the failure to acquire recognition by the state sanctions various forms of policing by both formal and informal actors, with great detriment to trans people. "Sex-classification policies are also harmful because they send a strong message to the public at large that we are not only justified in policing the gender expressions of others, but that doing so may in fact be our civic duty."[94] As the next chapter demonstrates, when trans individuals attempt to navigate public spaces, de facto policing of gender by the public works to constrain their movements in harmful and costly ways.

Chapter 4

"No Men in Women's Bathrooms"

De Jure and De Facto Policing of Sex-Segregated Bathrooms as a Means of Social Control

Introduction

Throughout U.S. history, battles for civil rights for marginalized and intersectionally subjected populations frequently have implicated access to bathrooms. As Harvey Molotch reminds us, "peeing is political, and so is taking a shit and washing up."[1] This is precisely because the decisions that public actors and private facilities make about the location of and access to restrooms govern individuals' movements and access to public spaces. This chapter examines how regulating and policing access to bathrooms becomes a way to punish trans individuals for "inappropriate self-presentation" in order to forcibly locate trans individuals in the right sex, and subsequently controls their movements.[2] These processes of governmentality are not happenstance and have combined over time to remove trans bodies from public spaces and the public realm in order to mitigate the challenge that they pose to governing gender norms and to foreclose individuals' investigations of gender.

These forces of governmentality work in various ways. First, public spaces are socially constructed and embedded with meanings by those in a position to do so. Then, trans individuals who challenge or contest these governing principles are marked as transgressive in order to empower others to police and marshal public spaces in the absence of or as a supplement to government surveillance. Finally, access to these spaces is controlled and dictated based on these socially constructed meanings which quickly become operationalized as governing norms. This works to manage individuals' abilities to access public spaces and facilities, and enables systemic denial of trans people's existence.

This chapter begins with a brief review of the history of bathroom hysterias in the United States before proceeding to a discussion of the social construction of sex-segregated spaces to include public bathrooms as sites of gender discipline. Then, attention is focused on how the promulgation of stereotypes and inaccuracies about trans people simultaneously marks them as transgressive bodies and empowers others to police their bodies in public spaces, to include public restrooms. Next, the consequences of this policing are examined, including the effects it has on trans individuals' abilities to access and navigate public spaces as well as the costs to their physical and mental health. This chapter concludes with an analysis of how these practices facilitate gender normativity and work to reify the sex binary and further marginalize trans individuals in the United States.

Bathroom Hysterias and Governmentality

During the Black Civil Rights movement, the opposition to desegregation included the argument that white women should not be forced to share restrooms with Black women because of the fear that the former would be exposed to and catch venereal diseases from the latter.[3] Similarly, during the campaign to ratify the ERA, opponents utilized fear mongering about integrated bathrooms and the threat of sexual violence against women and children that would accompany the end of sex-segregated bathrooms.[4] The Eagle Forum—an anti-ERA group led by Phyllis Schlafly—drew on racist and sexist stereotypes about Black male sexuality and deviance to advance its campaign against "integrated" bathrooms.[5] Then, again, during early campaigns for gay civil rights there was a concerted effort to depict gay men as child molesters congregating and hiding out in public restrooms in order to assault children in these spaces.[6] As such, bathroom hysterias have proven to be powerful discursive tools and management tactics for exercising social and political control over marginalized and disenfranchised populations. In this way, the articulation of "heterosexual genital insecurity" in debates surrounding access to public restrooms facilitates governmentality and simultaneously works to privilege heterosexual white bodies via segregated bathrooms and mark other bodies as transgressive and a threat to the former.[7] Bathrooms operate as sites of gender discipline, but also racial and sexual discipline as well.[8] The effect is to deny the physical needs and vulnerabilities of transgressive bodies in order to constrain their ability to access public spaces.

The recent public and political debates about trans individuals and restroom access are consistent with this prior history. For example, the 2015 Houston Equal Rights Ordinance (HERO) was a local civil rights law that advanced the interests of the LGBT community broadly defined, but it was quickly operationalized as a threat to heterosexual genital security. Opponents of this referendum reframed the legislation to suggest that it would allow transwomen, and men masquerading as women, to enter public restrooms in order to sexually abuse women and children.[9] While this argument is a red herring, it worked and HERO was defeated 61–39 percent.[10] In 2016 alone, nineteen states considered bathroom bills and North Carolina passed House Bill 2 (HB2) which specified that individuals are prohibited by law from using restrooms that do not correspond with their sex assigned at birth.[11] While HB2 was repealed in 2017, the alternative House Bill 142 is highly problematic as well because it prohibits locales from passing antidiscrimination measures, and it is the subject of ongoing litigation.[12] In 2017, sixteen states considered legislation that would require individuals to use restrooms, locker rooms, and other sex-segregated public facilities that correlate with an individual's "biological sex" or sex assigned at birth, and fourteen states introduced legislation intended to restrict the rights of trans students in schools.[13]

This bathroom hysteria and the associated bathroom bills need to be understood as tools of disciplinary power that are implemented through the combined and intersecting efforts of formal and informal institutions. These controversies are centered on public spaces where the state has the power to limit access through regulatory controls, but the use of public space implicates multiple actors within the public who simultaneously may be empowered to surveil others and supplement the disciplinary power of the state.

> [P]ower under disciplinary conditions "is no longer exercised through ritual, but through permanent mechanisms of surveillance and control." Those mechanisms—instantiated in institutions as diverse as prisons, factory workshops, schools, barracks, hospitals and monasteries—are deployed in order to inculcate certain patterns of behavior and self-understanding in the individual subjects who live or work there. The inculcation of the relevant behavioral norm is achieved through a

> series of disciplinary interventions . . . the subject of discipline is produced through the iterative application of the norm.[14]

The sex binary as a "relevant behavioral norm is achieved through a series of disciplinary interventions," one of which is the creation and perpetuation of sex-segregated public facilities. The sex binary is inculcated via sex segregation and acts to discipline all bodies in order to achieve compliance. As such, "it is crucial to recognize that the bathroom problem is much more than a glitch in the machinery of gender segregation and is better described in terms of the violent enforcement of our current gender system."[15]

Recognizing bathroom hysterias as tools of governmentality, it is no coincidence that the recent uproar about trans individuals and public facilities such as bathrooms and locker rooms coincides with advances in LGBT rights—including marriage equality, the expansion of protections for LGBT federal government employees under the Obama administration, and various local and state legislative attempts to expand civil rights protections for LGBT citizens—and may be characterized as a backlash against this progress. As mentioned above, debates about the integrity and safety of bathrooms come up time and time again in the context of civil rights battles as marginalized and intersectionally subjected populations start to make progress and then find that obstacles have been erected and discourses diverted. The politics of resentment may be offered as an explanation and description of these countermobilization efforts as majority populations attempt to shift the discourse away from the articulation of marginalized populations' interests to the articulation of majority values.[16] Considering that HB2 in North Carolina was introduced in the context of gradual advancements in civil rights for LGBT individuals, including the city of Charlotte's passage of a public accommodation law to include protections for gays, lesbians, and trans individuals, one could argue that HB2 is consistent with the politics of resentment.

That being said, in order to accurately understand how the policing of gender via the maintenance of sex-segregated spaces operates as a tool of population management and social control, "[w]e must escape from the limited field of juridical sovereignty and State institutions, and instead base our analysis of power on the study of the techniques and tactics of domination."[17] The discourse and tactics surrounding bathroom bills go beyond the politics of resentment to act as forces of governmentality—they synthesize both de jure prohibitions but also de facto techniques and tactics—that effectively regulate the bodies, movements, and functions of certain people but not others. The emphasis on sex segregation in public facilities, including but not limited to bathrooms, utilizes forces of governmentality to mark as transgressive those bodies that pose a challenge to the sex binary and the status quo, and then works to deny their existence by curtailing their ability to move freely in public space. Through the maintenance of sex-segregated bathrooms, including using the debates about and passage of laws such as HB2 as tactics, it is possible to enact and enforce social norms that validate privileged bodies and stigmatize transgressive bodies, particularly those fluid and dynamic bodies that are the most threatening to the governing binaries.[18]

Social Construction of Public Space

All public spaces are socially constructed and embedded with meaning and significance, and the bathroom space is no different. Throughout the world, people relieve themselves of urine and excrement in different types of spaces. In rural locations in Africa and Asia public restrooms do not exist, because people utilize outside lavatories and there are no sex-segregated facilities, whereas in many European locales bathrooms are marked as unisex.[19] Yet, as explained above, in the United States the public bathroom "has regularly been a location of consternation for the puritanical, puri-panic-al United States: an American conundrum resulting from American sensibilities and American history."[20] The creation and maintenance of sex-segregated bathrooms, however, must be understood as a social construct that derived from early attempts to maintain the subservient and marginalized positions of women in the public realm.

Sex-segregated bathrooms did not become institutionalized in the United States until the late 1800s in response to growing "social anxieties about women's places in the world."[21] As women began to transition out of the private sphere and into the public sphere traditional norms and expectations about women's behavior and social location reflected

> a reluctance to integrate them fully into public life. Women, policymakers argued, were inherently weaker and still in need of protection from the harsh realities of the public sphere. Thus, separate facilities were introduced in nearly every aspect of society: women's reading rooms were incorporated into public

> libraries; separate train cars were established for women, keeping them in the back to protect them in the event of a crash; and, with the advent of indoor bathrooms that were then in the process of replacing single-person outhouses, separate loos soon followed.[22]

Thus, the very fact that we have sex-segregated public bathrooms in the United States today is because policymakers and those with the power to influence the legislative process in the late 1800s resisted integrating women into public spaces. Policymakers created sex-segregated locations in order to maintain a separate sphere for women and thereby preserve divisions among men and women, but also because they were invested in maintaining all-male domains.[23]

Today, sex-segregated bathrooms continue to operate as sites of gender discipline for maintaining both a binary difference between the sexes and for perpetuating the hierarchy that accrues to the sexes. One need only witness the lengthy lines that women regularly navigate in order to gain access to public restrooms in comparison to the lineless men's restrooms to see this hierarchy confirmed.[24] Similarly, as women integrate more and more public spaces that used to be exclusively the domain of males, sex-segregated bathrooms are one of the few "male-only" sites remaining. In a patriarchal society, male-only spaces are locations of power where networking opportunities are shared and privileges distributed.[25] In fact, as fewer and fewer sex-segregated public spaces exist, bathrooms may become even more important as locations of power, but it is important to recognize that "the access to power offered by an all-male and all-female space continue to differ enormously."[26] As such, the ongoing maintenance of sex-segregated bathrooms works to defend and maintain heterosexist male privilege.

As architect Barbara Penner explains in *Bathroom*, a critical analysis of bathroom space, "I do not intend to consider the bathroom as a discrete and enclosed site. I want to make sense of how the bathroom meets the world outside, how it moves between different sites, scales and conditions, and how it hooks the human body up to technology, individuals to infrastructure and private to public realms."[27] The physical and social constructions of bathroom spaces matter precisely because bathrooms are not merely discrete sites, but rather are integrated into our daily lives via the linkages between individuals and infrastructure and private and public realms. Through the norms that govern the physical construction of bathroom spaces, bodies become objects of visual inspection, and "[g]aps between the perceived sex of the body, gender identity, and the insignia on toilet doors are subject to inquiry. The space is designed to authorize an invasive and persecutory gaze. Mirrors, fluorescent lighting, and metallic surfaces all invite voyeuristic attention . . . our gender is subject to survey every time we enter the lavatory. Prying eyes attend to the body and whether or not it is in the 'right place.'"[28]

It is through the social construction of bathroom space in the United States that these facilities come to operate as sites of gender discipline that link the individual private elimination of human excrement to public norms and expectations about gender. Bathrooms are not sex segregated out of necessity related to biology or culture, but this myth serves as a powerful discursive tool for connecting individual bodies and private acts with governing norms and social control. As Juang explains, "Segregation is material in nature insofar as public spaces are physically cordoned off and defended as the private reserve of certain privileged subjectivities. Segregation is symbolic insofar as the material act of exclusion attempts to convey the message and bolster the illusion that the boundaries of proper identities and the attribution of value, as well as dignity, are fully and solely in the hands of those privileged subjects."[29] As such, the debates about trans individuals in bathrooms misrepresent bathroom space in intentional and problematic ways that are intended to facilitate the forces of governmentality that privilege some and marginalize others.

First and foremost, bathrooms are not, in practice, sex segregated. Gender is a complicated physiological and cultural issue and the practice of having male and female bathrooms oversimplifies sex in ways that necessitate that people make individual decisions about which bathroom to utilize when forced to do so. This means that people, including but not limited to trans individuals, utilize the public restrooms of their choosing with regularity, thereby creating bathroom spaces that are not in effect single sex. Furthermore, people who require additional assistance using public facilities, such as children, often transgress the sex line when using public restrooms, whereas the disabled are degendered by bathroom signs affixed to sex-neutral handicapped facilities.[30] As such, the idea that bathrooms are sex segregated and/or that they have to be is inaccurate. Recognizing that many public restrooms are unisex further complicates this narrative.

Second, the discourse surrounding trans individuals and public bathrooms creates a threat where no threat exists. Commenting on HB2, "Deborah Thompson, who owns the Simply NC gift shop in downtown

Clinton, says she finds the bathroom debate to be a 'very confusing issue.' 'A lot of people don't understand what the whole transgender thing is,' she said. Thompson says the safety concern has been at the front of her mind as she's considered the issue. 'On the side of safety, I approve of what the governor did,' she said."[31] Yet, the trans threat is a social construct, and the argument that individuals must use the restroom that correlates with the sex assigned to them at birth in order to mitigate violence and sexual assaults against women and children in public restrooms is based on inaccurate stereotypes. The security issue in bathrooms is not real, and there is no evidence whatsoever that transwomen pose a threat to others in bathrooms or that men are dressing up as women in order to enter public restrooms to assault women and children.[32] In fact, it appears that trans people are the individuals most at risk of verbal and physical assaults in and around restrooms. According to the National Center for Transgender Equality survey conducted in the summer of 2015, 12 percent of respondents reported being verbally harassed, 1 percent reported being physically assaulted, and 1 percent reported being sexually assaulted when accessing a bathroom in the prior year, and this was before the increased public attention focused on trans people in restrooms that followed bills such as HB2 in 2016.[33] In addition to misrepresenting the bathroom space itself, bathroom bills such as HB2 further facilitate governmentality by socially constructing and de-subjectivating trans people in order to exclude them from public spaces and keep them decentered and located in the margins of the public.

Construction of Transgressive Bodies

The social construction of trans people as objects, frauds, and deviants is a tool of governmentality that not only ignores the facts but effectively distorts the truth in order to maintain the privileged position of some at the expense of others. These various tropes all work to socially construct trans individuals as transgressive bodies not worthy of public recognition at best and/or totally deny their existence at worst. For example, the public's obsessive fixation on the genitalia of trans individuals and the emphasis on "biological sex" and sex as "genitalia at birth" desubjectivates trans people by making them into objects.[34] Individuals become a penis or a vagina instead of a human being. As Flynn explains, "In adhering to the view of sex as genitalia-at-birth, the majority of courts simultaneously 'de-sex' and hypersexualize trans men and women. Given the centrality of sex and gender in our lives, both are dehumanizing moves."[35]

This fixation on genitalia as the defining characteristic of individuals' complex identities then becomes a mechanism for perpetuating the myth that trans individuals are frauds or deceivers because they are trying to "pass" as something they are not.[36] At a North Carolina rally in support of HB2, Bishop Patrick Wooden said, "Everyone knows that a transgender woman is a man. Everybody knows that a transgender man is a woman. And, we have allowed common sense to go out of the window."[37] This statement evidences the mischaracterization of trans individuals as fakes—they are misrepresenting themselves but the public knows better—and these concocted arguments about deception enable the public to blame trans people for their own marginalized position because it is their deception that renders them transgressive, as opposed to the intolerance or transphobia of the dominant public.[38] Furthermore, the fraud trope aids in the creation and maintenance of the mythology that trans individuals are sexual deviants, and sanctions violence against and the subjection of the trans community as legitimate processes of governmentality intended to protect society from these transgressive bodies.[39]

Individuals who do not easily pass as male or female are especially susceptible to being accosted as frauds in public spaces.[40] Accusations of "gender trickery" sanction harassment and violence against trans individuals in public bathrooms. As one genderqueer bisexual explained: " 'It's a gendered space, and so being in that space, people have implicitly agreed that they are one thing or another. When others start believing that somebody is in the wrong bathroom and that they've lied, are trying to pretend to be someone who they're not, or are in a place that they shouldn't be, then it opens up the door to harassment.' "[41]

Throughout U.S. history, the criminalization of certain populations has been an integral tactic of governmentality, as exemplified by the criminalization of the Black population in the United States.[42] In this way, the construction of trans individuals as objects evolves into the fraud trope and then the sexual deviance stereotype that justifies the need to protect the public from transgressive bodies, and becomes part of the discourse surrounding bathroom bills and substantiates the criminalization of trans people. This body-centric focus interacts with some individuals' disgust sensitivity to exacerbate their opposition to trans rights.[43] In North Carolina, a father of two teenage daughters agreed that HB2 was a necessary response to the city of Charlotte's public accommodation law because he was worried that "'some guy dressing up' might take advantage of an ordinance like Charlotte's to enter the women's bathroom. 'I don't want my daughters put in jeopardy'" he said. Tart said he doesn't think he's ever met a transgender person. Asked what he pictures when he hears the term, he described a man 'all dolled up with makeup and clothes.'"[44] This brief commentary exemplifies how the fraud trope—men dressing up as women—morphs into the fear of sexual predators to justify de jure sex segregation legislation such as HB2 as well as de facto community policing of public spaces.

Denial of Access to Space

The failure to accommodate and/or make space for transgender individuals in public facilities affirms that they are not bodies that matter with physical needs and/or vulnerabilities. In this way de jure sex segregation in bathrooms via legislation such as HB2 and de facto sex segregation of bathrooms via the policing of public spaces work to facilitate processes of governmentality by making it difficult for trans people to access and utilize public space. This systemic denial constrains and threatens trans individuals by making it difficult, if not impossible, for them to utilize public facilities, thereby controlling their movements in the public realm and subjecting them to physical danger and violence when they enter into public facilities.

According to the National Center for Transgender Equality survey of trans individuals conducted in the summer of 2015—before bathroom hysteria and bathroom bills took off later that year—9 percent of respondents reported that they had been denied access to a restroom,[45] and 24 percent of respondents reported that someone questioned their presence in a restroom in the prior year.[46] More than one-quarter (26%) of respondents reported that they were either denied access, verbally harassed, physically attacked, and/or sexually assaulted in a restroom in the prior year, and these experiences were exacerbated for intersectionally subjected trans individuals, with 50 percent of undocumented respondents, 39 percent of respondents who work in underground economies, 36 percent of Native American respondents, and 32 percent of multiracial respondents reporting one or more of these events.[47] Prior research similarly demonstrates that trans people of color experience greater difficulties in gaining access to restrooms than white trans individuals, and lower-income individuals experience greater difficulties than individuals who are more affluent.[48] Furthermore, individuals who reported that others "could always or usually tell they were transgender without being told (45%) or sometimes tell they were transgender (38%) were more likely to report one or more of these experiences, in contrast to those who said that others could rarely or never tell that they were transgender (16%)."[49] These statistics confirm that trans individuals are denied access to public restrooms via de facto and de jure prohibitions, but that some individuals are more vulnerable to the policing that occurs in public spaces than others. Race, class, masculinity, and femininity intersect with one's trans identity to make it more difficult for some individuals to move freely in public.

Limits Access and Constrains Movements in the Public Realm

The fact that trans individuals are denied access to public spaces such as restrooms and that they are vulnerable to verbal and physical attacks in these (and various other) locations works to constrain their movements in the public realm. This regulation is consistent with Foucault's work on governmentality as "the operation of power as the government of conduct."[50] According to the NCTE survey, 20 percent of respondents chose not to use one or more places of public accommodation in the prior year because they feared being mistreated on the basis of their trans identity,[51] and 59 percent avoided using a public restroom at some point in the prior year due to fear.[52] The inability to move freely through public spaces causes a great deal of stress that causes some individuals to "hide from public life."[53] In a survey of trans individuals in Washington, D.C., Herman found that participants experienced "absences from work and school, poor performance at work or school, choosing to not participate in public life, avoiding particular places or events, and having to develop strategies to navigate gendered restrooms," and she concludes that "it is reasonable to assume there is an impact on the mental health of those who suffer this type of minority stress."[54] In addition to the mental health toll that accompanies stress and anxiety, individuals report health issues such as kidney and urinary tract infections that derive from being forced to hold one's urine for lengthy periods of time as well.[55]

Among those NCTE survey respondents who avoided public restrooms in the prior year, the fears and vulnerabilities are not evenly distributed.

For example, 75 percent of transgender men reported that they always or sometimes did so, in comparison to 53 percent of transgender women and 53 percent of nonbinary respondents.[56] These differences might reflect the different perceived risks and vulnerabilities among trans individuals. Limited statistical evidence suggests that transmen may be at greater risk for verbal and physical attacks in restrooms than transwomen—a fact that may reflect the greater likelihood that males will attack a transman than females will attack a transwoman in the actual restroom facility—and this may make some transmen more wary of using public facilities.[57]

Similarly, individuals who reported that people could usually or always tell that they were trans reported very high rates of avoiding public restrooms (80 percent) as did those who said that others sometimes can tell they are trans (72 percent).[58] In contrast, those who said that other people could rarely or never identify them as trans were less likely to avoid public restrooms (48 percent).[59] Again, individuals' perceptions of their vulnerabilities in restrooms dictated the extent to which they avoided these facilities. Those individuals who indicated that they were likely to be identified by others as trans are more likely to avoid public restrooms, out of the greater fear that they will be profiled and challenged in these spaces. Not surprisingly, 72 percent of the respondents who are undocumented residents reported that they had sometimes or always avoided using a public restroom in the prior year.[60] Again, this statistic likely reflects the unique concerns and fears of undocumented trans individuals. Many undocumented individuals are cautious to avoid situations where they may attract unwanted attention, and they are especially vulnerable to harassment and violence because they have limited recourse when they are the victims of crimes.

Interestingly, the National Center for Transgender Equality surveyed 686 transgender individuals in North Carolina during the summer of 2015—months before HB2 was passed—and found that 62 percent of those surveyed "avoided using a public restroom in the past year because they were afraid of confrontations or other problems they might experience," and 32 percent "limited the amount that they ate or drank to avoid using the restroom in the past year."[61] Recognizing that this data was gathered prior to HB2 suggests that these statistics were even higher when HB2 was in effect, because individuals within the public were legally empowered to police bathroom spaces for trans individuals. De jure segregation such as HB2 makes individuals who transgress the sex binary into criminals. By violating the laws and using the bathroom, trans individuals risk being accosted by not just individuals but also the police. As one individual reported:

> I had just started transitioning and I met this guy who was trans and. . . . He went to the men's washroom and this cop followed him in and said, "Let me see your ID—you're in the wrong washroom." He said that he wasn't in the wrong washroom and that he was just going to use the washroom and that was it . . . and then the cop slammed him against the wall, handcuffed him, and dragged him out and arrested him. He had already had chest surgery but they brought him to the women's jail and ordered him to take off his clothes and said, "Why don't you have any tits," and all these things to him. So he was very traumatized.[62]

Interactions with the police are extremely problematic for trans individuals, as documented in the next chapter, and increase the likelihood that individuals will wind up in the criminal justice system, which is a dangerous sex-segregated public space as well.

The aforementioned statistics demonstrate that trans individuals avoid utilizing public restrooms, and one cannot underestimate the extent to which access to adequate restroom facilities governs people's movements. Thirty-two percent of respondents to the National Center for Transgender Equality survey reported that they had limited their consumption of liquids and foods in order to avoid using the restroom in the prior year,[63] and 55 percent reported that they "held it" to avoid using a public restroom when they needed to do so.[64] One respondent explained, "I either have to 'hold it' or break down and use a male restroom in a public place. I'm not allowed to use the female restroom and have been confronted multiple times when attempting to."[65]

Trans students who are forced to utilize separate designated bathrooms or those that match their sex as assigned at birth at school may find that the "anxieties of basic bodily needs impact the ability to gain an education or livelihood."[66] As Grace Dolan-Sandrino, a Black transgender teen explained, "I know how it feels to have to use a separate bathroom. In eighth grade I wasn't allowed to use the girls' bathroom because I am a trans girl. I had to walk down two floors and across an outdoor courtyard to the nurse's office. It took me so long to get to and from the bathroom that teachers stopped letting me go because it 'took too much time out of class.' "[67] Similarly, Gavin Grimm, a transgender male high school student who was forced to use the bathroom in the nurse's office stated, "seeing that the nurse's office is in one place in a very large school, it took a lot of time away from my education."[68] For these students, the challenges associated with using designated bathrooms interfered with their educations in comparison to their peers. Gavin Grimm then explained that "[a]ll I want to do is be a normal child and use the restroom in peace," and described the mistreatment he was experiencing as "bullying."[69]

This bullying acts as a form of de facto control of one's movements in public spaces, and the degradation and shame that accompanies having to use separate designated bathrooms may discourage trans students from using those spaces. As one trans individual explained, "I spent high school having to use the nurse's bathroom, because if I used the boys' bathroom, I would get reprimanded, and the same would happen if I went into the girls' bathroom since I was living as a boy. Going to the nurse's office always felt like a walk of shame, like there was no dignified place for me simply because I'm transgender."[70] Furthermore, because sex-segregated bathroom policies often result in the creation of separate accommodations for trans students, as described above, those individuals who contest restrictive bathroom policies and/or utilize designated restrooms are more likely to be outed as trans, thereby making them more vulnerable to bullying. A recent survey reported that 77 percent of students who are out as trans reported some form of mistreatment during K-12 education, including 54 percent who reported being verbally harassed, 24 percent who reported being physically assaulted, and 13 percent who were sexually assaulted.[71] In fact, 17 percent of respondents reported that the treatment was so severe that they left school.[72] Bathroom policies likely interact with these statistics to the extent that these policies out students in the schools and render them more susceptible to mistreatment by their peers and administrators. Thus, the people whose safety is actually jeopardized by bathroom policies in these environments are the trans students who are singled out for differential treatment, public shaming, and bullying.

Subjection to Physical Danger and Violence

De facto and de jure sex segregation in restrooms not only affects the movements of trans individuals, but those individuals marked as transgressive are subject to verbal and physical threats and danger when they challenge governing norms and expectations. One student reported that they were harassed extensively at school: "I'd get hit by soda cans, spit balls, and paper airplanes of hate mail. Teachers weren't there or didn't care. I had to avoid social interactions like buses and school bathrooms because I didn't feel safe."[73] The public attention focused on bathroom bills heightens these risks because this legislation empowers citizens to police bathroom spaces, and in the case of HB2 it legally empowered the public to do so while effectively criminalizing trans individuals who violated the law.

The fears that deter trans people from using public restrooms are real. As noted above, trans individuals are subject to verbal harassment, physical attack, and sexual assault when accessing or using public restrooms, and some intersectionally subjected individuals are more vulnerable than others.[74] Among the 1 percent of individuals (139 respondents, unweighted) who reported being sexually assaulted in a restroom in the prior year, trans women of color, including Asians (3.2%), Middle Easterners (3.2%), Native Americans (2.8%), and multiracial individuals (2.4%), were more likely to report these attacks, as were individuals employed in underground economies (4%).[75]

In this way, de facto sex segregation is implemented via actual or hypothetical policing of restrooms by members of the public. "Public restroom facilities stage gender so that non-experts—the general public—can decide if it is pure and intelligible or impure and indecipherable in heteronormative and cis-sexist landscapes."[76] These practices make it difficult for trans people to use the bathroom. For example, masculine or butch women regularly confront the "bathroom problem . . . [which] severely limits their ability to circulate in public spaces and actually brings them into contact with physical violence as a result of having violated a cardinal rule of gender: one must be readable at a glance."[77]

The policing of bathrooms need not involve law enforcement officers because the construction of bathroom space lends itself to vigilante justice. "Precisely because the toilet operates somewhat in hiding, those who plan, manage, and control its use often act on their own, without a public to which they must provide detailed and explicit accounts of what they are doing."[78] As one transman reported, "I went into the men's bathroom, being a man and all. I was using a stall, and I came out only to find one person who apparently thought it was okay to go after me. I was just washing my hands when he first punched me in the back and then went for my vagina. I nearly passed out due to the blow."[79] In this instance, a member of the general public took it upon himself to enforce the "heteronormative and cis-sexist landscape" that characterizes bathroom space.[80] In other instances, law enforcement may defer the policing of bathroom space to the public as exemplified by the following experience: "I walked into a stall to do my business like I had done so many times before. This time, though, someone recognized me. He and his buddies circled around me as I tried to exit the restroom and pushed me around between them. A police officer walked into the restroom and tried to protest their harassment. The men responded by ripping my pants down. The officer shot me a disgusted look and left the room."[81]

Sex-Segregated Public Spaces Facilitate Gender Normativity

The social construction of sex-segregated bathroom spaces and the policing of the sex binary that follows are tools of governmentality that are intended to maintain separations and hierarchies predicated on sex in the interest of maintaining patriarchal power, but they also are operating to maintain the privileges that currently accrue to non-trans individuals located in the center of discourse and power in the United States. Sex-segregated public facilities not only validate the sex binary, but subsequently maintain the marginalized position of trans people in order to mitigate the threat that trans individuals pose to the sex binary. As such, any attempt to challenge the institutionalization of the sex binary by extending legal recognition or civil rights protections to trans people requires a swift and decisive response that discursively and tactically maintains the privileged position of those in the public at the expense of those located in the margins.

While North Carolina is the only state to pass a bathroom bill, bathroom hysteria continues to grow and, as the foregoing analysis makes clear, with or without bathroom bills many trans individuals are fearful of utilizing public restrooms, which constrains their access to public spaces. This is because "the disciplines operate according to a form and logic irreducible to law and sovereignty. Not only does the disciplinary distribution around a norm mark a break with the binary juridical logic of the law, but these very disciplinary practices and procedures operate in the shadows and the interstices of law and formal state apparatuses. Discipline, Foucault insists, more than once, is a kind of 'infra-law' and exists on the 'underside of the law.'"[82] In this way, trans bodies are disciplined and their movements contained and constrained via a type of infra law that sanctions the policing of those bodies marked as transgressive when they enter public spaces. It is this combination of formal and informal institutional apparatuses and actual and threatened de jure prohibitions combined with de facto embargoes that intersect and work in tandem as tools of governmentality operating on trans people.

Furthermore, one of the reasons that these forces of governmentality are able to operate on trans bodies is because those in the public sanction the policing of public space. Some do this by policing space themselves or via explicit support and transphobic articulations of alleged security threats, whereas others facilitate these processes of governmentality by willful ignorance. " '[T]he bathroom problem' . . . illustrates in remarkably clear ways the flourishing existence of gender binarism despite rumors of its demise. Furthermore, many normatively gendered women have no idea that a bathroom problem even exists and claim to be completely ignorant about the trials and tribulations that face the butch woman who needs to use a public bathroom."[83] This ignorance is an essential component of governmentality because it indicates that trans individuals are invisible to the majority, and they are omitted from consideration. Absent the recognition that there is a systemic or institutional problem that disadvantages trans individuals in accessing and using public facilities, there is no need for discussions and solutions. In this void, powerful elites are now able to construct a problem that recognizes trans individuals as a threat to heterosexual gender security, as opposed to addressing the actual difficulties that trans people confront on a daily basis. It is through both omission and recognition that the "disciplinary subject" is controlled "by an ensemble of techniques and knowledges that is subjacent to the formal juridical armature of law."[84] These techniques and knowledges—either through omission or the recognition of trans individuals as objects, frauds, and deviants—are sufficient to control the movement of trans people and deny their access to public spaces via de facto prohibitions even in the absence of de jure prohibitions.

A brief analysis of the current debates surrounding bathroom bills demonstrates how this discourse privileges the articulated interests of the public over the real needs of trans communities, and then sanctions procedural tactics that maintain the former at the expense of the latter. In the discourse, the articulated interests of privileged and dominant populations within the public are always front and center. This was exemplified when North Carolina governor Pat McCrory defended HB2 to Fox News anchor

Megyn Kelly as follows: "It's the basic expectation of privacy that I hear from moms and dads and families that when their daughter or son goes into a facility, a restroom, they expect people of that gender . . . to be the only other ones in that. That's the expectations that we've had for many, many years."[85] In this way, the dominant population's expectations are privileged over the real and pressing needs of trans individuals, and the justification for doing so need only be the fact that this is how it has been done in the past. Yet, this commitment to upholding long-held expectations about gender reflects the fact that those in the public are deeply invested in the maintenance of the categories of male and female and are similarly committed to writing off as aberrations anyone who does not fit into this binary.[86] The practice of creating and then defending public policies based on the public's expectations comes with real costs for trans individuals, as discussed above, and also constructs problems where none exist, as exemplified by the following statement from a trans individual: "In high school, the staff told me I could not use the men's bathroom because I'd make other students uncomfortable, even though I was out to everyone and none of the students were bothered by my gender."[87]

At other times, tactics are utilized that explicitly prioritize the health and safety of dominant populations over marginalized populations. For example, in New Hampshire when there was debate about the Anti-Discrimination Bill HB 478, Representative Jess Edwards argued that the bill should be pulled and not voted on because "[t]he public is not ready. The number of people who have written stating that this bill essentially offers their children up to sexual predators is outrunning by 5 to 1 the number of emails stating that it's time to end the daily beatings of transgendered people. The passionate are yelling past each other with worst-case scenarios. I don't think this is an environment in which the legislature should pick a side. Society needs to evolve further on its own I think."[88] In this instance, Representative Edwards was willing to explicitly state that the dominant population's hypothetical and unsubstantiated fears based on inaccurate stereotypes trump the real and actual violence experienced by trans people.

When marginalized populations and their allies attempt to decenter the dominant public in the discourse or in policy by organizing for civil rights protections or in opposition to discriminatory laws, these arguments are rejected as political correctness or a grab for special rights. This discursive maneuver whereby demands for legal protections are recast as political correctness and/or fights for equal rights are rewritten as special rights works to recenter the dominant public any time that it is challenged from the margins.[89] In an interview after he was defeated in his reelection campaign for governor of North Carolina, Pat McCrory criticized the opponents of HB2 as follows, " 'It's almost Orwellian,' McCrory told Smith, 'that if you disagree with the thought police, the politically correct thought police on this new definition of gender, you're a bigot, you're the worst of evil. It's almost as though I broke a law!' "[90] McCrory's comment recasts the targets of HB2 as powerful Orwellian actors and reframes himself—the former governor of the state of North Carolina—as the center of the discourse and the actual victim of the events surrounding HB2.

Similarly, North Carolina state senator Buck Newton explained his support for HB2 as follows: "It is my honor to stand for law and order. . . . I can't believe we're having to talk about this. I cannot believe that we're having to pass bills like HB2. But we must, we must. The other side insists on the fight. The other side insists that we bow to their politically correct agenda."[91] Once again, a politically powerful elite facetiously positions the dominant public as David to the trans movement's Goliath and suggests that legislation such as HB2 is necessary to protect the public's threatened existence. The discourse is reframed to recenter the public and, tactically, legislation such as HB2 is offered as a mechanism for returning power to the public as well. The irony, however, is that HB2 does not return power to the public because it has never been lost to those at the margins. Instead, it reifies the power already located in the public. Thus, the underlying message of the public's discourse on political correctness and its use of tactical maneuvers such as HB2 appear to be to signal to those in the margins that if they dare to challenge the public and the dominant power structure they will be on the receiving end of bills like HB2. As a woman in North Carolina said about HB2: "Everybody's got a right to be whatever they want to be, but they can't push their rights on us."[92]

Furthermore, the dominant public is able to utilize its power to frame the discourse to pursue its broader policy priorities. For example, it is worth noting that HB2 was a large bill that advanced a number of neoliberal priorities, including undermining various employment protections and leave policies in addition to the restrictions on LGBTQ rights. Yet, in comments posted to Twitter on the night he signed the bill into law, North Carolina governor McCrory tweeted: "I signed bipartisan legislation to stop the breach of basic privacy and etiquette, ensure privacy in bathrooms and locker rooms. Ordinance defied common sense, allowing men to use women's bathroom/locker room for instance. That's why I signed bipartisan bill to stop it."[93] Interestingly, the governor immediately drew attention to the one specific aspect of HB2 that would prove to be most controversial, and in doing so, distracted attention from all of the other facets of the legislation. In this way, bathroom bills are not only bathroom bills, but may also be pieces of legislation that serve as Trojan horses for advancing a broad array of policies that work to advance the neoliberal agenda. Heterosexual genital security and bathroom hysteria can serve both as tools for killing legislation, as was the case with the Houston Equal Rights Ordinance, and for justifying and defending bills, as was the case with HB2. In both instances, bathroom hysteria is a mechanism for distracting and manipulating the discourse and public attention in order to reify the power and privilege that accrues to some bodies while maintaining the marginalized positions of others. Finally, the debates about bathroom space and legislative action distract time and resources from issues and threats that are real, including the ongoing discrimination and violence against trans people. This is both a tactical and a discursive maneuver that works to maintain the power and privilege of some at the expense of others.

Conclusion

By marking trans individuals as deviant and dangerous the public is able to simultaneously police and protect the sex binary and marginalize trans individuals via the systematic denial of their access to public spaces, which has major consequences for one's ability to obtain a quality education, get and keep employment, and function as an individual in contemporary society. The forces of governmentality that mark and then operate on trans bodies need not come from the state via formal laws, but may derive from infra law and the de facto prohibitions on transgressing the sex binary in public spaces that result when the public takes it upon itself to identify and discipline transgressive bodies. "Not having a door (or a sign) is a pertinent metaphor for those who have their gender identities rendered invisible subject to erasure, or expunged from the social field. To be unseen, to be unrecognizable, to be interrogated by indignant onlookers upset about gender 'impurity' or incoherence, and to lack legibility in a cissexist and heteronormative landscape is to have one's legitimate access to public participation thrown into question."[94] These de facto prohibitions create a culture of fear that predates the recent legislative forays into bathroom bills and effectively undermines the ability of trans individuals to move freely in public space. At the same time, however, these forces of governmentality enable those in the public to "transform bathrooms from a ubiquitous public convenience into extensions of their own gender, sexualities, and institutional positions."[95] In this way, forces of governmentality work to maintain existing supremacies and hierarchies. As the next chapter makes clear, when trans individuals do enter public spaces other forces of governmentality are sanctioned to remove these transgressive bodies from view.

Chapter 5

The War on Solicitation and Intersectional Subjection

How Quality of Life Policing Is Used as a Tool to Control Trans Populations

Introduction

Trans individuals are frequently targeted by law enforcement and charged with intent to solicit or solicitation even when all evidence makes clear that they are not sex workers.[1] In some jurisdictions the mere possession of condoms by trans individuals is accepted as evidence of the intent to solicit sex.[2] This practice has become so commonplace that it is referred to as "walking while trans," an analogy to "driving while black." When law enforcement officers repeatedly charge trans individuals with solicitation this creates and perpetuates the myth that this population is pathologically inclined to engage in sex work in much the same way that the selective enforcement of drug laws has worked to create and substantiate the myth of the "blackmancriminal."[3] In this way, ostensibly neutral "quality of life" policing laws are used to criminalize the existence of trans individuals and facilitate their incarceration and deportation, and the war on solicitation is transformed from sovereign state actors enforcing law in the interest of regulating crime and promoting public safety into a tactic for trans-profiling that implicates a more diffuse and multifaceted understanding of disciplinary power as a tool for governing. This latter mode of power is consistent with Foucault's concept of governmentality,[4] which can be understood as "an art of managing things and persons, concerned with tactics, not laws, or as that which uses laws as part of a broader scheme of tactics to achieve certain policy aims."[5] Accordingly, the selective enforcement of solicitation laws on trans individuals may be understood as a tactic of social control utilized to manage the movements and actions of this population. The effect of this process of governmentality is to relegate trans individuals to the margins of the public while simultaneously privileging white heteronormative values and identities. In this way, law becomes a tactic for managing the behavior and actions of a population, as opposed to a mechanism for prohibiting solicitation.

The war on solicitation is especially dire for trans people of color, immigrants, and the poor because intersectional subjection[6] increases the likelihood that trans individuals will be marginalized by society and approached by law enforcement and subject to harassment, violence, and/or criminal charges. Due to the fact that trans people of color and the poor are more likely to live in areas with extensive police surveillance there is an increased likelihood that they will be subject to transprofiling. In addition, trans immigrants are especially vulnerable to profiling by local law enforcement and immigration officials, and in these instances the risk of being charged with solicitation is magnified by the potential to be deported. Thus, while the war on solicitation works to simultaneously stigmatize and control all trans people it has an especially pernicious effect on those who are intersectionally subjected, forcing these people even farther into the shadows of American society or out of the country altogether. This chapter examines the war on solicitation and its effect on those who are intersectionally subjected, with particular attention focused on immigrants and people of color, in order to demonstrate how the harassment and criminalization of individuals "walking while trans" is a tool of social control that not only privileges heteronormative experiences and exacerbates transphobia but furthers racism and xenophobia as well.

Walking While Trans: Quality of Life Policing and the Enforcement of Solicitation Laws

Studies of trans populations in various U.S. cities—including New York,[7] San Francisco,[8] Washington, D.C.,[9] Los Angeles,[10] New Orleans,[11] Chicago,[12] and San Antonio[13]—document that they are regularly profiled and approached by law enforcement in public spaces for the crime of being trans. According to one survey, 28 percent of non-LGBTQ residents reported police stops compared to 59 percent of transgender individuals,[14] and the 2015 National Center for Transgender Equality survey reported that 11 percent of respondents reported that the police thought they were sex workers.[15] Women of color are particularly vulnerable to transprofiling, and of those survey respondents who interacted with law enforcement in the prior year, 33 percent of Black, 25 percent of Latina, 23 percent of Native American, 20 percent of Asian, and 30 percent of multiracial transgender women said that law enforcement officers assumed they were sex workers.[16] Trans individuals profiled by law enforcement officers often are verbally and physically harassed, and many times they are defaced by police officers, who forcibly remove their breasts and wigs in public spaces.[17] Frequently these interactions take a more sinister turn when police officers utilize trans identity as a pretext to profile individuals for violating solicitation laws. As one transgender woman put it, "'To the police, all transgenders are prostitutes.'"[18] One particularly disturbing account was reported by Cristina, a transgender Latina woman living in New York, who described how she was profiled while walking home from a nightclub with her boyfriend:

> One night I was with my boyfriend at a club in Jackson Heights, Queens. At around 4AM we left the club together and walked home. We were walking next to each other. At one point an undercover police van stopped next to us. Eight undercover cops got out from the van and some of them threw me against the wall. While they were handcuffing me, my boyfriend was also thrown to the wall and they frisked him. They told me I was being arrested for sex work. I told them that I was not doing anything like that. After they frisked my boyfriend, they frisked me and found 3 condoms, after seeing the condoms they asked if I was sure that I was not working. I told them that I was with my boyfriend and they said that he was not my boyfriend. I told one of the female cops to help me and that I was not doing anything wrong. She said that she couldn't help me out. My boyfriend came to the 110th Precinct where I was held and spoke to the captain; he tried to explain that I was his girlfriend and that I was with him. But the captain said that he couldn't do anything. I was taken to court and was accused of sex work.[19]

Cristina's experience is not an aberration. Many transwomen report being targeted repeatedly by law enforcement for prostitution while engaging in routine affairs in their communities.[20] According to a 2011 survey, 21 percent of male-to-female transgender respondents reported having been sent to jail as did 10 percent of female-to-male respondents.[21]

Profiling trans individuals engaging in the mundane activities of everyday life enables law enforcement to elicit fear and exercise control over trans individuals. This social control is demonstrated when Natalia, a transgender Latina woman residing in New York City, describes how she

> avoided going out in the day and night. They [the police] did not care who they saw you with, partners or family, to accuse you of sex work. I remember two times when coming out of a yellow taxi from Manhattan, there was a police car stationed outside my house waiting for me. I would leave the taxi in fear because I knew that I would be arrested and accused of sex work. They would tell us to go to them, we would ask why, they would not answer. We felt that they did not meet their numbers for the night and were waiting for us to have a record of arrest. I feel that precinct has something against us.[22]

In order to detain and/or criminally charge trans individuals, law enforcement officers frequently identify the possession of condoms as evidence that they intend to solicit sex.[23] For example, a transgender Latina woman reported the following interaction with the police in Jackson Heights, New York: "I was just buying tacos. They grabbed me and handcuffed me. They found condoms in my bra and said I was doing sex work. After handcuffing me they asked me to kneel down and they took my wig off. They arrested me and took me away."[24] This demonstrates how trans individuals, in particular transgender women, are targeted for stop and frisk so that police can look for condoms during searches. It is difficult to understand this practice as anything besides discrimination against trans people. As Andrea Ritchie, an attorney who represents trans clients, argued, "The use of condoms as evidence of prostitution is a good example of 'reasonable suspicion' becoming blatant discrimination. 'When was the last time you were arrested for carrying condoms?' "[25] In this way, transprofiling operates as a powerful tool of social control that governs the behavior of trans individuals.

Transprofiling as a Tactic of Governmentality

In order to understand how walking while trans—trans individuals walking in public spaces—becomes "walking while trans"—a criminal activity—requires an understanding of governing that goes beyond the state. This is reflected by the fact that legislatures pass laws criminalizing prostitution—thereby prohibiting certain acts—but there are no state laws that make it a crime for trans people to walk in and occupy public spaces. Rather, it is the governing authority bestowed upon and exercised by law enforcement officers, prosecutors, judges, community members, and others intersecting with modes of power such as capital and wealth, racial privilege, citizenship, and heteronormativity that works to criminalize trans communities via the selective application of quality of life policing laws. Notably, an Amnesty International investigation found that police report that they often are responding to community complaints when they initiate targeted enforcement of morals statutes including solicitation laws, indicating that nonstate actors are complicit in allowing transprofiling to operate as a tool of transphobia.[26] Society's tacit acceptance of questionable policing practices sanctions transprofiling as a legitimate use of state authority within the realm of governmentality.[27] Thus, it is the ways in which a neutral criminal prohibition intersects with myriad other governing entities and modes of power in the United States that enable it to become a tactic for marginalizing and stigmatizing trans communities.

While one tactic available to dominant groups is to utilize the power of the state to pass laws that substantiate their privileges, these laws are open to legal challenges if they target specific populations for differential treatment, as demonstrated by North Carolina's experience with HB2. Via governmentality, however, it is not necessary to pass discriminatory state laws because neutral laws are a sufficient tactic for managing different populations. Throughout U.S. history, dominant groups have utilized their power to maintain their privileged positions in this way. In particular, the process of designating certain acts as crimes is infused with issues of power and social control. While eradicating crime and promoting public safety are offered as justifications for facially neutral criminal laws, the reality is that these laws are imbued with historical biases and work in effect to disproportionately burden certain populations.

For example, in *The New Jim Crow: Mass Incarceration in the Age of Colorblindness*, Michelle Alexander argues that the mass incarceration of Black males resulting from the facially neutral policies promulgated in the War on Drugs is a form of racialized social control akin to Jim Crow laws.[28] Key to Alexander's argument is a recognition that the selective application of drug laws to Black individuals is not an inadvertent byproduct of overzealous or prejudiced law enforcement but rather reflects "a set of structural arrangements that locks a racially distinct group into a subordinate political, social and economic position, effectively creating a second-class citizenship. Those trapped within the system are not merely disadvantaged . . . the system itself is structured to lock them into a subordinate position."[29] The mass incarceration of Black males is then offered as evidence that Black men are criminals. Yet, as Alexander explains: "The temptation is to insist that black men 'choose' to be criminals. . . . The myth of choice here is seductive, but it should be resisted. African Americans are not significantly more likely to use or sell prohibited drugs than whites, but they are *made* criminals at drastically higher rates for precisely the same conduct. . . . And the process of making them criminals has produced racial stigma."[30] Thus, the process by which individuals are *made* to be criminals reflects existing biases while simultaneously creating and perpetuating new stereotypes that are used to validate the former and justify future regulations. Here, the concept of governmentality is useful for understanding how Black Americans are governed in ways that go far beyond hierarchical state control of their behavior.

Similarly, contemporary solicitation laws and prostitution-free zones are facially neutral criminal laws that are advanced in the interest of promoting public health and safety and eradicating crime. Yet, the process by which some individuals are made criminals while others are not reflects the historical biases of dominant groups operating within the realm of governmentality. The practice of profiling, arresting, and incarcerating trans individuals walking in public spaces works to make trans people criminals and promulgates a stigma that they are sex workers, in effect marking them as a sexually deviant population that exists outside of the margins of contemporary American society.

In addition to making trans individuals criminals, transprofiling impedes their ability to move freely and exist in public spaces. As Butler explains, "The public sphere is constituted in part by what can appear, and the regulation of the sphere of appearance is one way to establish what will count as reality, and what will not."[31] The removal of trans bodies from public spaces works to force a population into the shadows. If trans people do not "count as reality" there are numerous consequences.

First, their negation absolves the state and society from any obligations to these communities, including, but not limited to, taking action to address systemic violence and discrimination against trans people, providing social services and support to individuals in and considering transition, and accommodating the needs of trans individuals. Second, their erasure means that they are unable to challenge the gender binary that serves as a powerful organizational and privileging mechanism in contemporary patriarchal heteronormative American society, as demonstrated in the preceding chapters.

Throughout U.S. history, processes of governmentality have enabled certain populations to be marked as sexually deviant and outside of the margins of society. While LGBTQ individuals have been systematically marginalized and punished for deviating from the patriarchal heteronormative principles on which the nation was founded, allegations of sexual deviance have been projected onto Blacks, Native Americans, Asians, and various immigrant groups throughout the country's history to locate them at the margins of the public and/or keep them outside of the United States altogether.[32] Consistent with this history, transprofiling as a tool of governmentality implicates racist and xenophobic prejudices with dire consequences for those who are intersectionally subjected.

Intersectional Subjection of Trans Individuals

Intersectional subjection makes some individuals more vulnerable to transprofiling than others. According to the National Center for Transgender Equality survey conducted in the summer of 2015, the intersection of transphobia and structural racism is devastating for trans people of color. While 12 percent of respondents reported that they had engaged in prostitution, including 9 percent in the past year, the numbers were higher for transwomen of color.[33] Similarly, in a 2011 survey, "[d]iscrimination was pervasive throughout the entire sample, yet the combination of anti-transgender bias and persistent, structural racism was especially devastating. People of color in general fare worse than white participants across the board, with African American transgender respondents faring worse than all others in many areas examined."[34] Notably, "Black (fifty-three percent) and Latino/a (thirty-four percent) respondents had extremely high rates of underground work [including sex work (forty-four percent for Black and twenty-eight percent for Latina/o respondents)],[35] likely related in part to barriers and abuse within educational systems and dramatically higher rates of employment discrimination."[36] Thus, systemic racism intersects with heteronormative biases to increase the likelihood that trans people of color will be forced to resort to underground work in the first place, thereby making them more vulnerable in the war on solicitation.

As demonstrated in chapter 2, trans people often live in extreme poverty, and this means that they are more likely to live in poor and high crime neighborhoods, thereby subjecting them to increased opportunities for transprofiling. Rather than waiting to approach individuals engaged in criminal activities, law enforcement officers utilize proxy measures such as location, or the way a person looks and dresses, to proactively approach and detain individuals.[37] Yet, the reality is that trans people profiled by law enforcement oftentimes are walking in high crime neighborhoods because they live there, not because they are traveling there to engage in criminal activity. Juan David Gastolomendo, the executive director for the Latino Commission on AIDS, explains that many transgender Latinas are falsely arrested for prostitution because, "It ends up boiling down to being a trans woman in a place where known sex work is happening. The arrest is based on the client's identity and where the arrest happens. These are places where prostitution happens, *but they are also places where people socialize.*"[38]

Furthermore, in poor communities and majority-minority neighborhoods the pervasive police presence that exists enables extensive surveillance of trans residents. Due to the fact that stop and frisk practices disproportionately burden poor communities and communities of color, trans people living in those same communities are more likely to be subject to quality of life policing stops than those living in other neighborhoods.[39] Yet, it is important to understand how increased enforcement of quality of life policing on trans individuals implicates both racial and sexual norms in ways that intersectionally subject targeted populations. As Ritchie explains, " '[Q]uality of life' policing has dramatically increased the tools available to officers to enforce racialized norms of sexual and gender conformity."[40]

In addition, national immigration legislation passed in the aftermath of 9/11 increased opportunities for law enforcement to legally profile individuals based on one's perceived immigrant status, resulting in increased racial profiling as described in chapter 3.[41] While the selective enforcement of solicitation laws has negative consequences for all trans people of color, it is especially dire for trans immigrants. As crimmigration policies proliferate, both documented and undocumented immigrants are at increased risk of deportation. In particular, the government's ability to deport individuals detained and/or convicted of engaging in crimes of moral turpitude subjects trans immigrants to increased risk due to the practice of profiling these individuals for walking while trans.[42] For many trans immigrants, deportation means that they will be forced to return to countries they fled because of discrimination and violence based on their trans identities.[43] At the same time, some trans immigrants who have qualified for asylum or relief from removal because of their trans identity have subsequently lost these protections after prostitution convictions.[44]

In addition to fears about deportation, the challenges faced by many immigrants to the United States—such as finding sustainable employment and housing—are compounded for those who identify as trans. Due to their intersectional identities they are more likely to be subject to discrimination and violence, and many undocumented trans individuals experience workplace discrimination that makes economic security elusive.[45] According to the 2011 National Transgender Discrimination Survey, "[U]ndocumented trans people (thirty-nine percent) reported lost jobs due to bias more often than U.S. citizens (twenty-six percent)."[46] These employment challenges often drive undocumented trans immigrants to seek work in underground economies, thereby increasing their exposure to criminal charges and deportation proceedings.[47]

Transprofiling as a Tool for Removing and Erasing Trans Bodies from Public Spaces

The erroneous enforcement of solicitation laws, accompanied by the creation of prostitution-free zones, effectively controls the movements of the trans population with the intention of marginalizing and, perhaps more insidiously, erasing this population from the public realm.[48] Drawing on the work of Foucault, Butler argues that the managing of populations often implicates two dimensions: "a process through which regulatory power produces a set of subjects . . . [and] the process of their de-subjectivation, one with enormous political and legal consequences."[49] Both aspects of population management are present when individuals are profiled for walking while trans. While solicitation laws may be defended as attempts to regulate crime and promote safety, their selective application to trans individuals leads a population to be physically removed from communities and rendered invisible. While law enforcement's treatment of trans communities reflects the role that the state plays in enforcing and maintaining sexual, racial, and political hierarchies, the concept of governmentality suggests that these prejudices cannot be explained away as police officer bias that can be corrected via education and training.[50] Instead, the criminalization and incarceration of individuals for walking while trans is "intrinsic to the system itself. Prisons are designed to insulate society from those who fall outside the 'proper' functioning of the formal political economic order, as well as those who threaten the status quo or are marked as socially deviant."[51] The profiling of trans individuals effectively creates a criminal population whose incarceration substantiates the image of a state that is tough on crime while simultaneously subordinating all trans individuals and reifying existing hierarchies.[52] Not surprisingly, these costs are born disproportionately by those who are intersectionally subjected. For example, the intersection of race and trans identity results in increased incarceration rates for trans people of color. Specifically, "While seven percent of study participants reported being arrested or held in a cell strictly due to bias of police officers on the basis of gender identity/expression . . . [t]his experience was heightened for respondents of color. Black and Latino/a incidences of being incarcerated due only to gender identity/expression were much higher than the overall sample's experience, at forty-one percent and twenty-one percent respectively."[53]

Transprofiling does not always culminate in the incarceration of these individuals and their removal from public spaces. Oftentimes, trans individuals are not made into subjects of the regulatory state but rather are de-subjectivated. This occurs when law enforcement officers harass transgender women, including defacing them in public by forcibly removing their wigs and prosthetic breasts and exposing their genitals. These actions serve to publicly expose transgender individuals as deviant frauds. Similarly, many transgender women report being called "it" by the police or referred to in male terms.[54] As Butler explains, "It seems important to recognize that one way of 'managing' a population is to constitute them as the less than human without entitlement to rights, as the humanly unrecognizable."[55] Victoria D., a transgender woman, described how the abuse she suffered at the hands of law enforcement did just that:

> All my arrests always came from just walking on the street, coming out of a club, or just because a cop identified me as transgender. They would always look for condoms. They don't care about you, they take your purse, throw it on their car,

> your stuff they throw it on the floor, they pat frisk you, they ask if you have fake boobs, take them off right there, if you have a wig, take it off. It's humiliating. Right there in the street, *they take your identity right there*. When they find condoms, they say "what are these for . . . how many dicks did you suck today? How much money did you make today?"[56]

The costs of transprofiling are magnified in poor and predominantly minority neighborhoods. As previously discussed, many members of trans communities are socioeconomically disadvantaged and reside in lower-income neighborhoods. This location provides law enforcement with a pretext for being in the very neighborhoods where many trans individuals are likely to reside, thereby increasing opportunities for transprofiling. According to Human Rights Watch:

> Many members of the Queens Latina transgender community experienced being stopped and searched by the police on suspicion of prostitution while walking in their own neighborhoods. Alexa L., a transgender woman from Mexico, said, "Eight days ago I wasn't working because I was sick. I left my house to get a coffee, and had two condoms in my pocket. The police stopped me and said 'what are you doing?' I said I was getting coffee. They searched me and found two condoms. They asked 'what are you doing with two condoms, what are they for?' I said they were for protection. They took the condoms. I couldn't get coffee, I was so scared. I felt very bad. I'm not a delinquent, I didn't steal. When they searched me and found them, I was shaking, I was so scared."[57]

When trans individuals are physically monitored and threatened and/or forcibly removed from the communities in which they reside they are both metaphorically and physically left with nowhere to go.

In particular, the creation of prostitution-free zones poses a unique threat to trans individuals residing in lower-income communities recognized as high crime areas. Prostitution-free zones are an explicit attempt to remove certain people from designated areas backed up with the force of law. It is important to keep in mind that sex work is already prohibited and criminalized in the towns and cities where prostitution-free zones are implemented. As such, within these zones law enforcement is essentially encouraged to profile individuals in order to remove them. Furthermore, community members are empowered to profile and report to police those individuals deemed to be outside of the character of their neighborhoods.

For example, as Elijah Adiv Edelman explains, in Washington, D.C., the impetus for prostitution-free zones was the Metropolitan Police Department's desire to promote public safety and health.[58] As such, the Metropolitan Police Department's policy allows for the creation of prostitution-free zones in those areas where local residents complain about the prevalence of prostitution, but, as Edelman notes, "these areas do not necessarily constitute the areas of greatest sex work within the city; rather, they constitute spaces of liminality and contested use, nearly always situated along gentrifying borderlands."[59] In this way, residents that are rapidly gentrifying neighborhoods historically occupied by minority communities are able to exorcise those long-term residents that do not conform to the neighborhood's new racial and sexual hierarchies. These practices have the nefarious effect of removing trans people of color from their own neighborhoods. When cities couple the creation of prostitution-free zones with the selective enforcement of solicitation laws in areas known for sex work (often poor neighborhoods), the spaces open to poor and racial and ethnic minority trans people rapidly evaporate and cease to exist. In this way, quality of life policing laws become a tactic of governmentality and assist in gentrifying neighborhoods and insulating white residents from the poor and racial and ethnic minorities.[60]

Transprofiling increases the likelihood that trans immigrants will be charged with a crime, resulting in arrest records that may reveal one's sex as being different than that reported on other documents. For trans immigrants, any discontinuity in one's official gender identity may result in job loss (e.g., if one's employer reports an identity that does not match the Social Security Administration's information) or expulsion from the country if the government perceives one as hiding his or her "real" identity, as discussed in chapter 3.[61]

In addition, while many trans individuals charged with a crime are anxious to negotiate and/or accept plea agreements in order to avoid the extreme dangers posed to trans people while incarcerated, trans immigrants must weigh their personal safety and immigration status when evaluating the consequences of accepting a plea bargain. As Natalia, a transgender Latina woman, explains, "Being transgender women we live in fear of the police. . . . Many times when I was arrested remarks were made that I might be deported because I am an immigrant."[62] According to Congress's Illegal Immigration Reform and Immigrant Responsibility Act of 1996,[63] individuals convicted of crimes are subject to deportation, but as Gehi explains, "Congress defined 'conviction' to include much more than a formal judgment of guilt or a conviction under relevant state or federal criminal law. . . . [A]ny admission of . . . a CIMT [crime involving moral turpitude], regardless of whether the person knew it was a crime or whether the charge was dismissed in court, constitutes a conviction and renders an immigrant deportable."[64] Many immigrants may plead guilty or enter a plea of no contest to avoid incarceration and not realize that in doing so they may be subjecting themselves to deportation proceedings. Due to the fact that immigration status often intersects with poverty and language barriers, it is not unusual for immigrants absent any legal representation to be pressured into pleading guilty to a crime they did not commit. In this way, immigrants profiled for walking while trans—regardless of whether or not they were actually soliciting sex work—are at risk of and subject to deportation.

Furthermore, once an individual is deported, convictions for sex work make legal reentry difficult for trans immigrants. Individuals who have engaged in sex work in the past ten years are denied legal entry to the United States. As Jeanty and Tobin explain:

> This rule applies regardless of whether the individual was convicted of any crime, is no longer engaged in sex work, or whether the sex work occurred in a jurisdiction where it is legal. . . . The ban's unintended harmful effects were highlighted in 2012 when the International AIDS Conference was held in Washington, DC . . . leading activists from around the world—many of them transgender—were prevented from attending because their history of sex work barred them from even entering the country.[65]

The erasure and removal of trans people of color and trans immigrants from public spaces is not happenstance. It is a form of disciplinary power that subjects trans individuals and implicates various nonstate actors and entities.[66] As Edelman explains, the crime that trans people of color commit is the act of being visible.[67] Solicitation laws are utilized to remove these individuals from public spaces in order to render moot the challenge that their existence poses for existing racial and sexual hierarchies. For trans people of color and trans immigrants, the multiple subjections that accompany being trans and a racial or ethnic minority or noncitizen open up numerous opportunities for state-sanctioned control and violence against them.

Transprofiling and the Enforcement of Gender Normativity

In addition to controlling the movements of trans individuals, transprofiling acts as a tool for privileging the fixed gender binary consistent with the understanding that "'sex' is a regulatory ideal whose materialization is compelled . . . through certain highly regulated practices."[68] As Currah and Moore explain, "The identification of citizens or subjects is as vital a function of modern statehood as establishing and policing territorial borders."[69] Thus, the state has a vested interest in maintaining the existing gender binary and promulgating administrative regulations that make it difficult for trans individuals to deceive the public and the state, as described in chapters 3 and 4.[70] Due to the fact that trans individuals challenge existing gender norms, they are understood to be an affront to the state's authority to regulate identity and protect the public from fraud and security risks.[71]

This governing of people's sexual identities reflects the extent to which bodies are understood to be part of the public domain.[72] As such, attempts to exercise autonomy over one's body, particularly by people of color, may be understood as a threat and/or an affront to the interdependence of the community.[73] Keeping in mind that the dominant narrative privileges the white heterosexual body, any suggestion that gender might be fluid or that gender attributes are performative as opposed to expressive challenges the status quo.[74] As such, regulatory norms develop "to materialize the body's sex, to materialize sexual difference in the service of the consolidation of the heterosexual imperative."[75] Individuals who fail to abide by regulatory norms and reject being governed in this way will be systematically marginalized in order to reify the regulatory norms of sex.

For example, as previously noted, police officers often identify condom possession as evidence of intent to solicit, but only when those condoms are possessed by certain bodies. As an outreach worker in Manhattan told Human Rights Watch, "I have never had any young men afraid to take condoms, only black and Latina trans women who have refused to take them. I've had people not take condoms, people who do go through a rigorous routine of hiding them. They were wrapping them in paper, so they were gift-wrapped. . . . They took a couple, but consciously limit themselves, even though they know they are working and would need more, because they couldn't hide them."[76] Implicit in these comments is an understanding that non-trans males are "allowed" to have condoms because male bodies are allowed to be sexual bodies (and entitled to protection from the health risks associated with unprotected sex), whereas transgender women of color are made into criminals for possessing condoms because trans male-to-female bodies are not allowed to be sexual bodies (and are not worthy of public health protections). As Butler explains, "The materialization of a given sex will centrally concern *the regulation of identificatory practices* such that the identification with the abjection of sex will be persistently disavowed."[77] To the extent that trans individuals are understood to be abject beings as opposed to materialized bodies/subjects, their identities and existence are not viable. As one gender nonconforming Black Puerto Rican sex worker asked, "Why do they take your condoms, do they want us to die, do they want us to get something?"[78] In this way, governmentality's regulation of trans bodies in the interest of enforcing gender norms poses a tangible threat to the health and safety of trans people.

At the same time, the proliferation of transprofiling is not only a tool for criminalizing trans individuals, but also a tactic for maintaining the privileges of those "bodies that matter."[79] As more individuals publicly identify as trans, public awareness that sex and gender are social constructs increases, which in turn threatens the solvency of a social and political system that is predicated on the gender binary and "the forced reiteration of sexual and patriarchal norms."[80] Transprofiling, then, not only acts as a tool for removing trans people from public spaces, but discourages people from deviating from the regulatory and cultural norms that dictate how sex is materialized in order to keep individuals in the right sex. In this way "the law is not only that which represses sexuality, but a prohibition that generates sexuality or, at least, compels its directionality."[81] By making trans identity itself a crime, transprofiling discourages people from identifying as trans.

Furthermore, governmentality and the enforcement of gender normativity implicate norms governing race, ethnicity, citizenship, and socioeconomic status. Given the United States' history of legally and socially controlling the bodies and sexual availability of racial and ethnic minorities, efforts by trans people of color to assert their sexual autonomy are especially threatening.[82] Stereotypes about gender roles, femininity, masculinity, and hypersexuality have been projected onto racial and ethnic minorities throughout U.S. history to justify acts of sexual violence against these individuals as well as their fetishization and ostracization. Thus, it is essential to understand transprofiling as a tool for promoting a raced and classed conception of gender normativity. This is exemplified by police treatment of individuals who are intersectionally subjected. "The National Coalition of Anti-Violence Programs reported in 2011 that transgender people of color in particular were more than three times as likely to experience hate violence from police as compared to the general population."[83]

One of the ways that governmentality operates on trans bodies is subjecting them to violence as punishment for their attempts to circumvent the gender binary, including law enforcement harassment and abuse of trans individuals. According to the National Center for Transgender Equality's 2015 survey, 58 percent of respondents reported mistreatment by the police in the prior year, and among those who were arrested by the police 22 percent reported that they believed they were arrested because they are trans,[84] and 20 percent reported that they were verbally harassed, 4 percent physically assaulted, and 3 percent sexually assaulted by police.[85] These numbers are higher for racial and ethnic minorities, as demonstrated by the fact that 74 percent of Native American, 71 percent of multiracial, 66 percent of Latinx, and 61 percent of Black respondents reported mistreatment by law enforcement.[86] Given the criminal archetypes associated with racial and ethnic minorities, combined with the sexual deviance assigned to trans individuals, the aforementioned statistics should not come as a surprise.[87]

For transwomen of color, stereotypes and assumptions about their sexuality and the idea that their bodies are sexually available to white males might increase the likelihood of sexual abuse by police officers. Many individuals report being forced to perform sex acts on police officers or extorted to do so in exchange for the police not taking them into custody,[88] and "[r]espondents who were currently working in the underground economy (27%) and those who were homeless in the past year (17%) were more likely to report one or more of these [physical attacks, sexual assaults, or sexual extortion by a police officer] experiences."[89] Furthermore, trans immigrants may be especially vulnerable to police extortion and assault because of their fears of being arrested and deported. As Yesenia, a transgender Latina woman residing in Jackson Heights, explains:

> Being a transgender woman during the day, I interact with people and live my life normally and feel safe in my neighborhood. But at night it's different because the police are really transphobic and racist. I myself had a bad experience with the police some years ago. It was 3AM and the cops were doing a sweep and they arrested around eight girls, including me. They took us to the 110th Precinct. Once in the precinct a tall, white, Italian-looking police officer came inside my cell. He asked me to "wipe something off from his butt" and I told him "no, because that is not my job." He took me to the back of the precinct and started touching my breasts. He told me that if I performed oral sex on him that he would let me go, that I wouldn't have to go to court. I told him no, that I wasn't gonna do it. Then he asked me again if we could have this deal and I told him no again. Then he brought me back to the cell with the other girls. I was really scared and I knew I hadn't done anything wrong, but I felt humiliated. I didn't want to say anything or report him because of my legal status. But these types of situations shouldn't be happening to us with the people that are supposed to protect us.[90]

This violence is only possible because other actors and institutions ignore police abuse of trans individuals thereby empowering law enforcement officers to perpetrate abuse with impunity.[91] As such, trans individuals often are uncomfortable seeking assistance from law enforcement when it is needed. According to the National Center for Transgender Equality survey, 57 percent of respondents reported that they would not be comfortable seeking assistance from law enforcement.[92] The reality is that a sizeable portion of trans individuals do not believe that they may seek the help of law enforcement officers when needed. Trans victims of assaults and crimes often opt out of reporting these incidents because they do not want to interact with legal authorities,[93] but this is highly problematic given the high rates of violence experienced by trans individuals. These fears are exacerbated for trans people of color and trans immigrants, who are inclined to be wary of law enforcement based on their racial, ethnic, and/or immigrant identities.[94] Notably, the increased interactions among local police departments and U.S. Immigration and Customs Enforcement post-9/11 make it less likely that trans immigrant victims of violence and crimes will seek local police assistance because of fears of deportation.[95]

The fact that trans individuals often are uncomfortable seeking assistance from the criminal justice system makes them susceptible to violence by both strangers and their intimates. Perpetrators of hate crimes as well as domestic abusers may be confident that their actions will not be reported because of the common fear among trans victims that they will be ridiculed, ignored, or further violated by law enforcement officers. Among those interacting with law enforcement, 20 percent of respondents who sought police assistance reported that they were denied equal treatment by law enforcement,[96] and racial and ethnic minorities (35 to 47 percent) were more likely to report being treated by law enforcement with disrespect than white respondents (25 percent).[97] Furthermore, many trans individuals may fear that they will become the focus of criminal justice inquiries because of their intersectional identities. For example, Mogul et al. discuss as typical "an incident in which an Asian Pacific transgender woman reported a hate crime to police who refused to photograph her injuries. The Internal Affairs Bureau officer to whom she complained told her, 'You're not a victim of violence. If you didn't tell people you're a transsexual, people would leave you alone.' "[98] The suggestion here and elsewhere is that the deception perpetrated by trans individuals negates, or in many instances legitimates, the violent actions of others.[99]

Trans individuals pose a challenge to a society that continues to organize itself both legally and socially according to gender norms. Throughout the United States, people and institutions identify an individual's sex and then locate him or her in the appropriate spaces and narratives according to the right sex. Due to the fact that trans individuals often are misunderstood as concealing their real sexual identities and/or are perceived as embodying gender fluidity, their existence threatens the gender binary that is essential to organizing and maintaining a patriarchal, heteronormative society. These deceptions are exacerbated by trans people of color because they fail to conform to existing racial/ethnic stereotypes and gender norms, thereby confounding the dominant narrative. Furthermore, this perceived duplicity legitimizes and sanctions violence against trans individuals as well as their exclusion from society. As described above, transprofiling exposes trans individuals to various threats—sexually transmitted diseases, sexual and physical violence, incarceration and its associated dangers—and sends a clear message that those who deviate from raced and classed gender norms are abject beings. In doing so, white heterosexual bodies are marked as those bodies that matter and maintain their privileged position.[100]

Conclusion

The criminalization of trans people via the selective enforcement of solicitation laws controls the movements of trans people and removes them from public spaces. While transprofiling has especially nefarious effects on transwomen of color, all trans people are vulnerable when forces of governmentality conspire to facilitate the movement of some, but not others, into the criminal justice system. The risks to trans people in their interactions with local, state, and national law enforcement are well documented, and the potential of incarceration and/or deportation is a powerful mitigating force in trans people's lives. In this way, a neutral criminal prohibition is operationalized and implemented as a raced, classed, and sexed disciplinary tool that targets trans people, and clearly signals that those who deviate from gendered norms will be profiled as abnormal and transgressive criminal beings.

These practices work in concert with the forces of governmentality described in chapters 3 and 4 to relegate trans people to the margins of the public, and it is difficult to imagine how these forces of discrimination and infrahumanization can be remedied via a trans politics of rights alone. In fact, the tendency of rights recognition to work in tandem with the sociolegal construction of binary identities suggests that a trans politics of rights risks becoming a transnormative politics of right sex. Given the way that forces of governmentality work to privilege and reify the sex binary, a politics of right sex may actually work to extend rights to transgender people who are able to successfully pass and permanently transition to the right sex while implicitly sanctioning new and creative disciplinary mechanisms that continue to obfuscate trans individuals' abilities to transition as described in chapter 3, the exercise of de facto policing of gender and sex as described in chapter 4, and/or continue to marginalize those who do not meet the raced, classed, sexed, gendered expectations for transnormativity as discussed above. The chapter that follows explores the viability and efficacy of a trans politics of rights in light of the obstacles posed by the forces of governmentality that govern the public.

Part Three

The Limits of Trans Rights

Chapter 6

The Viability and Efficacy of a Trans Politics of Rights

Introduction

Attempts to mark trans individuals as abnormal beings and "frustrating political subjects" occur via myriad forces of governmentality that effectively locate trans people at the margins of the public.[1] These forces of governmentality include the designation of trans bodies as transgressive, administratively impossible, and/or queer security threats via state and social regulations of identity documents in order to deny or undermine their existence, the maintenance of sex-segregated facilities, including bathrooms, that enable both de jure and de facto policing of the sex and gender binaries in public places, which constrain trans individuals' access to public spaces and subject them to violence, and the criminalization of trans people via the selective enforcement of solicitation laws, which sanctions their removal from public spaces. The combined effects of these forces of governmentality are to regulate trans bodies in order to marginalize and stigmatize these individuals, and maintain the privileged positions of some relative to others in the public.

As chapters 3, 4, and 5 demonstrate, governmentality works by, first, denying trans people's existence in order to force them into compliance with the expectations of the public or relegate those who dare to challenge these norms to the margins of the public, then it constrains the ability of trans individuals to enter and move through public spaces, and, finally, it removes trans individuals from public spaces if they dare to enter them at all. The policing and surveillance of trans bodies also takes on raced and classed dimensions because the threats posed by trans individuals are further exacerbated when they are trans people of color and trans immigrants. These threats, however, are socially constructed by a dominant population that identifies those who are intersectionally subjected by multiple sources and locations of social and state control as appropriate targets of disciplinary power. Via the processes of governmentality, laws governing identity documents, access to public accommodations, and solicitation laws are used as tactics to transprofile and manage trans individuals of color and immigrants to mitigate the threats they pose to the dominant narrative, norms about sex, and the maintenance of raced and classed gender norms.

In this context, it is difficult to imagine how rights-based strategies are going to be able to overcome the processes of governmentality that operate on trans people. To that end, this chapter will explore two potential shortcomings of rights recognition as a mechanism for resisting the processes of governmentality described in the preceding chapters. First, understanding that political mobilization is an essential component for crafting and executing rights-based movements, it is essential to elucidate the challenges associated with mobilizing trans individuals given the high rates of poverty and socioeconomic marginalization within these communities as well as the interlocking and systemic forces of oppression that operate on trans individuals, rendering them one of the most intersectionally subjected populations in the United States.[2] Forces of governmentality have been remarkably effective in erasing, criminalizing, delegitimating, and denying the existence of transgender individuals as demonstrated by chapters 3, 4 and 5, and these facts may interfere with the political mobilization of trans individuals. In particular, those trans individuals best situated to assume leadership roles within trans rights organizations may not be representative of the diversity of identities and experiences within the trans communities.[3] At the same time, trans communities may be in a position to capitalize on their preexisting alliance with the gay rights movement to overcome some of these obstacles to mobilization, but this strategy comes with both pros and cons to be discussed below. Notably, it raises questions about whether or not a successful trans rights movement is likely to be more beneficial to some portions of trans communities than others.[4] As discussed throughout this book, a trans politics of rights is most likely to be successful as a transnormative politics of right sex, but this will enable the recognition of rights for a privileged portion of the trans community—those transgender individuals able and willing to meet the requirements for a successful transition from male to female or female to male as specified by the state—while leaving many others including intersectionally subjected, nonbinary and gender fluid, and socioeconomically disadvantaged trans people outside of the protections of the law.

Second, the forces of governmentality described in the prior chapters are not merely tools of state control that can be remedied via rights-based litigation.[5] Much of the de jure and de facto policing of the sex and gender binaries that occur on a daily basis are instances of infrahumanization enabled by infra laws. Furthermore, in those instances in which formal laws are at issue, the laws themselves often are neutral and do not specifically state that trans people should be the targets of government surveillance and regulations. As such, it is not clear how the recognition of rights by the courts and/or the expansion of protected identities and extension of rights via local, state, and national legislation will be effective in mitigating the forces of governmentality that operate on trans individuals and locate them at the margins of the public subject to ongoing discrimination and infrahumanization.

Central to the discussion of the politics of rights is the idea that "rights can be useful political tools" because

> [i]t is possible to capitalize on the perceptions of entitlement associated with rights to initiate and nurture political mobilization—a dual process of *activating* a quiescent citizenry and *organizing* groups into effective political units. Political mobilization can in this fashion build support for interests that have been excluded from existing allocations of values and thus promote a *realignment* of political forces.[6]

The analysis that follows will first examine the activation and organization of trans individuals in pursuit of rights recognition, including the pros and cons of working with liberal gay rights groups versus going it alone. Then, attention will be dedicated to evaluating whether or not these mobilizations will culminate in the realignment of political forces in ways that are advantageous to trans individuals. Finally, this chapter concludes with the recognition that a trans politics of rights may result in substantive benefits for some individuals within trans communities, but collective liberation for all trans people will require alternative strategies that move beyond the constraints of the politics of rights. That being said, in light of the fact that rights movements are proceeding, it is useful to explore the pros and cons of the different alliances and strategies available to activists working on behalf of trans rights.

The Political Mobilization of Trans Individuals

Recognizing that "rights are most sensibly thought of as agents of political mobilization rather than as ends in themselves," it is essential to examine the pros and cons of different social movement configurations for advancing trans interests.[7] One pressing question is whether or not trans interests are best served via alliances with liberal gay rights groups or alternative arrangements that prioritize and privilege trans individuals and interests. As noted in the introduction, the tenuous alliances among gay rights groups and trans people have been fraught with difficulties for decades given that trans interests were long neglected by gay rights groups, leading Dean Spade to refer to the umbrella acronym LGBT as "LGB-fake-T."[8] While the challenges associated with subsuming different intersecting identities under a single umbrella "movement" have been well documented,[9] a brief review demonstrates how the politics of respectability have informed these interactions since the aftermath of World War II, as "homosexuals, transvestites, and transsexuals began to develop a mutual aversion to one another, each believing that the other groups hurt their cause for public acceptance."[10]

Throughout the history of the modern gay rights movement, historical events have been subject to whitewashing and normalizing to exclude the participation of people of color and trans individuals, consistent with the politics of respectability. For example, the celebration of the Stonewall riots in 1969 as the pinnacle event that established a gay resistance neglects the history of trans activism and resistance, including the Compton's Cafeteria riots of 1966, and the associated whitewashing of Stonewall erases the leadership roles and participation of many trans people of color in the riots. These patterns of omission have been replicated in the creation of social movement organizations and their articulation of social, political, and legal priorities. As explained in the introduction, early gay rights groups such as the Gay Liberation Front (GLF) and Gay Activists Alliance (GAA) formed in New York City, but transwomen of color such as Sylvia Rivera reported that they felt ostracized and marginalized when they attended GLF and GAA meetings.[11] As such, Rivera and Marsha P. Johnson, another transwoman of color, worked to organize the Street Transvestite Action Revolutionaries (STAR) as an offshoot of GLF in order to advocate for the interests of trans individuals, in particular those who were homeless and/or runaways.[12]

These class-based conflicts played a major role in the marginalization of the T in LGBT in the post-Stonewall era and the subsequent development of an independent trans movement:

> These class-based conflicts are also apparent in the increasing invisibility of transsexuals, cross-dressers, and drag queens in the decades after Stonewall, as "gay liberation" gave way to "gay rights" and to an emphasis on "dispelling the stereotypes" that lesbians and gay men are all bull dykes and flaming fairies. In an important sense, the mainstream gay rights movement defined itself and emerged as an organized political and legal movement by embracing an explicitly nontransgender, or gender-normative, model of gay identity. Over time, the increasing hegemony of this gender-normative model has resulted in the increasing isolation of gender-variant lesbians and gay men within the mainstream movement, and increasing tensions between gay and transgender people. Eventually, these tensions permitted gender-variant people to emerge as a distinct constituency, or as what is now known as the "transgender" movement.[13]

In light of this history, the social movement strategies employed by liberal gay rights groups become clearer. The politics of respectability intersects with liberal gay rights movements' emphases on assimilation to privilege the interests and priorities of those who are able and willing to assimilate. These strategies, however, come with consequences for those who do not want to acclimate to the expectations and norms of the public and/or those who are unable to do so.[14] "The ostracism of transgender people from the mainstream assimilationist movement for gay rights—i.e. marriage, military, and employment non-discrimination legislation—has functioned as a way for white, homonormative, non-trans gays and lesbians to gain social recognition and state benefits."[15] As such, when liberal gay rights groups such as the Human Rights Campaign (HRC) began to advocate on behalf of trans interests, including playing a large role in organizing the corporate boycott of North Carolina in response to its passage of

HB2, it is not surprising that questions arise about the sincerity of their commitment to trans interests.[16]

The Pros of Working with Liberal Gay Rights Groups

At the same time, however, recognizing that favorable political conditions must converge with preexisting organizational resources to provide activists with a context for effective collective action, there is an argument to be made that trans interests may be best advanced by working within or in conjunction with existing gay rights organizations and capitalizing on their resources to advance trans rights.[17] By capitalizing on their preexisting alliances with the gay rights movement, trans activists may be able to overcome some of the obstacles to political mobilization. In fact, one of trans advocates' earliest strategic calculations was to lobby lesbian and gay rights groups to include trans issues in order to raise their profile and link them with a larger social movement. In this way, trans activists sought to emphasize the collective struggle shared by gays, lesbians, and trans people.[18] While the fight to get the "T" included in LGBT was contentious and many gay and lesbian organizations systematically marginalized trans individuals and their interests, as described above, the history and connections exist and provide opportunities for bridge building.[19]

In fact, as explained in the introduction, beginning in the 1990s and into the twenty-first century, leading liberal gay rights groups began to adopt trans-inclusive mission statements and started to identify and work on behalf of trans rights.[20] Post-*Obergefell*, many liberal gay rights organizations stated that lobbying Congress to pass a gender-identity inclusive nondiscrimination act such as the Equality Act, which would prohibit discrimination in housing, employment, public accommodations, and so on, is a priority.[21] This verbal commitment and the decision to focus resources on pursuing legal protections for the LGBTQ community broadly defined, as opposed to only seeking prohibitions on employment discrimination on the basis of sexual orientation, is an improvement over prior missteps when, for example, HRC supported an Employment Non-Discrimination Act (ENDA) that did not include protections for gender identity. Given HRC's historic marginalization of trans interests, it is noteworthy that, as noted above, HRC took a leading role in the fight against HB2.[22]

Similarly, numerous liberal gay rights groups have been active in the litigation on behalf of trans individuals, such as the case of Gavin

Grimm, the transgender high school student who challenged his school's refusal to allow him access to male restrooms as a violation of his civil rights as protected by the Fourteenth Amendment and Title IX of the 1972 Education Amendments.[23] As such, trans individuals may benefit from the expertise and resources that accrue to existing liberal gay rights groups and legal advocacy organizations such as Lambda Legal and GLBTQ Legal Advocates & Defenders.[24]

Cons of Working with Liberal Gay Rights Groups

At the same time, however, given the liberal gay rights movement's contentious history with and mistreatment of trans communities and their interests, it is logical for trans individuals to question the merits of investing in a movement and its organizations that historically have not wanted them as members. In 2001, Sylvia Rivera said, "One of our [STAR's] main goals now is to destroy the Human Rights Campaign, because I'm tired of sitting on the back of the bumper. It's not even the back of the bus anymore—it's the back of the bumper."[25] Furthermore, despite the positive advancements described above, antagonisms toward trans individuals by liberal gay rights groups are not historic relics. Individual gays and lesbians continue to question whether or not their interests are commensurate with those in trans communities, and some even suggest that trans people are an embarrassment to the gay rights movement.[26] In addition, some gay rights advocates argue that "as a 'new' group, transgender people must wait their turn and cannot expect to 'piggyback' or 'ride on the coattails' of the gay movement."[27] In other instances, strategic calculations regarding the likelihood of passing trans-inclusive policies may lead some LGBT advocacy groups to exclude gender identity from state-level policy efforts, thereby favoring "pragmatic incrementalism" over "full inclusion."[28]

In addition to their history of marginalizing the interests of trans people, liberal gay rights groups have tended to underrepresent and marginalize the viewpoints and interests of minorities. As Spade explains, "Feminist, anticapitalist, and antiracist analysis has been notably absent from mainstream discourses about LGBT rights, and low-income people, people of color, and gender-transgressive people have been notoriously underrepresented from leadership and decision-making power in these movements."[29] Thus, the mainstream liberal gay rights agenda has prioritized issues that are important to the most affluent and privileged within

LGB populations, including marriage equality and the associated socioeconomic benefits such as access to shared health care, property, and so on, as opposed to affordable housing for all or universal health care.[30] Efforts by liberal gay rights groups on behalf of trans interests risk replicating the normative strategies associated with the push for gay rights.

These assimilationist strategies are especially problematic when adapted to a trans politics of rights because of the significant burdens and intersectional subjections imposed on the most marginalized within trans communities. When trans activism is constructed as an appeal for acceptance into the extant neoliberal regime, it privileges those bodies that "are the most productive and most effortlessly absorbed into capitalist employment pools" and comes with costs for "those within trans communities who cannot be easily assimilated into normative categories, such as those who do not pass as men or women or those who are physically or mentally ill or incarcerated."[31] Thus, rather than eradicating the norms that privilege some and marginalize others, assimilationist strategies fight for some to be normalized in order to gain access to the public, while others are left behind and the forces of governmentality that work on those bodies marked as transgressive remain unchallenged.

Furthermore, the "homonormative narratives of queer history" that are so closely associated with and often promulgated by liberal gay rights groups "construct a limited horizon of queer futurity that is in alignment with the anti-queer, anti-trans, capitalist, and white supremacist state."[32] In this way, the success of the liberal gay rights movement and its emphasis on homonormativity now means that many assimilated gays and lesbians are implicated in the operation of forces of governmentality and engage in the policing of gender that works to the detriment of trans individuals.[33] As such, those LGBTQ constituencies who have felt excluded or underrepresented by liberal gay rights groups often have formed their own organizations and may be reticent to partner with the very entities that have excluded them in the past, thereby making it difficult to coordinate and articulate a consensus set of priorities and interests.[34] This distrust is difficult if not impossible for some to overcome. As Bassichis, Lee, and Spade remind us, "We know that when those in power say they will 'come back' for those at the bottom of the social and economic hierarchy, it will never happen. . . . We've all seen painful examples of this in LGBT politics time after time—from the abandonment of transgender folks in the Employment Non-Discrimination Act (ENDA) to the idea that gay marriage is the first step toward universal health care."[35]

Finally, in addition to prioritizing homonormative gay and lesbian interests, many liberal gay rights groups emphasized litigation as a primary form of legal mobilization and argued that discrimination on the basis of sexual orientation should be recognized as a violation of constitutional guarantees because sexual orientation is a fixed identity and not a preference, as described in chapter 1. By analogizing sexual orientation to other immutable characteristics such as race and sex, gay rights groups utilized a legal strategy modeled on the successful tactics of prior civil rights movements, but this emphasis on immutable characteristics as the means to legal protection has significant consequences for trans communities given the emphasis that many place on the fluidity of gender identity and the argument that sex and gender are social constructs and not immutable characteristics, as noted in chapter 2.[36] Thus, much like earlier civil rights movements, the gay rights movement is an identity-based movement, and the emphasis on identity lends itself well to and "reinforces its dominant orientation toward civil rights rather than facilitating its adoption of other approaches to social change."[37] As Minter explains, the liberal gay rights movement's resistance to incorporating trans interests into its policy agenda may reflect "genuine confusion and concern about how to reconcile transgender issues with the modern, nontransgender model of gay identity that has dominated legal and political advocacy on behalf of lesbians and gay men for several decades."[38]

Furthermore, these identity-based appeals that culminate in civil rights strategies including litigation have gained the support of affluent donors, whereas broader appeals or different approaches and strategies may not attract the resources that these liberal gay rights groups depend on for their existence.[39] The utilization of rights-based appeals predicated on the construction of a heterosexual/gay binary has proved to be a persuasive tool for changing public perceptions and creating opportunities for legal change that favor the interests of liberal gay rights groups thereby confirming the efficacy of the politics of rights. As such, liberal gay rights groups are unlikely to abandon litigation, because it has proven to be a successful strategy and, as noted above, they are now beginning to litigate on behalf of the rights of transgender individuals. Their emphases on binary and immutable identities, however, may prove problematic if that paradigm is accepted by the courts in the context of litigation surrounding transgender rights and validates a transnormative politics of right sex. As such, challenges to traditional identity politics and disagreements about the nature of identity may hinder the opportunities for trans individuals to articulate their interests within the confines of existing liberal gay rights movements.

Going It Alone: A Trans Social Movement and Political Mobilization

Given the increased attention to trans individuals, interests, and causes, and the growing emphasis on pushing for trans rights by those within liberal gay and civil rights groups as well as segments of the broader public, it is useful to explore how trans individuals can best position themselves to define their own wants and needs as opposed to having them articulated by others on their behalf. Recognizing the liberal gay rights movement's history of marginalizing trans interests, its emphasis on immutable characteristics and the binary operationalization of sexual orientation, and the possibility that its attention to trans rights may be occurring in part because mainstream advocacy groups are confronting waning support in the aftermath of the marriage equality victory, it may be advantageous for advocates of trans rights to channel efforts and resources into growing the existing independent trans rights movement, which is distinct from the gay rights movement.[40]

It is important to acknowledge that trans individuals and groups consistently have been fighting for their rights with or without the support of liberal mainstream gay rights groups, and many of them have been rejecting assimilationist and transnormative strategies in the process of doing so.[41] "By the mid-1990s, transgendered individuals and groups were protesting when their peers were murdered, lobbying Capitol Hill and state legislatures for civil rights previously denied them, and engaging in vigorous letter-writing campaigns and political demonstrations when they were slandered or slighted by those in power."[42] As such, while the public may be paying greater attention to the wants and needs of trans people at this moment in time, within trans and certain LGBTQ communities these individuals have been present, organized, and active for decades.[43]

Mobilizing to create new trans-centric rights organizations or supporting existing ones such as the National Center for Transgender Equality may open opportunities for trans advocacy groups interested in pursuing the recognition of rights to work to leverage a politics of trans rights that "politicize[s] needs by changing the way [transgender] people think about their discontents," and challenge the homonormative priorities and conventional legal tactics such as the binary operationalization of immutable characteristics associated with liberal gay rights organizations.[44] A trans politics of rights that profiles and gives voice to the broad array of trans identities and perspectives will be in a better position to offer an alternative location for mobilization and offer a substantive challenge to the dominant homonormative values that inform and dictate the policy priorities of liberal gay rights organizations, and recognize and challenge the discriminatory legal and bureaucratic classifications that work to marginalize and subject trans individuals in ways that are distinct from the contemporary treatment of gays and lesbians.[45]

Yet, similar to other social movements, trans mobilization and organization has been facilitated by a shared collective identity that may come with later costs and risk promulgating transnormative policy priorities and strategies. As Nownes's extensive research on transgender rights interest group formation demonstrates, while the growth of a collective transgender identity—a "we"—enabled group formation, "after determining who they *were not*, transgender people had (and continue to have) a more difficult time determining who they *are*. This battle over collective identity has led to the founding in recent years of several 'niche' groups . . . [and] splintering, infighting, and conflict among actors within the larger transgender social movement."[46] The risk here is that the mainstream transgender rights interest groups successfully advance a transnormative policy agenda for a raceless, classless, gender-binaried, transgender "we" while "niche" groups advance the interests of intersectional trans communities.

Instead, it is imperative that trans rights movements avoid the dangers associated with replacing liberal gay rights groups' homonormative rights strategies with transnormative ones. In order for a trans rights movement to produce substantive and meaningful change in the lives of all trans individuals, it will be necessary to acknowledge and validate the complexity and fluidity of gender and explicitly challenge the ways that law and society seek to suppress challenges to the sex and gender binaries, as opposed to advancing a politics of right sex. Challenging narrow conceptions of gender creates space for the inclusion of a broader array of identities, including intersectionally identified, nonbinary and gender-fluid, and socioeconomically disadvantaged individuals. "Historically, clinging to a narrow and exclusive conception of gender identity has not only marginalized transgender and gender-variant gay people, it also has exacerbated divisions based on race and class."[47]

The Recognition of Rights and the Realignment of Political Forces

Recognizing that the best option for an authentic and viable trans politics of rights is for trans individuals and activists to grow independent trans movements for change that are distinct from liberal gay rights groups, the section that follows evaluates the likelihood that this political mobilization will produce an efficacious trans politics of rights that culminates in the "realignment of forces within the political arena" including the courts and legislatures.[48]

Despite the foregoing discussions of the limitations of rights recognitions and the dangers associated with continuing to perpetuate the myth of rights, rights-based arguments implicate symbolic and substantive goals. As Kylar W. Broadus explains:

> As a former litigant in a transgender discrimination case, I am keenly aware of the law's tremendous power to reflect and shape larger societal messages of acceptance or rejection. When I lost my case, I was devastated not only by the loss of my job and my career but, even more profoundly, by the terrible message that loss conveyed—that as a transgender person, I was not worthy of legal protection or recognition. For many years, progressive scholars and activists have cautioned against placing too much emphasis on the law and on the discourse of "rights" in particular, based on well-founded concerns that doing so can channel our political energies too narrowly and render us too fixated on the chimerical goal of achieving normalcy and approval from the state. At the same time, other progressive voices—and particularly those of people of color—have cautioned against jettisoning the notion of rights altogether. . . . Rights both empower transgender people to contest discrimination and allow us to envision ourselves, and to be seen by others, as fully human. As lawyers and litigants continue to struggle to win individual cases and to set precedents that will benefit the community as a whole, we must not lose sight of this fundamental dimension of legal advocacy.[49]

Broadus's description of rights as both a source of empowerment and a limited resource for pursuing social change via litigation gets directly to the heart of the politics of rights. "The politics of rights, therefore, involves the manipulation of rights rather than their realization. Rights are treated as contingent resources which impact on public policy indirectly—in the measure, that is, that they can aid in altering the balance of political forces."[50] Thus, the power of rights discourse and recognition is located in their ability to change the distribution of political force and power in incremental ways that ultimately may work to favor the interests of trans people.

Declarations of Trans Rights from the Courts

As discussed throughout this book, the courts are unlikely to be a great resource for trans communities, although litigation may prove useful for some transgender individuals if the latter are able to persuade judges that transgender identity is analogous to other protected characteristics. Yet, these types of civil rights strategies that privilege binary identities and litigation in the courts are unlikely to further the interests of trans individuals who cannot locate themselves in the existing categories of male and female, and risk perpetuating the reification of socially constructed binary identities.

As discussed in chapters 1 and 2, courts are going to be of limited utility for trans rights movements because trans individuals will have a difficult time persuading courts that gender identity in all of its complexity is entitled to the legal protections that accrue to immutable binary characteristics such as race, sex, and, perhaps, sexual orientation. At the same time, however, the trans movement's goals are multifaceted, and while some priorities—eliminating laws that target trans individuals for differential treatments, eradicating systemic institutional transphobia in public institutions, etc.—may be similar to the goals of prior civil rights social movements, eradicating discrimination on the basis of gender identity might require different strategies than those commonly associated with the politics of rights. As argued in chapter 2, while trans activists may have some success in the courts by challenging society's and government's mistreatments of trans individuals in comparison to non-trans individuals, this strategy perpetuates a binary construction of gender and necessitates an emphasis on immutable characteristics that will leave many trans individuals outside of the protection of the law. As such, while litigation may be a venue for securing some immediate short-term victories, the trans movement's long-term interests are not likely to be well served by emphasizing litigation as a mechanism for advancing trans rights.

At the same time, the ideological composition of the federal courts, and the U.S. Supreme Court in particular, is not amenable to progressive interests and civil rights at this time, and it is doubtful that it will change anytime in the future. While some federal district and appellate courts may be open to transgender rights claims, the hostility such litigation is likely to face at the U.S. Supreme Court may deter litigation as a viable strategy for change. In fact, the likelihood that a majority of the justices will reject transgender civil rights claims suggests that there may be significant costs associated with pursuing litigation in this current hostile legal environment.

Instead, a more optimal strategy may be to pursue legislative remedies, including lobbying to add the category of gender identity to the list of protected characteristics in civil rights laws. This strategy may create space for a broader array of gender identities and fluidities in the future, given that legislation may be updated and executive actors exercise discretion when interpreting and implementing legislation, and may circumvent the institutional and jurisprudential constraints associated with litigation, including the binary construction of gender identity. "Such a view of identity as unstable and potentially disruptive, as alien and incoherent, could in the end produce a more mature identity politics by militating against the tendency to erase differences and inconsistencies in the production of stable political subjects."[51] Finally, a successful strategy of rights that includes protections for gender identity in concert with existing protections for sex offers an alternative path for legal recourse. "Designating gender identity as a freestanding classification sends a powerful message that transgender people are entitled to full equality and legitimacy."[52] At the same time, the definition of gender identity and the language utilized in legislation is significant, and considering that terminology is constantly evolving—transsexuals versus transgender versus trans—it is essential to craft legislation that is inclusive and captures the diversity within trans communities, or the disruptive potentialities may be lost in favor of a default politics of right sex.[53]

Finally, adding gender identity to the list of protected characteristics need not preclude litigation implicating sex discrimination as a means to address discrimination against trans individuals. Recognizing the complexity of identities and intersectionalities and the nuances of de facto and de jure discrimination and gender policing, it is possible to imagine instances in which some trans individuals may be positioned to argue that they have been discriminated against on the basis of gender, whereas for others in different situations it may be appropriate to allege differential treatment on the basis of sex. "Like many other types of discrimination, anti-transgender discrimination may fall under more than one category of discrimination and thus may be cognizable under more than one statutory provision. There is no reason to hold anti-transgender discrimination to a different standard in this regard."[54]

Congressional Legislation: Adding and Including Gender Identity

Similar to the symbolic power associated with the political mobilization of individuals into movements and the use of litigation as a tool for facilitating change, the push to include protected identity categories in national, state, and local legislation has substantive and representational significance as well. Given the many ways in which trans people are legally, politically, economically, and socially marginalized, government recognition of gender identity as a protected category is a powerful discursive and substantive antidote. "There is a symbolic element to the passage of these laws, a statement that trans lives are meaningful, often described by proponents as an assertion of trans people's humanity."[55]

At the national level, attention has been focused on passing legislation extending civil rights protections to LGBTQ individuals in the form of the Employment Non-Discrimination Act (ENDA) or the Equality Act and securing a federal hate crime law. While the former has proven elusive, the Matthew Shepard and James Byrd Jr. Hate Crimes Prevention Act was passed in 2009 and includes gender identity as an enumerated and protected characteristic.[56] Since 1994, civil rights legislation has been introduced regularly in Congress in the form of ENDA or the Equality Act, but both have failed to gain majority support.

Initially, ENDA only prohibited discrimination on the basis of sexual orientation in employment,[57] and it was not until 2007 that gender identity was added to the legislation.[58] The 2007 ENDA clearly stated that it "[p]rohibits employment discrimination on the basis of actual or perceived sexual orientation or gender identity by covered entities,"[59] but after it failed to make it out of committee, Representative Barney Frank introduced a new bill that did not include prohibitions on discrimination on the basis of gender identity, which passed in the House of Representatives by a vote of 235–184.[60] This maneuver incited massive disagreements and fissures among LGBT advocacy groups and individuals. As a result, each time ENDA was introduced after 2007 it included prohibitions on discrimination in employment on the basis of sexual orientation and gender identity. Yet, majority support within Congress remained elusive.

Furthermore, there were substantive issues associated with ENDA. In order for ENDA to be truly effective and address the vast array of discriminations experienced by LGBTQ populations it needed to be expanded to include not just employment but education, housing, and health care as well. In addition, the religious exemptions that were included in the most recent iterations of ENDA created a loophole that enabled ongoing individual and systemic discrimination that is problematic and dangerous, and greatly limited the reach of ENDA. As a result, beginning in 2015, the Equality Act was offered as a replacement for ENDA, and it has been introduced in each Congress since. The Equality Act covers a far broader array of sites of discrimination than ENDA—e.g., it includes housing, public accommodations, schools, juries—and offer more expansive coverage to include protections for sex, sexual orientation, and gender identity discrimination. Yet, it continues to meet with resistance in Congress and has yet to acquire majority support.

While Congress has failed to pass legislation prohibiting discrimination on the basis of sexual orientation and gender identity, Title VII of the 1964 Civil Rights Act has been used as a tool to protect trans individuals from employment discrimination as both the Equal Employment Opportunity Commission (EEOC) and various federal courts have interpreted Title VII's prohibition on sex discrimination to include prohibitions on gender identity discrimination as described in chapter 1. At the same time, however, private employers are not bound by these interpretations at this time, and not all federal courts agree that Title VII should be understood in this manner, thereby limiting the reach of this approach and validating the need for the Equality Act or similar legislation moving forward.[61]

Thus, at the national level, the expansion of rights for trans individuals remains stalled because the Equality Act is unlikely to be passed in Congress in the current political climate. In fact, recent legislative battles surrounding attempts to repeal the Patient Protection and Affordable Care Act (ACA) (including the nondiscrimination provisions that prohibited any facilities receiving funds under the ACA from discriminating on the basis of sex, to include gender identity and expression) and the reauthorization of the Violence Against Women Act (VAWA) (which introduced protections for trans individuals in the 2013 reauthorization) suggest that Congress remains inhospitable to trans interests. As such, if the past few decades are an accurate depiction of congressional politics, it is going to require Democrats to control both houses of Congress and the White House in order to see national legislation that includes protections for trans individuals. Given the current political climate it might be difficult, albeit not impossible, for Democrats to gain control of both houses of Congress and the White House, thereby making the passage of the Equality Act unlikely in the near future and exposing the vulnerabilities of existing protections under Title VII, the ACA, and VAWA.

State and Local Legislation: Laboratories of Democracy?

At the state and local levels there is a great deal of variation. Minnesota was the first state to pass a nondiscrimination law that extended protections to trans individuals, in 1993, and in 2017 twenty states had laws prohibiting employment and housing discrimination against trans people, and nineteen states prohibit discrimination against trans people in places of public accommodation.[62] In addition, a number of municipalities have extended civil rights protections to gender identity including some of the largest cities in the country.[63]

At the same time, however, other states have taken up and passed legislation prohibiting cities and counties from passing nondiscrimination laws, and twenty-one states have passed laws or constitutional amendments that allow for religious exemptions from compliance with state laws.[64] Similarly, some states have passed "don't say gay" laws that prohibit educators and school employees from discussing anything LGBT in the schools, and others have passed laws forbidding local school districts from passing nondiscrimination policies that would prohibit bullying or discrimination on the basis of one's trans identity.[65] During 2016, approximately two hundred anti-LGBT bills, including HB2, were introduced in more than twenty states.[66] Many of these bills contain dire consequences for trans individuals, including a Mississippi "license to discriminate" law that allows government actors, doctors, and businesses to deny services and care to LGBT people.[67]

Thus, while increased media and public attention to the issues and challenges that trans people confront have been heralded as positive developments that enable growing awareness as a means for facilitating a trans politics of rights, the reality is that the political atmosphere remains quite hostile to trans interests. Thirty-one states "have a low or negative overall rating in terms of legal equality for transgender people,"[68] and "51% of LGBT people live in states that have a hostile or low gender identity tally."[69] In fact, "[a] shocking 23 states have negative policy tallies for gender identity, meaning they have more laws that actively harm transgender people than laws that help or protect them. No state has a high level of equality across all major policy areas affecting transgender people. And there is no major policy area in which even half of states have a medium or high tally."[70]

More specifically, thirty states received a low or negative rating for failure to prohibit discrimination on the basis of gender identity in employment, housing, and/or public accommodations, forty-three states received low or negative ratings for their policies governing an individual's ability to change one's identity on documents, thirty-seven states received low or negative ratings for their failure to protect trans youth, and thirty-four states received low or negatives ratings for their failure to protect the health and safety of trans individuals.[71]

One of the areas where states have the farthest to go to protect trans rights is in modifying laws that make it difficult for individuals to change their identity documents. "Eighty-four percent of states have negative or low rankings in Identity Documents compared to 59% of negative or low ranking states in Non-Discrimination."[72] As the analysis in chapter 3 demonstrates, state policing of gender via the control of identity documents facilitates and enables myriad other forms of de jure and de facto discrimination, and the fact that this is the area where the states score the worst demonstrates how much work still remains to be done in order to change these laws.

To date, legislative activity at the local, state, and national levels has come with pros and cons for trans people, because while there have been successful attempts to recognize trans rights there also have been numerous bills and statutes that have targeted trans individuals for discriminatory treatment. This push and pull for trans rights recognition reflects the messiness of the politics of rights, and it is important to recognize that the hostility toward trans people that is expressed and codified in legislation might foment a powerful countermobilization, as demonstrated by the political, economic, and legal response to North Carolina's HB2. "[P]roponents of both anti-discrimination and hate crimes laws argue that the processes of advocating for the passage of such laws, including media advocacy representing the lives and concerns of trans people and meeting with legislators to tell them about trans people's lives, increases positive trans visibility and forwards the struggle for trans equality."[73] As such, the struggle is likely to continue, as proponents of trans rights—ranging from independent trans advocacy groups to liberal gay rights and civil rights groups—fight for recognition in the courts and legislatures and opponents work to maintain and create discriminatory laws.

The Limitations for a Trans Politics of Rights

While the myth of rights is predicated on the belief that "when the judges talk the politicians listen,"[74] the politics of rights more accurately characterizes the complexity of the relationships among judges/courts, politicians, and social change. Recognizing that "[w]ithout support of the real power holders, then, litigation is ineffectual and at times counterproductive. With that support, litigation is unnecessary. While this conclusion indicates that the *direct* impact of litigation on implementation is likely to be minimal, it does not exclude the possibility of *indirect* influence—in particular, the use of litigation as a means of altering the balance of power."[75] Thus, the efficacy of the politics of rights is to alter the balance of power in indirect and incremental ways.

As the foregoing discussion makes clear, the institutional environments at the national level are not particularly conducive to a trans politics of rights at this time, whereas there is greater variation across the states and locales. Even in this hostile environment, one could argue that a trans politics of rights has the ability to start to change the balance of power in indirect ways even if and when individuals are losing cases in the courts and/or struggling to pass and extend civil rights protections to trans people. While these environments are contested, the growing attention to trans people and the discourses surrounding trans rights have the potential to increase mobilization, raise the saliency and power of the movement, and culminate in legal and political change in the future. Yet, when the institutional environments become more hospitable and responsive to the political and mobilization strategies of trans rights organizations, "[r]ights are declared as absolutes, but they ripple out into the real world in an exceedingly conditional fashion. The declaration of rights is ordinarily the prelude to a political struggle, and according to the evidence that struggle is primarily coercive. When it comes to getting large numbers of people to conform to norms they oppose, power is indispensable; it is necessary although it may not be sufficient."[76] Understood this way, a declaration of rights may be the beginning of the struggle for the expansion of rights.

The problem, however, is that the people within the public who are most resistant to new norms have the power, and they are not surrendering that power to marginalized groups, as demonstrated by the analysis of the discourse surrounding the passage of HB2 reviewed in chapter 4. Recognizing that "power is indispensable," while a trans politics of rights may culminate in greater recognitions of civil rights for trans individuals, these processes are not intended to and do not change the distribution of power in American society. In fact, as argued throughout this book, a trans politics of rights that culminates in a declaration of rights by the courts or a recognition of rights by Congress is likely to be a transnormative politics of right sex, because stakeholders will sanction this incremental advancement of transgender rights when it suits their interests. In this way, the recognition of rights for transgender individuals will lead to changes in the mechanisms that are utilized for social control and population management with no reallocation of power. Thus, a fundamental shortcoming of the politics of rights is the perpetuation of the mythology that political forces and power may and/or eventually will be redistributed, when in fact the recognition of rights acts as a cathartic valve that provides some gains but effectively maintains the position of the powerful. The push to extend civil rights protections to Black Americans demonstrates how "our system of civil rights law and enforcement ensures that racial progress occurs at just the right slow pace. Too slow would make minorities impatient and risk destabilization; too fast could jeopardize important material and psychic benefits for elite groups."[77] The same forces are at play in the efforts to advance a trans politics of rights. If anything, threats to the status quo facilitate countermobilization and force dominant populations within the public to get creative and increase their dependence on tactics of governmentality and infrahumanization, as opposed to law and de jure discrimination, to maintain their power.

For example, as chapter 5 demonstrates, the war on solicitation utilizes neutral criminal prohibitions on solicitation to selectively target and criminalize trans women. The successful implementation and execution of this war on those who deviate from gender norms is possible because various social and institutional actors act in concert with state actors to legitimate and sanction these discriminatory practices. Law is used as a tactic for pursuing broadly accepted raced and classed transphobic goals. Consequently, the recognition of rights will not be sufficient for overcoming the processes of governmentality that utilize the force of law—a war on solicitation—to pursue what may be more accurately understood as a form of population management—a war on those who deviate from gender norms.

Similarly, expanding legislation to include protections for gender identities and expressions does not mean that trans individuals are going to be in a position to initiate litigation and challenge discrimination when it occurs.[78] In fact, due to the socioeconomic marginalization of many trans people, legislation such as the Equality Act or other nondiscrimination laws may only benefit the most privileged within these communities. Effectively, many nondiscrimination and hate crimes laws gesture toward improving the lives of trans individuals while actually failing to do so. In this way, these types of legislation serve as a balm for treating discontents—those of trans people as well as those members of the public who want to be on the "right side of history" and periodically push to expand civil rights protections because it is the right thing to do—without actually addressing the injuries themselves and/or their systemic causes.

Furthermore, the reliance on government to identify, articulate, and enforce legislation is problematic. There are limitations associated with pursuing rights recognition via legislatures and asking executive actors to enforce these protections, because, absent a fundamental transformation of the hegemonic power structures themselves, these institutions will continue to privilege some while marginalizing others, even while engaging in the advancement of rights. While liberals and conservatives, Democrats and Republicans may disagree about the content of legislation and policies, dominant populations within the public benefit from legislation that is understood to offer government/state remedies to ongoing discrimination, marginalization, and violence against marginalized and transgressive bodies. Each time new legislation is passed and heralded for addressing these issues, this works to "reaffirm and internalize the very state that was and remains in significant ways a primary cause of the now-outlawed violence."[79]

Thus, the manner in which the rights of marginalized populations are advanced via the legislative process works in tandem with the maintenance of hegemonic power and governmentality. For example, Chandan Reddy argues that the inclusion of the Matthew Shepard and James Byrd Jr. Hate Crimes Prevention Act in the National Defense Authorization

Act (NDAA) of 2010 "dramatizes the inextricability of civil, political, and social rights from the martial obligations of citizenship. In this perspective, the state's enforcement of norms and behaviors, such as tolerance in the case of hate-crimes laws, is predicated on the achievement of homogeneity in political society—whether that is homogeneities of blood, race, tradition, and culture, or simply a set of defining values, as in the case of US exceptionalism."[80] These processes privilege and validate the liberal state "as the ultimate embodiment of the values that enable and guarantee equality."[81] In this way, when the state extends protections to members of LGBTQ communities and people of color it simultaneously maintains itself and those who benefit from its preservation. Even in those instances in which the state is "the source of a grievance, injury, or horrific exposure to arbitrary violence, its epistemological assumptions ultimately affirm the value of that very state foundation."[82]

Ultimately, civil rights legislation fails to deliver on the promise of eradicating and ending discrimination. It has been more than fifty years since the 1964 Civil Rights Act was passed, and yet discrimination on the basis of race, national origin, and sex continues, as does discrimination against the disabled in spite of the Americans with Disabilities Act.[83] As such, the allocation of time, energy, and resources in pursuit of national, state, and local legislation that prohibits discrimination on the basis of gender identity "invites caution when assuming the effectiveness of these measures."[84] Similar to litigating in pursuit of rights recognition, legislating rights comes with significant costs and limitations. Much like the former, the latter will be unable to reach the forces of governmentality that will continue to mark trans bodies as transgressive and locate them at the peripheries of the public. Truly transformative change and collective liberation will require more than the politics of rights.

Conclusion

One of the limitations of the politics of rights is that it understands the obstacles to the recognition and integration of marginalized populations as political and legal ones that can be remedied, albeit incrementally, via political and legal channels. Thus, the social movements described above—both liberal gay rights groups and independent trans rights organizations—are political and legal organizations working within the hegemonic institutions and structures in pursuit of the recognition of rights. While an independent trans politics of rights that is distinct from liberal gay rights organizations is offered as a more attractive alternative than operating within the confines of the latter, such a movement and its attendant organizations will be forced to work within the language and institutions of hegemony and likely will find that these barriers constrain their discourse and tools, thereby fomenting a politics of rights sex as opposed to collective liberation for all trans people. Fighting for recognition of the complexities of gender identities in the courts seems futile if not impossible, and while legislation appears to be a more viable option for adding gender identity to the litany of protected identities and has the benefits of adaptability over time, gaining political and legal recognition is not sufficient to facilitate the transformative change that is required in order to overcome the combined effects of discrimination and infrahumanization that work to subject trans people. Absent the reallocation of power, a trans politics of rights is likely to meet the same fate as prior civil rights movements where some individuals benefit but collective liberation remains elusive for all.

To be clear, winning litigation and the expansion of civil rights via the courts or passing legislation that expands individual liberties for trans people will have positive effects, but social movements that have successfully pursued their civil rights in the United States often find that rights accrue to those individuals best able to exercise them; oftentimes the most privileged within a protected group or class. If the pursuit of trans rights culminates in a transnormative politics of right sex, those who are normalized may gain limited rights, but those who continue to be marked as transgressive will not, and they will continue to be subjected by forces of governmentality and located at the margins of the public. In particular, those trans individuals who are located at the intersection of race, ethnicity, nationality, and poverty experience discrimination and governmentality in ways that distinguish their experiences from other members of the trans population. For example, the freedom to change one's identity on one's documents might be easily facilitated via legislative change, but that legal protection is not sufficient for trans liberation, because access to hormone treatments, surgeries, and so on will remain beyond the reach of many individuals in a system that continues to be predicated on racism, capitalism, and intersectional subjection. Similarly, passing a law that says that individuals may use any bathroom that they choose will not end the policing of sex/gender that occurs on a regular basis in public places, and cannot address the fact that some individuals are forced to navigate traditionally sex-segregated public spaces, including restrooms, locker rooms, prisons, homeless shelters, domestic violence facilities, and so on, more than others.

The reality is that legal change via the courts or legislative bodies might improve some people's lives and increase individual rights and liberties, but these developments do not constitute liberation for all trans people and cannot get at the ongoing myriad forces of governmentality that will continue to operate on trans individuals, particularly the most vulnerable, moving forward. Bassichis, Lee, and Spade write: "We know that freedom and justice for the most oppressed people means freedom and justice for everyone and that we have to start at the bottom. The changes required to improve the daily material and spiritual lives of low-income queer and transgender people of color would by default include large-scale transformation of our entire economic, education, healthcare, and legal systems. When you put those with the fewest resources and those facing multiple systems of oppression at the center of analysis and organizing, everybody benefits."[85]

As such, it is imperative to identify the ways in which intersectional subjection works as a tool of social control that repeatedly decenters certain populations and not others. A truly transformative and radical resistance would seek to put "those facing multiple systems of oppression at the center of analysis and organizing."[86] This requires both moving away from traditional rights-based social movements that privilege certain types of experiences and not others in favor of more open and less hierarchical organizational entities as well as challenging the public about its complicit participation in and/or sanctioning of those processes for discrimination and infrahumanization of trans people in order to reify the regulatory norms of sex and the associated distributions of power, privileges, and costs. This awareness may open up spaces to build bridges across local communities and identities, to unite those who want to challenge the privileged narratives that dominate discourse in the public and reconstitute power to craft a viable political resistance to these existing tactics of governmentality.[87] As the following chapter will demonstrate, however, facilitating the redistribution of power within the public in pursuit of collective liberation for all will require disruptive discursive and mobilization strategies.

Chapter 7

Trans and Queer Counterpublics and Transformative Change

Collective Liberation not the Politics of Right Sex

Introduction

The preceding chapters demonstrate the challenges that trans individuals and their allies will confront as they seek to craft a trans politics of rights. In the event that a trans politics of rights is able to triumph in the courts of law, the benefits that a legal recognition of rights will confer are limited by the fact that rights are exercised within a hegemonic paradigm that implicitly and explicitly enables the continued practices of governmentality on trans people, and effectively privileges some within the protected communities but not others. As past civil rights movements have demonstrated, the legal recognition of rights does not relieve historically marginalized groups from the myriad forces of governmentality that operate on them in the public realm. Similarly, legislative victories predicated on the expansion of rights are likely to be of limited utility in overcoming the forces of governmentality operating on trans people if these strategies are constrained by the extant frames of identity politics. Merely adding gender identity to the "alliance politics of the slogan, 'race, class, and gender,' " will not challenge the hegemonic power structure.[1] To the contrary, the "reification of identity" that follows such recognition will continue to identify trans people as a distinct category defined in opposition to the dominant population (i.e., transgender versus cisgender).[2] "The point here is that the naming [of a protected class] may be *simultaneously* a form of empowering recognition and a site of regulation."[3] As such, while a traditional politics of rights approach to eradicating discrimination against trans people may have the benefit of extending legal recognitions to some within a marginalized and vulnerable population, it cannot eradicate the forces of governmentality that will continue to operate on trans people or facilitate the collective liberation of all trans people. Recognizing the limits of the politics of rights as discussed in chapter 6, it is useful to evaluate alternative strategies for empowering trans individuals and transforming the hegemonic public.

To that end, this chapter makes the case that the pursuit of collective liberation for all trans people via the cultivation of counterpublics has the potential to disrupt the governing hegemony. This requires recognizing that a successful trans politics of rights may eradicate de jure discrimination, such as the bathroom bills discussed in chapter 4, but cannot get at the forces of governmentality that sanction transprofiling, violence against trans individuals in public and private spaces, and transphobia. Furthermore, a recognition of trans rights will privilege those individuals best situated to take advantage of a legal recognition of rights, and likely leave intersectionally identified trans men and trans women as well as gender nonconforming individuals behind. While the analysis in chapter 6 illustrates the costs and benefits of a trans politics of rights and the potential gains that a rights-focused trans social movement might extract from the courts and legislatures, the recognition of rights will not transform the discourse and hegemonic power structure. As such, trans people will continue to suffer subjection via governmentality. In contrast to the pursuit of rights for some, fighting for collective liberation for all trans people may provide a stark challenge to governing hegemony.

To that end, this chapter proceeds as follows. First, different alternatives for pursuing the advancement of trans interests will be reviewed and evaluated. Then, counterpublics will be introduced as an alternative mechanism for challenging the forces of governmentality that work to constrain trans individuals in the contemporary American context. Particular attention will be paid to the different strategies available to trans and queer counterpublics, including the efficacy of education and persuasion versus agitation and disruption. As this chapter seeks to make clear, while many trans and LGBTQ rights and advocacy groups utilize education and persuasion to pursue change within existing institutions, their interests may be better served by working to challenge the system itself via the politics of agitation and disruption.[4] Counterpublics are uniquely situated to cultivate new discourses and strategies that can be utilized to disrupt extant power arrangements.

To overcome governmentality and eradicate discrimination and infrahumanization, trans people need power. Power is necessary to transform the hegemonic public and dominant systemic and institutional mechanisms of power. As such, trans movements and other marginalized groups must find ways to gain power in both the public and the apparatuses of power, including the government, economy, and other privileging institutions in contemporary American society. Counterpublics provide a viable mechanism for growing and cultivating power within marginalized populations.[5] Vibrant counterpublics enable the development of new discourses and dialogues, validate a broad array of identities, and create space for the cultivation of new strategies for challenging the hegemonic power structure and the associated forces of governmentality. Recognizing that the continued and ongoing subjection of people of color, gender and sexual minorities (GSM), and the intersectionally identified is not going to be eradicated within the confines of our existing hegemonic system, the analysis that follows explores how counterpublics might empower trans individuals and enable potentially transformative alternative discourses and systemic change focused on collective liberation as opposed to individual rights.

Strategies for Advancing Trans Interests

In order to eradicate governmentality, groups that are subjected to its forces need more than just the recognition of rights as sanctioned by the hegemonic powers. As long as the articulation of rights as a discursive strategy in the public sphere and the demand for rights via apparatuses of power take place within existing paradigms it will be impossible to overcome the forces of governmentality that continue to subject trans people. Understanding the recognition of rights as a tool of hegemony—the privileged will sanction the expansion of rights in order to alleviate the fomenting unrest and frustration among marginalized populations while simultaneously guaranteeing that the recognition of rights via court decisions and legislative developments does not transform the distribution of power in the public—makes clear that while rights have the potential to change public policy, they are not sufficient for transforming "the space of public life itself."[6] As the analyses in chapters 3, 4, and 5 demonstrate, governmentality works as a powerful tool for subjecting targeted populations within public spaces in order to deny them power in the public. Absent a transformation of the public, trans people and other marginalized groups are unable to overcome the forces of governmentality that will continue to subject and remove them from these spaces even if and when rights recognition transpires.

Existing political science research has examined the different tools available to trans populations to challenge prejudice and reduce discrimination. While these strategies may marginally advance trans interests, they do not challenge governing power arrangements and the forces of governmentality that operate on trans people. For example, research demonstrates that the descriptive representation of LGBT individuals in elected office correlates with pro-LGBT public policies, suggesting that increasing the numbers of LGBTQ officeholders might translate to increased rights recognition for LGBTQ individuals, including protections for trans communities.[7] This is certainly a strategy worth pursuing for both the descriptive and substantive benefits that may accrue, but it is also worth noting that seeking access to and representation within the hegemonic power structure is going to be of limited utility for trans interests in the current context because legislative reforms are not able to reach the panopticon of disciplinary forces that operate on trans people in the contemporary United States, as discussed in chapter 6. As such, increased representation of LGBTQ individuals in local, state, and national legislatures is not in and of itself sufficient to dismantle the underlying norms and practices that not only enable, but substantiate, a system of power that enables the infrahumanization of trans people.

That being said, scholars have found evidence that increased personal contact with and/or exposure to marginalized populations can reduce prejudice and may change public opinion and attitudes.[8] Recent research explores whether or not such interactions may counter the infrahumanization of trans people. Flores finds that education about trans individuals as well as contact with gays and lesbians may facilitate positive attitudes toward trans communities, and Tadlock et al. find that interpersonal contact with trans individuals themselves has a positive effect on public attitudes about trans individuals.[9] A variety of experimental research has explored different mechanisms for advancing trans interests, and Flores et al. found that "reducing transphobia is a key mechanism for garnering support for transgender rights . . . [and] a way to reduce transphobia is to humanize transgender people by exposing individuals to information about them and representations of them."[10] While these findings reflect the potential to change the dominant public's attitudes toward trans individuals and potentially increase support for pro-trans public policies, there are practical obstacles to facilitating these changes.

First and foremost, the trans population is small—it is estimated that 0.6 percent of U.S. adults or 1.4 million people identify as transgender—and many Americans will never come in contact with a trans individual.[11] Furthermore, because many trans individuals are not readily identifiable as trans, the benefits of contact may be further limited. Given the discrimination and violence perpetrated against trans people, it is unreasonable and unfair to expect that individuals will out themselves as trans in order to facilitate greater public awareness and acceptance. Ultimately, the small size of the trans population interacts with the policing and removal of trans bodies from public spaces via myriad forces of governmentality to limit the opportunities for interpersonal contacts in the current environment.

Notably, trans individuals face distinctive challenges in overcoming these forces of governmentality in comparison to other historically marginalized groups. While a key facet of governmentality throughout history has been to remove transgressive populations from public spaces—Black persons via segregation, women via the distinctions between private and public spheres, the use of violence and threats of sexual assault as a way to control the movements of Black individuals, women, and gays and lesbians—social and economic necessities mitigated these erasures in powerful ways. For example, while segregation was practiced as a tool for removing Black individuals from white public spaces, white homes were open to Black individuals as slaves and later as domestic workers. Similarly, while the sexes may have been segregated in the public sphere, men interacted with women in the private sphere as wives, mothers, sisters, and daughters. As such, while the public movements of Black persons and women have been controlled throughout U.S. history, they were visible and present in the public realm and oftentimes in the dominant population's private spaces as well. In contrast, as the analyses in chapters 4 and 5 demonstrate, trans people are forcibly removed and erased from public spaces through the combined effects of state-sanctioned discrimination and forces of governmentality, including transprofiling, bathroom bills, and transphobic violence. Furthermore, as the statistics offered in chapter 2 document, trans individuals suffer from extreme socioeconomic marginalization and experience incredibly high rates of homelessness and poverty precisely because so many trans people are ostracized by their families and communities. In this way, many trans people are excluded not only from the public realm, but from the private familial sphere as well. In these ways, the infra law of governmentality reduces the interpersonal contacts between trans individuals and dominant populations thereby limiting the efficacy of these strategies. As such, additional research is needed to determine how to upscale these experiments and studies in light of the unique circumstances of trans communities. In the meantime, it is imperative to find ways to address the ongoing discrimination, violence, and infrahumanization that subjects trans people.

In *Does Gender Matter*, Heath Fogg Davis criticizes the liberal tendency to prioritize assimilation and accommodation into extant institutions and norms, including the sex and gender binaries, and recommends a structural reform that seeks to dismantle one of the most powerful tools of governmentality available to dominant populations: the reification of the sex binary as a mechanism of control and power. Specifically, Davis proposes eliminating sex-classification policies utilizing antidiscrimination laws, because "sex-classification policies cause sex-identity discrimination."[12] Yet, instead of seeking recourse through the courts, Davis suggests that entities proactively engage in a gender audit in order to determine how and why they are using gender in their policies and practices, and then move to eliminate irrational and unnecessary sex classifications in a broad array of areas, including identity documents, restrooms, single-sex colleges, and sex-segregated sports.

This is a strong argument, and Davis's proposal is an elegant solution to one of the foundations of the politics of right sex. At the same time, however, it is not likely to be viable in the current sociocultural, political, and legal contexts. Instead, significant systemic changes must occur *before* Davis's recommendations can be successfully implemented, because the liberal tendency to accommodate or assimilate will continue to govern the different areas that Davis analyzes in his book because they are powerful tools for maintaining extant power arrangements.

For example, while Davis argues for eliminating sex markers on identity documents—a sound proposal—states are instead promulgating standards for assimilating transgender individuals into the existing gender binary or moving to add a third identity category that accommodates trans people. Similarly, Davis suggests that single-sex schools open their doors to all applicants while maintaining their historical missions, but instead many men's and women's colleges are revising their definitions of men and women, thereby reifying the gender binary. This trend is exemplified by Morehouse College's 2019 decision to open admission to all individuals identifying and living as men regardless of one's sex as assigned at birth while continuing to exclude women, expelling any individuals who transition from male to female while matriculated at the school, and requiring that all students use male pronouns.[13] Most recently, the May

2019 decision by the Court of Arbitration for Sport that Caster Semenya, discussed in chapter 1, can no longer compete in certain women's track and field events unless she and other similarly situated athletes suppress their testosterone levels to the equivalent of the amount deemed to be appropriate for a woman's body is demonstrative of recent efforts to reinforce sex as biology.[14]

Collective Liberation

Recognizing the limitations of pursuing change within the confines of the current system, and that "rights are but one available political means to contest those power relations and to perform that always-imperiled work of freedom," it is necessary to explore alternative approaches to facilitating transformative change to include the goal of remaking the space of public life itself.[15] Rather than seeking the recognition of rights for some via extant hegemonic institutions, trans interests may be furthered via the agonistic contestation of the distribution of power within the public in pursuit of the freedom and collective liberation for all. While this goal may seem elusive or impossible, the reality is that "[p]ower is not stable or static, but is remade at various junctures within everyday life; it constitutes our tenuous sense of common sense, and is ensconced as the prevailing epistemes of a culture. Moreover, social transformation occurs not merely by rallying mass numbers in favour of a cause, but precisely through the ways in which daily social relations are rearticulated, and new conceptual horizons opened up by anomalous or subversive practices."[16]

Recognizing that "the guarantee of freedom is freedom," freedom must be understood as a practice that requires the "constant work of critique, self-interrogation, and political struggle [over] power relations."[17] The challenge to power relations and the pursuit of freedom will not be facilitated via governing institutions and legal reform, but rather through the contestation of the public. The pursuit of collective liberation will require the existence and maintenance of vibrant counterpublics that reject the dominant discourse in the public and insist "that the grammar of justice be reconstituted so as to enable the subaltern to speak *in authoritative terms*,"[18] and occupy public spaces despite the public's efforts to remove trans people from accessing them, because "[i]t is in the spaces of the public that the discovery of *power* and *demos* is made, and it is in the contestation of public space that democracy lives."[19]

When the quest for rights is replaced by the pursuit of collective liberation, the goals shift from sociolegal policy reforms predicated on gaining access to equal opportunities and democratic participation to transforming the public via the redistribution of resources and power.[20] In this way, collective liberation requires agonistic challenges to extant systems of power, including the forces of governmentality that operate in the public, whereas rights require recognition by those institutions and, as demonstrated above, cannot get at governmentality. Recognizing the obstacles to institutional transformation and that "the emancipatory function of rights cannot be adjudicated in abstraction from the bureaucratic juridical apparatus through which they are negotiated," a move to collective liberation begins with an attempt to change the public discourse.[21] "This is not about rights, equality, or identity—it is about the speech of bodily groups that are the material foundations of the US nation-state. And, although we don't yet know the complex content of this speech, we are becoming aware of its multiple voices and forms," and the exercise of this speech may prove to be a powerful mechanism for remaking the public.[22]

Counterpublics as Sources of Power and Contestation

Counterpublics have always existed to contest the discourse in the hegemonic public. As Fraser explains:

> History records that members of subordinated social groups—women, workers, peoples of color, and gays and lesbians—have repeatedly found it advantageous to constitute alternative publics. I propose to call these *subaltern counterpublics* in order to signal that they are parallel discursive arenas where members of subordinated social groups invent and circulate counterdiscourses, which in turn permit them to formulate oppositional interpretations of their identities, interests, and needs.[23]

In this way, subaltern counterpublics make two significant contributions to discourse. First, by providing "subordinated social groups" with the space to develop their own counterdiscourses, these groups are empowered to craft their own "identities, interests and needs" in their own vernacular on their own terms.[24] Second, the existence of subaltern counterpublics means "a widening of discursive contestation, and that is a good thing in stratified societies."[25]

Subaltern counterpublics are a source of power for marginalized groups because they create a space for community, identity formation, and discourse that is not governed by the dominant norms found in the public. At the same time, however, the counterpublic is powerful because it is not simply a separate community or group. As Warner explains, a counterpublic

> comes into being through an address to indefinite strangers. (This is one significant difference between the notion of a counterpublic and the notion of a bounded community or group.) But counterpublic discourse also addresses those strangers as being not just anybody. Addressees are socially marked by their participation in this kind of discourse; ordinary people are presumed to not want to be mistaken for the kind of person who would participate in this kind of talk or be present in this kind of scene.[26]

The *counter* in counterpublic is not merely about crafting a discourse that is outside of or runs counter to the dominant discourse. Instead, counter is operationalized as the proactive embrace of the identity of "other" or "outsider," an appropriation of power that shifts the gaze from the hegemonic public to the others and outsiders themselves. "The subordinate status of a counterpublic does not simply reflect identities formed elsewhere; participation in such a public is one of the ways its members' identities are formed and transformed. A hierarchy or stigma is the assumed background of practice. One enters at one's own risk."[27] In this way, counterpublics have the potential to be sources of transformative power for those individuals who are subjected to governmentality. Individuals who make the decision to "enter at one's own risk," and participate in the counterpublic's alternative discourses and power arrangements often find "the poetic-expressive character of counterpublic discourse to become salient to consciousness."[28] Distinctive and oppositional identities become a basis for power, as that which is considered illegible, undesirable, unacceptable, and so on by dominant powers becomes a source of pride. This power is exemplified when Black individuals announce, "I am Black and I am proud," or when gender and sexual minorities state, "We are here. We are queer. Get used to it." While these discursive pronouncements are not sufficient for instigating widespread systemic change, as demonstrated by the ongoing racism and homophobia that exist in spite of Black power and gay pride, they remain powerful mechanisms for allowing individuals who have been systematically dehumanized to locate and articulate their humanity as well as cultivating the "out" groups' community power.

Trans and queer counterpublics may be especially important for trans people who are systematically removed and erased from public space via the forces of governmentality. These counterpublics provide trans people with an opportunity to literally be seen and heard by one another, and create a space to articulate one's own identities, priorities, and voice. Queer counterpublics may be valuable spaces for trans people, especially the intersectionally identified and trans people of color, because consistent with queer theory's rejection of identity politics, these entities prioritize self-determination, validate intersectional identities, and understand identity as fluid and unstable.[29] Trans and queer counterpublics exist across the United States and provide both a discursive space and a realm to cultivate and exercise power. These counterpublics take various forms ranging from national entities such as Familia: Trans Queer Liberation Movement to regional entities such as Southerners on New Ground (SONG) to state entities such as allgo to local entities such as FIERCE, and, finally, to informal publics throughout the United States. In addition, there are online counterpublics including chat rooms, Tumblr, Facebook communities, and YouTube channels as well as blogs such as *Black Girl Dangerous*.

While varying in size and focus, these entities have commonalities that suggest that they are appropriately identified as trans and/or queer counterpublics. These entities provide space for trans individuals who are erased from and denied access to public spaces to practice self-determination and self-identification, as exemplified by SONG's commitment to create "spaces in which all of a person's identities are honored and affirmed—no one is asked to prioritize one over the other, and no one is left behind," and an expectation "that members will not hinder the self-determination of others through acts of racism, sexism, classism, homophobia, hatred, and intolerance."[30] Likewise, Black Girl Dangerous provides a platform for queer and trans people of color to publish their writing in order to "amplify the voices, experiences and expressions of queer and trans people of color . . . on the issues that interest us and affect us, where we can showcase our literary and artistic talents, where we can cry it out, and where we can explore and express our 'dangerous' sides: our biggest, boldest, craziest, weirdest, wildest selves."[31] In this way, these counterpublics give trans people the space to speak and be heard in their own voices in their own terms, and validate self-determination and intersectional perspectives. This "[p]ublic space offers a spatial medium to the frustrations subalterns feel with regard to the systems of archy. It allows them to locate their anger in a material sense, thereby opening public space to new visualizations, which may initiate new organizations rooted in the idea of system and management without rule, and co-operation and contestation without repression."[32] This contrasts with the public, where trans people are marginalized and removed from public spaces via the forces of governmentality that operate on transgressive bodies, including gender surveillance, policing, and violence in order to prevent them from exercising self-determination and being themselves.

Relatedly, there is a shared emphasis on empowering individuals and growing the power of the individuals within the counterpublic. This inward-looking focus is exemplified by allgo's annual Statewide Queer People Of Color Activist Summit, which is intended to "build a movement coming from a place of engaging possibilities rather than a place of fighting, and that works to create *our own power*" via programming on "honoring *our history*; strengthening *our network*; growing and sustaining the movement; and creating possibilities for economic and social change in queer communities of color that lead to liberation *from the inside out*."[33] Similarly, FIERCE, an organization of LGBTQ youth of color in New York City, presents its organizing model on its website, which emphasizes building "our power" via base-building and leadership development in order to exercise "our power" via campaigns, community building, and youth development in order to sustain "our power."[34] By positioning themselves outside of existing hegemonic structures, counterpublics are able to cultivate and build their own power to be used for their own ends, or to leverage it in concert with other marginalized populations if they decide to do so.

In order to build self-empowerment, many of these entities offer trainings to give trans people the power and tools for survival that are denied to them in the public realm. For example, The Audre Lorde Project's TransJustice Community School is designed to "strengthen our community and ourselves and build participants' confidence and self-esteem" so that participants will, among other things, "learn how to and teach others to be self-advocates."[35] This programming by and for the counterpublic intends to give trans individuals the tools necessary to assert and/or protect themselves in their interactions with the dominant public and hegemonic power structures. Other types of trainings include

FIERCE's Education for Liberation Project (ELP) which is a "development program that provides comprehensive community organizing, political education, and anti-oppression trainings to new and active members of FIERCE. . . . Ultimately, ELP strives to help develop a new generation of community organizers dedicated to social justice work in historically underserved communities."[36] Reflecting values of mutual support and recognition, ELP trains individuals who are marginalized and subject to forces of governmentality in the public to work on behalf of others who are similarly situated in relation to the hegemonic power structure.

Finally, these counterpublics offer a counterdiscourse that prioritizes liberation and ending oppression, as compared to the dominant discourse on seeking equality through the politics of rights.[37] For example, Familia: TQLM's vision is to pursue "the *collective liberation* of trans, queer, and gender nonconforming Latinxs to build power and (re)imagine our communities free from oppression. We seek to abolish the systems that marginalize, criminalize, imprison, and kill our people. We are building on the legacy of racial justice and liberation movements."[38] By shifting the discourse toward collective liberation, trans and queer counterpublics signal that they want to be free from the hegemonic power structures that currently subject them as opposed to appealing to these structures for the recognition of rights. They want to be liberated from state and public control, not merely recognized by the government. This discursive move distinguishes trans counterpublics from mainstream gay rights groups such as the Human Rights Campaign and Lambda Legal Defense and Education Fund.

In addition to enabling the articulation of alternative discourses that empower those within the counterpublic, these counterdiscourses have the potential to "expand discursive space."[39] The challenge for all counterpublics is that dominant powers may pressure them to abandon their counterpositioning and enter the public to engage in an open dialogue when the latter fears that the former is gaining too much power and potentially poses a threat to the existing hegemony. If and when the counterpublic enters or engages the public, it often loses its counterpositioning because it is forced to adopt the vernacular of the dominant discourse and designated appropriate modes of behavior, and this mitigates its ability to challenge and transform the hegemonic discourse and power structure.

The belief that counterpublics can engage in dialogue with the public and play an educative function is premised on the idea that the public is "a discursive space characterized by symmetry, nonhierarchy and reciprocity, [which] both presupposes, and makes possible, plurality and so provides the opportunity for a politics based on mutual recognition and respect for difference."[40] This conception of the public suggests that counterpublics are welcome to introduce new discourses and challenges to the status quo within the public sphere in order to redefine the terms of public debate.[41] In fact, Livingston goes as far as to suggest that "[t]he work of counterpublics is to 'smooth' the striated space of public political culture so as to displace old prejudices and allow new identities and claims to flourish."[42]

If successful, the counterpublic potentially changes the public discourse and dominant consciousness in positive ways. As Livingston explains:

> When these experiments in consciousness-raising are successful, as with the feminist movement's introduction of "date rape," the queer movement's turn away from civil unions in favor or "gay marriage" . . . the terms of resonance in the public sphere change. Coining terms like "gay marriage" is not the same thing as institutionalizing it, but it does have the effect of redefining the terms of public debate around a now resonant experience of exclusion that had hitherto been simply invisible or erroneously seen as harmless.[43]

In this way, the introduction of new terms and concepts in the public may provide marginalized populations with the opportunity to name injustices and wrongs and consequently place demands on extant political-juridical institutions for redress. According to this perspective, the addition of "date rape" to the dominant lexicon validates that these rapes exist and provides rape victims with the discursive power to articulate the crimes against them in the social and legal realms. This works in much the same way that the second wave women's movement's use of the phrase "the personal is political" worked to open the private sphere to public discussion and political-juridical analysis, resulting in domestic violence laws, prohibitions on spousal rape, a recognition of the "second shift," and so on. Similarly, the discursive recognition of "gay marriage" enabled gays and lesbians to make the case that they wanted the same rights and recognitions as heterosexuals, and this shift in public discourse provided new tools for contesting the exclusion of gays and lesbians from the institution of marriage in the political and legal realms.

There are, however, numerous obstacles that counterpublics must navigate if they wish to change the public discourse and advance their interests. Notably, when counterpublics try to participate in the public discourse they are forced to adopt the appropriate decorum, sanctioned discursive strategies, and acceptable political and legal tactics as determined by the center. As Fraser explains:

> [Historically,] discursive interaction within the bourgeois public sphere was governed by protocols of style and decorum that were themselves correlates and markers of status inequality. These functioned informally to marginalize women and members of the plebeian classes and to prevent them from participating as peers. Here we are talking about informal impediments to participatory parity that can persist even after everyone is formally and legally licensed to participate.[44]

Under the best conditions, this means that in order for trans people to be seen and heard in the public they will be required to conform to the expectations of decorum established by those with power. If the power of the counterpublic is the ability to validate new identities, craft new discourses, and challenge the status quo, being forced to abandon these strengths at the threshold of the public sphere in order to engage the center necessarily robs it of its power and transformative potential. For trans and queer counterpublics, if the cost of recognition and legitimation in the public is compliance with cisgendered heterosexist white supremacist norms, then trans individuals will not be free to be themselves. Instead, they will be present, but invisible and silent because of the "informal impediments to participatory parity that can persist even after everyone is formally and legally licensed to participate."[45] All too often, when the counterpublic tries to participate in and engage the public, the price of admission is to surrender its very tools for contestation and this reframes the counterdiscourse.

As such, the idea that the counterpublic has the ability to educate the center and transform public discourse is highly problematic because discursive power is obfuscated the moment one is forced to surrender his/her/their discourse, vernacular, and perspective. Despite protestations to the contrary, "[w]e should question whether it is possible even in principle for interlocutors to deliberate as if they were social peers in specially designated discursive arenas, when these discursive arenas are situated in a larger societal context that is pervaded by structural relations of dominance and subordination."[46] Understanding that the public is hierarchical and constituted in favor of the powerful, even if trans and queer counterpublics could "smooth" public space to make their discourse more legible, these discursive victories are short-lived at best and illusions at worst because the center will coopt new terms and concepts in pursuit of its own ends. Whereas Livingston argues that the introduction of the term *date rape* into the American lexicon represents a victory for women's rights, one could argue that getting "date rape" introduced into the public discourse did not improve the lives of women and rape victims.[47] In fact, distinguishing between "date" rape or acquaintance rape and "stranger" rape created a hierarchy wherein the latter is considered "real" rape and the former is often made out to be a misunderstanding or an unfortunate thing that happens to a woman, especially if she have been drinking, in which case the woman is often blamed for the assault.[48] In this way, the creation of a new category of rape actually came with significant costs for women as their interests were coopted by a patriarchal system that still works to protect male sexual aggression and power at the expense of women. This reflects the fact that "Habermas' conception of communicative rationality may act ideologically by obscuring the power relations it contains."[49] Failing to recognize that some voices are privileged in the discursive public sphere works to reify the power that exists there.

As a result of the barriers to participation and the hierarchies that exist in the public, it is not surprising that many counterpublics inevitably morph or spin off into social movements operating within the constraints of the public and political apparatuses established by the powerful and privileged. This explains why post-marriage equality there is great momentum among progressives to prioritize the pursuit of trans rights culminating in pressure on trans activists to join the fight and coalesce as a trans social movement. On the day that the U.S. Supreme Court decided *Obergefell v. Hodges* (576 U.S. ___ [2015]), Evan Wolfson, founder and president of Freedom to Marry, stated that it was time to "get back to work" and fight for getting prohibitions on discrimination on the basis of sexual orientation and gender identity in employment added to the 1964 Civil Rights Act.[50] Yet, "when alternative publics are cast as social movements—they acquire agency in relation to the state. They enter the temporality of politics and adapt themselves to the performatives of rational critical discourse. For many counterpublics, to do so is to cede the original hope of transforming, not just policy, but the space of public life itself."[51] This is demonstrated by the split between liberal gay rights organizations operating within the public realm in pursuit of rights such as the successful quest for marriage equality and queer counterpublics interested in maintaining their outside positioning and alternative discourses and explicitly rejecting the gay public's prioritization of marriage equality.[52] This division is about more than just strategic priorities, but rather reflects competing ideas about the value of counterpublics themselves. As Warner explains:

> Counterpublics are "counter" to the extent that they try to supply different ways of imagining stranger-sociability and its reflexivity; as publics, they remain oriented to stranger-circulation in a way that is not just strategic, but also constitutive of membership and its affects. As it happens, an understanding of queerness has been developing in recent decades that is suited to just this necessity; a culture is developing in which intimate relations and the sexual body can in fact be understood as projects for transformation among strangers. (At the same time, a lesbian and gay public has been reshaped so as to ignore or refuse the counterpublic character that has marked its history.)[53]

While some would argue that the fight for marriage equality was a successful use of time and resources,[54] others criticize gay rights organizations for advancing the interests of privileged gays and lesbians over more pressing interests such as economic equality,[55] resent the framing of LGBTQ rights as a fight for access to heteronormative institutions as opposed to a demand for self-recognition and/or LGBTQ power,[56] and critique marriage equality for expanding the disciplinary power of the state over gays and lesbians.[57] When a counterpublic becomes a social movement, assertions of power are rearticulated as requests for rights, and demands for self-identification and self-determination are reframed within the constraining frames of identity politics that dominate the discourse in the public sphere as requests for the recognition and validation of binary identities. No matter the argument, the prioritization of marriage equality has complicated the pursuit of other LGBTQ interests, and demonstrates the costs and benefits of social movements' rights-based strategies and victories.

Counterpublics as Agitators: Radical Resistance

As discussed above, the educative function presupposes a receptive public that is nonhierarchical while simultaneously putting the responsibility for education on those operating at the margins of the public. Given the aforementioned challenges, it is difficult to imagine how trans or queer counterpublics transform the public discourse via educational engagement. While counterpublics have the ability to contest and change the discourse, and occasionally they expand the discourse in ways that actually facilitate policy changes, these discursive and policy changes are not tantamount to transformative change. As long as those with power and privilege act as gatekeepers and monitor the expansion of discourse and control the institutions of government, they will allow change only to the extent that it does not undermine their own interests. As such, the changes that are sanctioned are not transformative, because they do not redistribute power. As Kendi writes in *Stamped from the Beginning*, "Indeed, power creates freedom, not the other way around—as the powerless are taught."[58]

In addition, as previously noted, the challenges that confront all counterpublics as educators are exacerbated for trans counterpublics because one of the most nefarious effects of governmentality on trans individuals is to remove them from public spaces. The erasure of trans individuals in public spaces makes it exceedingly difficult for them to be in a position to educate the public in the first place. Recognizing that this form of discipline renders participation in the public realm extremely difficult, it is essential to recognize that there are different roles for trans counterpublics to play in relation to the public. In order to exercise their discursive power, counterpublics must resist the norms of dominant discourse and expectations in the public. As Springer explains, "If those 'from below' perceive those 'from above' as unwilling to listen, evidenced through a denial of public space and a refusal to recognize them as legitimate political adversaries, then tensions will mount and may erupt into violence. Contestation of public is paramount because, though elite challenges may be fierce, they are never insurmountable."[59]

As such, while contesting the dominant terrain will not lead to transformative change, rejecting the center's control over one's discourse, identity, and power in the public may do so. Put another way, while the counterpublic as educator still requires the counterpublic to address its concerns to the center in order to receive redress or recognition, a transformative discourse will decenter the center in the public and empower the counterpublic to speak to its needs and wants in its own terms. By actively rejecting the expectations and decorum of the public, such an approach maintains the counterpublic's outsider positioning. Rather than attempting to leverage its power to gain access to the existing public and/or morphing into a trans social movement, the counterpublic uses its power to disrupt the public by embracing the role of agitator and refusing to surrender its discursive power.

Due to the fact that subaltern counterpublics form in response to the subordination of marginalized populations in the public, they are uniquely situated to reject the dominant discourse:

> A counterpublic maintains at some level, conscious or not, an awareness of its subordinate status. The cultural horizon against which it marks itself off is not just a general or wider public, but a dominant one. And the conflict extends not just to ideas or policy questions, but to the speech genres and modes of address that constitute the public and to the hierarchy among media. The discourse that constitutes it is not merely a different or alternative idiom, but one that in other contexts would be regarded with hostility or with a sense of indecorousness.[60]

This hostility has the potential to be a source of transformative power. Rather than catering to the center and contesting the dominant discourse in the public, the indecorousness of the counterpublic acts as an affront to and rejection of the norms that characterize the public.

When "I Hate Straights" flyers were distributed at gay pride events in New York and Chicago in 1990, they challenged the dominant discourse in a way that was perceived as hostile. As Berlant and Freeman explain, the "I Hate Straights" polemic deployed rage "both to an 'internal' audience of gay subjects and an 'external" straight world."[61] In this way, the rage is intended to empower a radical gay counterpublic and contest the dominant public discourse and power arrangements in the straight world:

> In the face of an exile caused by this arrogant heterosexual presumption of domestic space and privilege, the speaker launches into a list of proclamations headed by "I hate straights": "I" hates straights on behalf of the gay people who have to emotionally "take care" of the straights who feel guilty for their privilege; "I" hates straights for requiring the sublimation of gay rage as the price of their beneficent tolerance. "You'll catch more flies with honey," the speaker hears; "Now looks who's generalizing," they say, as if the minoritized group itself had invited the "crude taxonomy" under which it labored. In response, the flier argues,

> "BASH BACK. . . . LET YOURSELF BE ANGRY . . . THAT THERE IS NO PLACE IN THIS COUNTRY WHERE WE ARE SAFE."[62]

More recently, in 2015, Jennicet Gutiérrez of Familia: Trans Queer Liberation Movement was escorted out of a White House event celebrating LGBT Pride when she challenged President Obama on his deportation policies. As part of Familia: TQLM's Not1More LGBTQ Deportation Campaign, Gutiérrez sought to draw attention to the deportation of LGBTQ individuals by speaking out during President Obama's remarks at the White House. Identifying herself as a transwoman, Gutiérrez implored the president to end "the abuse."[63] She was then audibly booed and heckled by the audience—comprised of other members of the LGBTQ community and gay rights advocates—and the president responded, " 'Shame on you,' " and proceeded to say, " 'Listen you're in my house . . . it's not respectful.' "[64] Security then escorted Gutiérrez from the event. This type of "hostile" or "indecorous" contestation demonstrates how trans and queer counterpublics work to expose the oppressive tendencies of the dominant discourse. Just as President Obama started to speak about the "civil rights of LGBT Americans," Gutiérrez interrupted him in order to draw attention to the mistreatment of LGBTQ immigrants at the hands of a presidential administration celebrating its own commitment to gay rights.

When interviewed afterward, Gutiérrez said that despite the risk of speaking out as an undocumented immigrant, it was worth "giving a voice to my community that does not have that voice,"[65] whereas President Obama commented, "If guests are 'eating the hors d'oeuvres and drinking the booze,' they're typically expected to listen respectfully."[66] The contrast between Gutiérrez's and Obama's after-the-fact comments could not be more clear. For Gutiérrez, rejecting the dominant discourses and power structures by articulating a "hostile" counterdiscourse was worth great personal risk whereas President Obama's comments reflect the expectation that people in the public will behave and speak consistently with the discourses and norms imposed on those entering those spaces. This pattern of behavior has existed throughout U.S. history: "Virtually from the beginning, counterpublics contested the exclusionary norms of the bourgeois public, elaborating alternative styles of political behavior and alternative norms of public speech. Bourgeois publics, in turn, excoriated these alternatives and deliberately sought to block broader participation."[67] Interestingly, if Gutiérrez had tried to engage President Obama in a "respectful" manner, there would have been no media coverage of her concerns. It is precisely because she disrupted the event and rejected the dominant discourse and norms that she was able to articulate and draw attention to her message in the public.

It is in these instances in which the counterpublic resists and refuses to comply with the expectations of the public that it derives its transformative power. While this counterpositioning may mean that it loses its ability to educate those in the public, the speaker maintains her power and may be able to harness publicity and awareness to educate other, like-minded allies in other counterpublics and raise awareness to grow a resistance. When Jennicet Gutiérrez entered the public realm, but refused to be silent and did not behave as expected, she was removed from the public. While the counterpublic's ability to engage and educate the public is mitigated by its refusal to comply with expectations, rather than write these engagements off as failures these encounters may resonate with other like-minded audiences. Counterpublics can and should build mutually supportive relationships with other counterpublics. While those with power may not cede power to the counterpublic in the public, allies within the public need to attune themselves to the discourse in the counterpublic, take responsibility for their roles and complicity in the systems of governmentality, and acknowledge that discourse when it bleeds into and/or interrupts the dominant discourse in the public. Imagine if gays and lesbians in the audience had not booed Gutiérrez's speech, but rather applauded and/or joined her. Instead of dismissing the speech of one "heckler," President Obama would have been forced to confront a discursive resistance.

Given that those with power and privilege control the discourse within the public, the only way to "enable the subaltern to speak in authoritative terms" and to change "the space of public life itself" is for those in the counterpublics to refuse to surrender their power and reject dominant discursive norms and expectations.[68] Those in the counterpublic are the authorities on their own identities, wants, and needs, and they need to maintain and wield that power through agitation and the rejection of the dominant discourse in pursuit of transformative change and liberation. It is essential, however, to move toward systemic change, as opposed to "celebrating abnormality for its own sake, as if contestation were itself liberation."[69] Given the right opportunity structure, this form of radical discursive resistance may have the capacity to facilitate change.

The Transformative Power of the Trans and Queer Counterpublics

As discussed in chapter 6, in the aftermath of *Obergefell v. Hodges* (576 U.S. ___ [2015]), liberal gay rights groups began to mobilize on behalf of trans rights, but if they are successful the political and legal recognition of rights will leave unchanged many of the obstacles to trans liberation and freedom, especially for intersectionally subjected individuals. This is not to suggest that there is no utility in pursuing equal rights for trans people, but rather to draw attention to the limitations of operating within an extant power structure that is predicated on hierarchy and invested in maintaining the privileged positions of some and the marginalized status of others. While rights organizations may be coordinating political and legal strategies to advance trans rights, queer and trans counterpublics also are out there fighting to end the discrimination, infrahumanization, and violence experienced by trans people.

In SONG's "2016 End of Year Report," the power of a transformative intersectional queer counterpublic is clearly exhibited in the following statement:

> How will we hold the weight of the thousands of immigrant people who have been deported or continue to sit in detention centers across the South? How will we hold the weight of the relentless attacks against Black and Brown communities in an election cycle that embodied the consolidation of white political power? How will we hold the weight of the very familiar white rage putting targets on our backs and those of our kinfolk? How will we hold the weight of the fight to protect natural water sources and our tribes from ongoing genocide? How will we hold the weight of escalated environmental disasters rocking our Gulf Coast, Caribbean and Pacific Islander political family? How will we hold the weight of every police shooting and every killing of our trans and gender non-conforming family? How will we rise together in resistance in times of uncertainty to take risks and live out our collective vision?[70]

This statement reflects SONG's embrace of intersectional identities as well as intersectional resistance. SONG locates its power in the people in the counterpublic as opposed to looking outward to the public for validation and recognition. In its annual report for 2016, SONG discusses the work it engaged in the past year and the co-directors explicitly thank the members of SONG for showing up time and time again, and not just to oppose and protest anti-LGBQT policies and legislation but to stand up against ICE raids on immigrant communities, mobilize in response to police violence and abuse of Black people, support the protestors at Standing Rock, and so on.[71] SONG's vision engages people across demographic groups as well as people sitting at the intersection of different identities, it crosses borders, it connects politics to power and violence, and it values the environment and natural resources. SONG's validation of intersectionality builds power within the counterpublic as well as bridges to and across counterpublics to foment local radical resistance, as exemplified by the broad array of work SONG members did in 2016. Finally, SONG is not pursuing rights within the confines of identity politics, but rather it is "longing for justice, kinship, love and sanctuary. Our story is not just of building kinship but of building power. Power concedes nothing without a demand . . ."[72]

Trans people have much to gain by working within groups such as SONG where their intersectional identities will be recognized and validated, and a demand for power as the means to collective liberation for all is prioritized over individual liberties and rights. Counterpublics such as SONG are well situated to fight for trans interests broadly defined because they are not constrained by the expectations and norms of the public. Furthermore, their privileging of intersectional resistance in and of itself serves as a rejection of the binary identities created and enforced by the hegemonic powers. Ongoing resistance will be required to decenter the center in the public, and while it is easy to be pessimistic about the opportunities for transformation, vibrant trans and queer counterpublics have been building their own power and using it for their own ends for decades. Wielding that power in the public not as educators but as agitators may facilitate discursive change, but allies need to be prepared and willing to surrender their power and make space for the counterpublics in the public. Imagine if audience members had responded to Jennicet Gutiérrez's discourse by saying, "Let her speak," or if President Obama had surrendered his power by ceding the floor or acknowledging that "his" house is actually the people's house.

Transformative change requires the voices of the counterpublic, but it also requires the silence of the public. "For those of us who, coming from another place, happen upon these realities and want to intervene, the task is not to bring 'light' or 'voice' somehow, presuming there was none before; it is to use the social mobility of our bodies and our language to transform relations—to treat people as legitimate subjects of rights, to mobilize the resources necessary for an intervention that makes sense to the people directly involved."[73] For those who are allies but are not trans, queer, or people of color it is essential to cede your power to others, your space at the center to make room for others, and to be quiet so that others may speak. It is only then that the contours of the public will change and forces of governmentality can be addressed and potentially remedied.

Conclusion

I want to conclude this book by recognizing that rights are powerful tools for mobilizing people and consolidating social movements, and when these political and legal actions culminate in the declaration of rights by courts and/or the recognition of rights by legislatures these affirmations become new tools in the politics of rights as marginalized populations leverage them to facilitate change across a broad array of institutions and social venues. We have witnessed the power of rights time and time again as different populations within the United States successfully challenge differential and discriminatory treatment by the state and a broad array of public and private actors and entities.[74] While the politics of rights is messy, arduous, and costly, one could argue that it has been a worthwhile investment of time, resources, energies, and blood, sweat, and tears for people of color, women, the disabled, gays and lesbians, and so on.

While the myth of rights suggested that aggrieved parties could take their cases to court, have judges declare their rights, and political and social actors would fall into line thereby providing rapid remedies to grave injustices, the recognition that the pursuit, declaration, and implementation of rights is significantly more complicated than the myth suggests remains an important contribution to our understanding of the mutually constitutive relationship between law and society.[75] At the same time, however, I believe that the politics of rights itself has become mythologized. The belief in the politics of rights is pervasive and tells aggrieved parties that they should mobilize, build a movement, target various points of entry across the political and legal systems, and eventually the recognition of rights and social change will follow. While there is disagreement about the ability of the courts to facilitate social change via declarations of rights, even skeptics agree that change occurs when the political, legal, economic, and social forces converge.[76]

Yet, as I argue in this book, all too often successful civil rights movements become coopted by the hegemonic power structures and dominant populations to limit their effectiveness and reach. While much attention has been dedicated to how opponents of civil rights seek to delay or obfuscate the implementation of rights, little attention has been given to those who silently accept or publicly celebrate the advancement of rights and then rely on other disciplinary measures to subject marginalized populations in order to maintain their own privileged positions. Given that many individuals within the public—including liberals and conservatives, Democrats and Republicans, wealthy and poor whites, men and women, heterosexuals and some gays and lesbians, and so on—are invested in the maintenance of the status quo, civil rights victories are often celebrated by the very parties that then utilize all of the disciplinary tools at their disposal to limit the breadth and depth of their reach.

As such, I fear that a trans politics of rights risks becoming a politics of right sex and a debate about how transgender individuals assigned the "wrong" sex at birth can secure legal protections, as opposed to a movement focused on the collective liberation of all trans peoples. While a politics of right sex that focuses on securing protections for transgender individuals either via existing prohibitions on sex discrimination or the recognition of gender identity as a new protected category will benefit those able or willing to make the case that they have transitioned to the "right" sex, these approaches are likely to promote transnormativity and privilege some within trans communities while doing nothing to eradicate the marginalized status of others, as discussed in chapter 2. Thus, a politics of right sex would provide trans communities with a symbolic rights victory and facilitate positive change in the lives of many transgender individuals while simultaneously maintaining patriarchy, male privilege, heterosexism, and heternormativity, and promulgating transnormativity.

The recognition and implementation of civil rights for trans individuals is not sufficient for remedying the legacies of de jure and de facto discriminations, intersectional subjection, and exploitation by legal, political, economic, and social institutions. While the politics of rights may provide trans individuals with the tools to advance their interests within extant political and legal institutions, like prior civil rights movements they will be constrained by the informal norms and formal procedures that govern these institutions. As such, operating within and asking for recognition from the very institutions and individuals who have played a dominant role in the subjection of trans populations and directly benefited from raced, classed, sexed, and intersectionally oppressive hierarchies is problematic. Absent a redistribution of power, those with power will continue to exploit the system in order to maintain their privileged positions, and trans people will continue to be marginalized and subjected.

One tool that dominant populations within the public are able to use to preserve their monopoly on power is to utilize forces of governmentality to designate, manage, and control frustrating political subjects. The use of governmentality supplements or works on the underside of law to facilitate the management and control of designated populations. As demonstrated throughout this book, the disciplinary and panoptic tools used by the public to marginalize trans people include but are not limited to: the designation of trans bodies as abnormal and/or illegible via mandatory reporting of gender markers on identity documents; the processes that grant individual administrators and state actors the discretion to designate trans people as administratively impossible, queer security threats, or sex workers; the creation and dissemination of damaging stereotypes such as the fraud trope or myth of sexual deviancy; the selective enforcement of neutral criminal prohibitions as exemplified by the discussion of solicitation laws; attempts to contain and/or remove transgressive bodies from public spaces as demonstrated by the surveillance of trans bodies enabled by incongruent identity documents, the gender policing that occurs in and around restroom facilities, and transprofiling; advancing norms of discourse and behavior within the public that disadvantage those trans people who speak in a different vernacular or prefer alternative forms of comportment; and so on. All of these forms of discipline, population management, and social control of trans individuals across various locations by myriad public and private actors are possible because those who possess power are able to exercise and wield their power in the public whereas those without power are subject to it.

The recognition of rights is of limited utility precisely because it fails to address, challenge, or redistribute power in the public. In fact, governmentality often works in tandem with the recognition of rights so that privileged populations within the public are able to maintain their power and prominence even if and when rights are conferred on marginalized groups. As civil rights movements develop and achieve successes, new disciplinary tools are crafted and implemented by the public in order to limit and undermine advancements in rights, as demonstrated by the experiences of prior successful civil rights movements. The stereotypes of Black criminality, Black welfare queens, Native American alcoholism, Central American and Mexican illegality, Asian docility, Muslim fundamentalism, and so on all work in tandem with the recognition of rights to maintain the marginalized positions of racial and ethnic minorities. Similarly, gender and sexual minorities continue to be stereotyped as sexual deviants and perverts in spite of advancements in civil rights, and women are subjected by a broad array of stereotypes that intersect with race, class, and sexuality that are too many to list, but involve everything from women of color's hypersexuality, working women's "real" desire to be stay-at-home mothers, and ongoing myths about women's emotional and physical fragility. These stereotypes are more than just overly broad generalizations and negative fictions, but rather are tools for managing populations in the public. They sanction the selective enforcement of criminal laws that make some people into criminals but not others, and make some people legible as victims but not others. They mark some as administratively possible and allow them to benefit from public programs and services and render others administratively impossible in order to deny them access to the same facilities and entitlements. They sanction violence against some and not others.

As such, it is difficult to imagine how a trans politics of rights might overcome the forces of governmentality that will continue to mark and operate on trans bodies. Instead, it is more likely that a successful trans politics of rights will emulate prior civil rights movements and put an end to most forms of explicit de jure discrimination, such as state laws that prohibit local governments and/or school districts from prohibiting discrimination against or bullying of trans individuals, and create some new legal protections by, for example, prohibiting discrimination in employment and places of public accommodations against trans individuals. To be clear, these are important and meaningful goals, but they are limited in their reach. In addition, the recognition of rights for trans people will come with costs as well. It is likely that the sex binary will be maintained as a powerful privileging identity category, and that trans people will be pressured to situate themselves in the categories of men and women by demonstrating that they have permanently transitioned to the right sex. In the event that gender identity is added as a new protected identity category it is likely to be operationalized as a binary—transgender versus cisgender—in order to validate the permanency of gender as a transition to one's right sex. Both the sex and gender binaries will erase those who do not fit in the categories of male and female and will deny them legal redress, and the maintenance of binary operationalizations of identity will continue to obfuscate the recognition of intersectional identities. The result will be to privilege some within trans communities over others thereby promoting transnormativity as opposed to the collective liberation of all trans people. Finally, as demonstrated throughout this book, because it will not redistribute power, a trans politics of rights will not reach the forces of governmentality that will continue to operate on trans bodies as well as the new tools that are likely to develop in concert with the recognition of trans rights.

As such, my aim with this book is to raise people's awareness of the myriad forces of governmentality that continue to mark and operate on transgressive bodies even if and when civil rights movements are successful. We must acknowledge and interrogate the existence of these disciplinary tools if we hope to mount a concerted effort to challenge them in the interest of actually facilitating substantive change in people's lives. Too often in the United States, the sins of the past have been cleansed via the recognition of rights, and people with power are relieved of their complicity in the operation of hierarchical and oppressive systems of power because the slate is wiped clean once legal obstacles to political, legal, economic, and social participation are removed. The discourses about equality of opportunity in the here and now and the mythology of a level playing field that accompany rights recognition absolve dominant populations of responsibilities and obligations to historically marginalized populations while simultaneously forces of governmentality are working to maintain the hegemonic system and the associated distributions of power, wealth, and privilege.

Thus, it is important to understand how the current attention focused on trans individuals and the battles for and against trans rights that are accelerating across local, state, and national governments come with significant pros and cons even if and when trans people are victorious in the courts and legislatures. Recognizing that a successful trans politics of rights will not eradicate governmentality and the ongoing marginalization of trans people, in particular those who are intersectionally subjected, this chapter makes the case for alternative forms of social and political mobilization via counterpublics. Trans and queer counterpublics exist across the United States and have been doing important work on behalf of trans and queer people for decades, but they often are ignored by the public and media in favor of rights groups. Yet, it is the former who have the potential to change the distribution of power within the public by explicitly challenging the discourse and norms within the public as described above. It is the dominant discourse and norms of behavior in the public that allow for those who deviate from these expectations to be marked as abnormal and which then sanction governmentality to work in tandem with and in the shadow of the law to locate these transgressive bodies at the periphery of the public. By virtue of their location outside of hegemonic power structures and the public, counterpublics have the ability to explicitly challenge the normativity that dominates the public and privileges whiteness, heteronormativity, homonormativity, cissexuality, patriarchy, and intersectional subjection.

Collective liberation requires the redistribution of power, not merely the recognition of rights and liberties that in practice can be exercised by some and not others. The ability to articulate one's identity free from the regulatory control of the state and the disciplinary measures of the public, and to define gender identity as fixed or fluid outside of the binary constraints of male and female or right versus wrong sex is essential for collective trans liberation. To that end, the interests of marginalized populations are best served by operating across multiple fronts in order to confront the multiple ways in which they are marginalized and subjected. In this moment, when trans rights are moving to the front of the discourse and action is being taken to achieve institutional declarations of trans rights, it is essential to recognize, validate, and support trans and queer counterpublics who are in a position to instigate and facilitate truly transformative change in pursuit of the collective liberation of all trans people, as opposed to the politics of right sex.

Notes

Preface

1. Courtenay W. Daum, "The War on Solicitation and Intersectional Subjection: Quality-of-life Policing as a Tool to Control Transgender Populations," *New Political Science* 37, no. 4 (2015): 562–81.

2. Jacob Hale, "Suggested Rules for Non-Transsexuals Writing about Transsexuals, Transsexuality, Transsexualism, or Trans______," Nov. 18, 2008; http://sandystone.com/hale.rules.html.

3. Marc Galanter, "Why the 'Haves' Come out Ahead: Speculations on the Limits of Legal Change," *Law and Society Review* 9, no. 1 (1974): 95–160.

4. Sandy Stone, "The *Empire* Strikes Back: A Posttranssexual Manifesto," in *Body Guards: The Cultural Politics of Gender Ambiguity*, ed. Kristina Straub and Julia Epstein (New York: Routledge, 1991).

5. Paisley Currah, "Gender Pluralism: Under the Transgender Umbrella," in *Transgender Rights*, ed. Paisley Currah, Richard M. Juang, and Shannon Price Minter (Minneapolis: University of Minnesota Press, 2006), 3–31; Susan Stryker, "My Words to Victor Frankenstein Above the Village of Chamounix: Performing Transgender Rage," *GLQ* 1, no. 3 (1994); Paisley Currah, Richard M. Juang, and Shannon Price Minter, "Introduction," in *Transgender Rights*, xiii–xxiv, xiv.

6. Susan Stryker, "(De)Subjugated Knowledges: An Introduction to Transgender Studies," in *The Transgender Studies Reader*, ed. Susan Stryker and Stephen Whittle (New York: Routledge, 2006), 3.

Introduction

1. See Dawn Ennis, "Why is *The New York Times* Suddenly Focused on Transgender People?" *The Advocate*, June 9, 2015; http://www.advocate.com/politics/media/2015/06/09/why-new-york-times-suddenly-focused-transgender-people; Alice Gregory, "Has the Fashion Industry Reached a Transgender Turning Point?" *Vogue*, April 21, 2015; http://www.vogue.com/13253741/andreja-pejic-

transgender-model/; Brandon Griggs, "America's Transgender Moment," *CNN.com*, June 1, 2015; http://www.cnn.com/2015/04/23/living/transgender-moment-jenner-feat/; Katy Steinmetz, "The Transgender Tipping Point," *Time Magazine*, May 29, 2014; http://search.time.com/results.html?Ntt=laverne+cox.

2. Stuart A. Scheingold, *The Politics of Rights: Lawyers, Public Policy and Political Change* (Ann Arbor: University of Michigan Press, 2004), 5.

3. See Heath Fogg Davis, *Beyond Trans Does Gender Matter?* (New York: New York University Press, 2017); Anthony Nownes, "Interest Groups and Transgender Politics: Opportunities and Challenges," in *Transgender Rights and Politics: Groups, Issue Framing, and Policy Adoption*, ed. Jami K. Taylor and Donald P. Haider-Markel (Ann Arbor: University of Michigan Press, 2014), 83–107; Mitchell D. Sellers, "Executive Expansion of Transgender Rights: Electoral Incentives to Issue or Revoke Executive Orders," in *Transgender Rights and Politics: Groups, Issue Framing, and Policy Adoption*, ed. Jami K. Taylor and Donald P. Haider-Markel (Ann Arbor: University of Michigan Press, 2014), 189–207; Jami K. Taylor and Daniel C. Lewis, "The Advocacy Coalition Framework and Transgender Inclusion in LGBT Rights Activism," in *Transgender Rights and Politics: Groups, Issue Framing, and Policy Adoption*, ed. Jami K. Taylor and Donald P. Haider-Markel (Ann Arbor: University of Michigan Press, 2014), 108–32; Jami K. Taylor, Daniel C. Lewis and Donald P. Haider-Markel, *The Remarkable Rise of Transgender Rights* (Ann Arbor: University of Michigan Press, 2018).

4. Malcolm M. Feeley, "Review: Hollow Hopes, Flypaper and Metaphors," *Law and Social Inquiry* 17, no. 4 (1992): 745–60; Matthew E. K. Hall, *The Nature of Supreme Court Power* (New York: Cambridge University Press, 2011); Michael W. McCann, "Review: Reform Litigation on Trial," *Law and Social Inquiry* 17, no. 4 (1992): 715–43; Gerald N. Rosenberg, "Hollow Hopes and Other Aspirations: A Reply to Feeley and McCann," *Law and Social Inquiry* 17, no. 4 (1992): 761–78; Gerald Rosenberg, *The Hollow Hope* (2nd ed.) (Chicago: University of Chicago Press, 2008).

5. Scheingold, *The Politics of Rights*, 5.

6. Ibid., 131; See also David M. Engel and Frank W. Munger, *Rights of Inclusion: Law and Identity in the Life Stories of Americans with Disabilities* (Chicago: University of Chicago Press, 2003); Charles R. Epp, *The Rights Revolution: Lawyers, Activists, and Supreme Courts in Comparative Perspective* (Chicago: University of Chicago Press, 1998); Jonathan Goldberg-Hiller, *The Limits to Union: Same-Sex Marriage and the Politics of Civil Rights* (Ann Arbor: University of Michigan Press, 2002); Lisa Keen and Suzanne B. Goldberg, *Strangers to the Law: Gay People on Trial* (Ann Arbor: University of Michigan Press, 1998); Michael W. McCann, *Rights at Work: Pay Equity Reform and the Politics of Legal Mobilization* (Chicago: University of Chicago Press, 1994).

7. Mark Tushnet, *The NAACP's Legal Strategy against Segregated Education* (Chapel Hill: The University of North Carolina Press, 1987); Mark Tushnet, *Making Civil Rights Law: Thurgood Marshall and the Supreme Court* (New York:

Oxford University Press, 1994) on Black civil rights; McCann, *Rights at Work* on pay equity; Scott Barclay, Mary Bernstein, and Anna-Maria Marshall, eds., *Queer Mobilizations: LGBT Activists Confront the Law* (New York: New York University Press, 2009); Patricia Cain, *Rainbow Rights: The Role of Lawyers and Courts in the Lesbian and Gay Civil Rights Movement* (Boulder: Westview Press, 2000); Craig A. Rimmerman, Kenneth D. Wald and Clyde Wilcox, eds., *The Politics of Gay Rights* (Chicago: University of Chicago Press, 2000) on gay rights; Susan Olson, *Clients and Lawyers: Securing the Rights of Disabled Persons* (New York: Praeger, 1984) on rights for the disabled.

8. Jefferson Decker, *The Other Rights Revolution: Conservative Lawyers and the Remaking of American Government* (New York: Oxford University Press, 2016); Jeffrey Dudas, "In the Name of Equal Rights: 'Special' Rights and the Politics of Resentment in Post–Civil Rights America," *Law & Society Review* 39, no. 4 (Dec. 2005): 723–57; Jeffrey Dudas, *The Cultivation of Resentment: Treaty Rights and the New Right* (Stanford: Stanford University Press, 2007); Amanda Hollis-Brusky, *Ideas with Consequences: The Federalist Society and the Conservative Counterrevolution* (New York: Oxford University Press, 2014); Steven M. Teles, *The Rise of the Conservative Legal Movement: The Battle for Control of the Law* (Princeton: Princeton University Press, 2010).

9. Nan Alamilla Boyd, *Wide-Open Town: A History of Queer San Francisco to 1965* (Berkeley: University of California Press 2003), 109; John D'Emilio, *Sexual Politics, Sexual Communities: The Making of a Homosexual Minority in the United States 1940–1970* (Chicago: University of Chicago Press, 1998), 49–50.

10. D'Emilio, *Sexual Politics, Sexual Communities*, 106.

11. Martin Duberman and Andrew Kopkind, "The Night They Raided Stonewall," *Grand Street* 44 (1993): 120–47; Susan Stryker, *Transgender History: The Roots of Today's Revolution*, 2nd ed. (New York: Seal Press, 2017).

12. Ibid.

13. Evan Greer, "Powerful Gay Rights Groups Excluded Trans People for Decades—Leaving Them Vulnerable to Trump's Attack," *The Washington Post*, October 29, 2018; https://www.washingtonpost.com/outlook/2018/10/29/trumps-attack-trans-people-should-be-wake-up-call-mainstream-gay-rights-movement/?utm_term=.34f1fda516b3.

14. Keegan O'Brien, "Tearing Down the Walls: The Story of the Stonewall Rebellion and the Rise of the Gay Liberation Movement," *Jacobin*, August 20, 2015; https://www.jacobinmag.com/2015/08/lgbtq-stonewall-marriage-equality-mattachine-sylvia-rivera/; Deborah Sontag, "Once a Pariah, Now a Judge: The Early Transgender Journey of Phyllis Frye," *The New York Times*, August 29, 2015; http://www.nytimes.com/2015/08/30/us/transgender-judge-phyllis-fryes-early-transformative-journey.html.

15. Jessi Gan, " 'Still at the Back of the Bus': Sylvia Rivera's Struggle," in *The Transgender Studies Reader 2*, ed. Susan Stryker and Aren Z. Aizura (New York: Routledge, 2013), 291–301, 298.

16. Stryker, *Transgender History*, 121.

17. Ibid., 166.

18. Ibid., 167.

19. Amin Ghaziani, *The Dividends of Dissent: How Conflict and Culture Work in Lesbian and Gay Marches on Washington* (Chicago: University of Chicago Press, 2008), 151.

20. Phyllis Randolph Frye, "History of the International Conference on Transgender Law and Employment Policy, Inc." *Transgenderlegal.com*, 2001; http://www.transgenderlegal.com/ictlephis1.htm.

21. Stryker, *Transgender History*, 167–70.

22. Anthony J. Nownes, *Organizing for Transgender Rights: Collective Action, Group Development, and the Rise of a New Social Movement* (Albany: State University of New York Press, 2019).

23. "Sylvia Rivera Law Project"; https://srlp.org.

24. Gan, " 'Still at the Back of the Bus,' " 292.

25. "Transcript: HRC President Chad Griffin Apologizes to Trans People at Southern Comfort," *The Advocate*, Sep. 5, 2014; http://www.advocate.com/politics/transgender/2014/09/05/transcript-hrc-president-chad-griffin-apologizes-trans-people-speech.

26. Scheingold, *The Politics of Rights*, 91.

27. Michael Warner, *Publics and Counterpublics* (New York: Zone Books, 2005), 124.

28. Jacques-Philippe Leyens, Paola M. Paladino, Ramon Rodriguez-Torres, Jeroen Vaes, Stéphanie Demoulin, Armando Rodriguez-Perez, and Ruth Gaunt, "The Emotional Side of Prejudice: The Attribution of Secondary Emotions to Ingroups and Outgroups," *Personality and Social Psychology Review* 4, no. 2 (2000): 186–97.

29. Michel Foucault, *Discipline and Punish: The Birth of the Prison*, trans. Alan Sheridan (New York: Vintage, 1995), 222.

30. Ibid., 223.

31. Ibid.

32. Kendall Thomas, "Afterword: Are Transgender Rights *In*human Rights?" in *Transgender Rights*, ed. Paisley Currah, Richard M. Juang, and Shannon Price Minter (Minneapolis: University of Minnesota Press, 2006), 312.

33. Warner, *Publics and Counterpublics*, 122.

34. Maria Ochoa, "Perverse Citizenship: Divas, Marginality, and Participation in 'Loca-lization,' " in *The Transgender Studies Reader 2*, ed. Susan Stryker and Aren Z. Aizura (New York and London: Routledge, 2013), 447.

35. Nancy Fraser, "Rethinking the Public Sphere: A Contribution to the Critique of Actually Existing Democracy," *Social Text* 25/26 (1990): 66.

36. Warner, *Publics and Counterpublics*.

37. Ochoa, "Perverse Citizenship," 447.

38. Chandan Reddy, *Freedom with Violence: Race, Sexuality, and the US State* (Durham and London: Duke University Press, 2011), 71.

39. Ibid.

40. Warner, *Publics and Counterpublics*, 124.

41. Wendy Brown, *States of Injury: Power and Freedom in Late Modernity* (Princeton: Princeton University Press, 1995), 27.

42. Courtenay W. Daum, "Marriage Equality: Assimilationist Victory or Pluralist Defeat? What the Struggle for Marriage Equality Tells Us About the History and the Future of LGBTQ Politics," in *LGBTQ Politics: A Critical Reader*, ed. Susan Burgess, Marla Brettschneider, and Cricket Keating (New York: New York University Press, 2017); Epp, *The Rights Revolution*; McCann, *Rights at Work*; Tushnet, *Making Civil Rights Law*.

43. Gary Mucciaroni, "Will Victory Bring Change? A Mature Social Movement Faces the Future," in *After Marriage Equality: The Future of LGBT Rights*, ed. Carlos Ball (New York: New York University Press, 2016), 23.

44. Michel Foucault, *Security, Territory, Population: Lectures at the College de France 1977–78* (London: Palgrave Macmillan, 2007).

45. Ibid., 247–48.

46. Ibid.

47. Judith Butler, *Precarious Life: The Powers of Mourning and Violence* (London & New York: Verso, 2006), 52.

48. Susan Stryker, "Kaming Mga Talyada (We Who Are Sexy): The Transsexual Whiteness of Christine Jorgensen in the (Post)colonial Philippines," in *The Transgender Studies Reader 2*, ed. Susan Stryker and Aren Z. Aizura (New York and London: Routledge, 2013), 550–51.

49. Jürgen Habermas, *The Structural Transformation of the Public Sphere* (Cambridge: MIT Press, 1989).

50. Simon Springer, *The Anarchist Roots of Geography: Toward Spacial Emancipation* (Minneapolis: University of Minnesota Press, 2016) 13, quoting Geoff Eley, "Nations, Publics and Political Cultures: Placing Habermas in the Nineteenth Century," in *Habermas and the Public Sphere*, ed. Craig Calhoun (Cambridge: MIT Press, 1992).

51. Ibid., 108.

52. Clare Sears, "Electric Brilliancy: Cross-dressing Law and Freak Show Displays in Nineteenth-century San Francisco," in *The Transgender Studies Reader 2*, ed. Susan Stryker and Aren Z. Aizura (New York and London: Routledge, 2013) 557.

53. Ibid.

54. Jordan T. Camp and Christina Heatherton, "How Liberals Legitimate Broken Windows: An Interview with Naomi Murakawa," in *Policing the Planet: Why the Policing Crisis Led to Black Lives Matter*, ed. Jordan T. Camp and Christina Heatherton (New York: Verso, 2016), 229–30.

55. Butler, *Precarious Life*, 60.

56. Michelle Alexander, *The New Jim Crow: Mass Incarceration in the Age of Colorblindess* (New York: The New Press, 2012); Daum, "The War on Solicitation and Intersectional Subjection."

57. Robin D. G. Kelley, "Thug Nation: On State Violence and Disposability," in *Policing the Planet: Why the Policing Crisis Led to Black Lives Matter*, ed. Jordan T. Camp and Christina Heatherton (New York: Verso, 2016), 28–29.

58. Ruth Wilson Gilmore and Craig Gilmore, "Beyond Bratton," in *Policing the Planet: Why the Policing Crisis Led to Black Lives Matter*, ed. Jordan T. Camp and Christina Heatherton (New York: Verso, 2016), 197.

59. Michel Foucault, *Discipline and Punish*, 199.

60. Kimberlé Crenshaw, "Demarginalizing the Intersection of Race and Sex: A Black Feminist Critique of Antidiscrimination Doctrine, Feminist Theory, and Antiracist Politics," *The University of Chicago Legal Forum* 1989.

61. Reddy, *Freedom with Violence*, 32.

62. Daum, "The War on Solicitation."

63. Shannon Price Minter, "Do Transsexuals Dream of Gay Rights? Getting Real about Transgender Inclusion," in *Transgender Rights*, ed. Paisley Currah, Richard M. Juang, and Shannon Price Minter (Minneapolis: University of Minnesota Press, 2006), 156.

64. Toby Beauchamp, "Artful Concealment and Strategic Visibility: Transgender Bodies and U.S. State Surveillance after 9/11," in *The Transgender Studies Reader* 2, ed. Susan Stryker and Aren Z. Aizura (New York: Routledge, 2013), 49.

65. Stryker, "We Who Are Sexy," 552.

66. Alexander, *The New Jim Crow*.

67. Melissa V. Harris-Perry, *Sister Citizen: Shame, Stereotypes, and Black Women in America* (New Haven: Yale University Press, 2011), 56.

68. Ochoa, "Perverse Citizenship," 450, quoting Dagnino (1998), 50–51.

69. Thomas, *Inhuman Rights*, 311.

70. Ibid.

Chapter 1

1. Judith Butler, *Bodies that Matter: On the Discursive Limits of "Sex"* (New York: Routledge, 1993), 1.

2. Ibid.

3. Paulo Freire, *Pedagogy of the Oppressed* (New York: Bloomsbury Academic, 2000), 141.

4. Warner, *Publics and Counterpublics*, 166–67.

5. Brown, *States of Injury*, 167.

6. Audre Lorde, "The Master's Tools Will Never Dismantle the Master's House," in *Sister Outsider: Essays and Speeches* (Berkeley: Crossing Press, 2007), 110–14.

7. Helena Silverstein, *Unleashing Rights: Law, Meaning, and the Animal Rights Movement* (Ann Arbor: University of Michigan Press, 1996), 9.

8. Freire, *Pedagogy of the Oppressed*, 145.

9. Ibid., 74.

10. Ibid.

11. Butler, *Precarious Life*, 52.

12. Kitty Calavita, *Invitation to Law and Society* (Chicago: University of Chicago Press 2010), 36.

13. Ian Haney López, *White by Law: The Legal Construction of Race* (New York: New York University Press, 2006), 19–20.

14. Ibid., 20.

15. Plessy v. Ferguson, 163 U.S. 537 (1896), 541–42.

16. Ibid.

17. Ibid., 543.

18. Brown v. Board of Education of Topeka, 347 U.S. 483 (1954), 495.

19. Plessy v. Ferguson, 163 U.S. 537 (1896), 551; emphasis added.

20. Brown v. Board of Education of Topeka, 347 U.S. 483 (1954), 494; emphasis added.

21. López, *White by Law*, 18.

22. Frantz Fanon, *Black Skin, White Masks*, trans. Richard Philcox (New York: Grove Press, 2008), 90.

23. López, *White by Law*, 20.

24. See, e.g., Crenshaw, "Demarginalizing the Intersection of Race and Sex"; Patricia J. Williams, *The Alchemy of Race and Rights* (Cambridge: Harvard University Press, 1992).

25. Daum, "Marriage Equality."

26. Chief Justice Burger's concurring opinion explicitly stated, "This is essentially not a question of personal 'preferences,' but rather of the legislative authority of the State. I find nothing in the Constitution depriving a State of the power to enact the statute challenged here" (Bowers v. Hardwick, 478 U.S. 186 (1986), 197).

27. Colo. Const., Art. II, 30b.

28. Justice Kennedy, majority opinion, Romer v. Evans, 517 U.S. 620 (1996), at 633.

29. Ibid., at 634.

30. Boulder Rev. Code 12-1-1.

31. Romer v. Evans 517 U.S. 620 (1996), 624; emphasis added.

32. Obergefell v. Hodges 576 U.S. ___ (2015), 4.

33. Ibid., 19.

34. Lisa Duggan, *The Twilight of Equality? Neoliberalism, Cultural Politics, and the Attack on Democracy* (Boston: Beacon Press, 2003).

35. Ibid., 50.

36. Currah, "Gender Pluralism," 15.

37. Daum, "Marriage Equality."

38. Lisa Arnold and Christina Campbell, "The High Price of Being Single in America," *The Atlantic*, Jan. 24, 2013; http://www.theatlantic.com/sexes/archive/2013/01/the-high-price-of-being-single-in-america/267043/.

39. Stephen M. Engel, *Fragmented Citizens: The Changing Landscape of Gay and Lesbian Lives* (New York: New York University Press, 2016).

40. Ibid., at 240.

41. Courtenay W. Daum, "Social Equity, Homonormativity, and Equality: An Intersectional Critique of the Administration of Marriage Equality and Opportunities for LGBTQ Social Justice," *Administrative Theory & Praxis*, forthcoming.

42. Judith Butler, *Gender Trouble: Feminism and the Subversion of Identity* (New York: Routledge, 1990).

43. Ibid., 23.

44. Jane Allison Sitton, "Introduction to the Symposium, (De)Constructing Sex: Transgenderism, Intersexuality, Gender Identity, and the Law," *William and Mary Journal of Women and the Law* 7, no. 1 (2000): 1–2.

45. Ibid., 2.

46. Butler, *Gender Trouble*, 23.

47. Muller v. Oregon 208 U.S. 412 (1908), 421.

48. Hoyt v. Florida 368 U.S. 57 (1961), 62.

49. Goesaert et al. v. Cleary et al., Members of the Liquor Control Commission of Michigan, 335 U.S. 464 (1948).

50. Dothard v. Rawlinson 433 U.S. 321 (1977), 336.

51. See, e.g., Schlesinger v. Ballard 419 U.S. 498, 508 (1975); Michael M. v. Superior Court of Sonoma County 450 U.S. 464, 472 (1981); Rostker v. Goldberg 453 U.S. 57, 74, 76, 79 (1981); Miller v. Albright 523 U.S. 420 (1998); Nguyen v. INS 533 U.S. 53 (2001).

52. Butler, *Gender Trouble*, 142.

53. Brown, *States of Injury*, 167.

54. Ibid., 178.

55. Diana Fuss, *Essentially Speaking: Feminism, Nature, and Difference* (New York and London: Routledge, 1989).

56. See, e.g. Crenshaw, "Demarginalizing the Intersection of Race and Sex"; Angela Y. Davis, *Women, Race and Class* (New York: Vintage, 1983); Audre Lorde, *Sister Outsider*; Cherríe Moraga and Gloria Anzaldúa, *This Bridge Called My Back: Writings by Radical Women of Color*, 4th ed. (Albany: State University of New York Press, 2015); Williams, *The Alchemy of Race and Rights*.

57. Fuss, *Essentially Speaking*, 3.

58. Cynthia Bowman, Laura Rosenbury, Deborah Tuerkheimer, and Kimberly Yuracko, *Feminist Jurisprudence: Cases and Materials*, 4th ed. (St. Paul, MN: West Academic, 2010), 8, 13.

59. Judith Halberstam, *Female Masculinity* (Durham: Duke University Press, 1998).

60. Jere Longman, "Understanding the Controversy over Caster Semenya," *The New York Times*, Aug. 18, 2016; http://www.nytimes.com/2016/08/20/sports/caster-semenya-800-meters.html.

61. Heath Fogg Davis, "Sex Classification Policies as Transgender Discrimination: An Intersectional Critique," *Perspectives on Politics* 12, no. 1 (2014): 48.

62. Mark Critchley, "Rio 2016: Fifth-placed Joanna Jozwik 'Feels Like Silver Medallist' after 800m Defeat to Caster Semenya," *Independent*, 2016; http://www.independent.co.uk/sport/olympics/rio-2016-joanna-jozwik-caster-semenya-800m-hyperandrogenism-a7203731.html.

63. Halberstam, *Female Masculinity*, 1.

64. Ibid.

65. Marc Stein, *City of Sisterly and Brotherly Loves: Lesbian and Gay Philadelphia: 1945–1972* (Chicago: University of Chicago Press, 2000), 202.

66. Halberstam, *Female Masculinity*; Minter, "Do Transsexuals Dream of Gay Rights?" 156.

67. Halberstam, *Female Masculinity*, 9.

Chapter 2

1. David Valentine, *Imagining Transgender: An Ethnography of a Category* (Durham: Duke University Press, 2007), 5.

2. Duggan, *The Twilight of Equality?*

3. Butler, *Gender Trouble*; Michael Warner, *Fear of a Queer Planet: Queer Politics and Social Theory* (Minneapolis: University of Minnesota Press, 1993).

4. Julia Serano, *Whipping Girl: A Transsexual Woman on Sexism and the Scapegoating of Femininity* (Emeryville, CA: Seal Press, 2007).

5. Sheila L. Cavanagh, *Queering Bathrooms: Gender, Sexuality, and the Hygienic Imagination* (Toronto: University of Toronto Press, 2010), 19; Stryker, "(De)Subjugated Knowledges," 7; Serano, *Whipping Girl*, 178.

6. Sears, "Electric Brilliancy," 556.

7. Julia Serano, "Skirt Chasers: Why the Media Depicts the Trans Revolution in Lipstick and Heels," in *The Transgender Studies Reader* 2, ed. Susan Stryker and Aren Z. Aizura (New York and London: Routledge, 2013), 226.

8. Ibid., 230–31.

9. A. Finn Enke, "The Education of Little Cis: Cisgender and the Discipline of Opposing Bodies," in *The Transgender Studies Reader* 2, ed. Susan Stryker and Aren Z. Aizura (New York and London: Routledge, 2013), 236.

10. Cavanagh, *Queering Bathrooms*, 113.

11. Ochoa, "Perverse Citizenship," 444–45.

12. Cavanagh, *Queering Bathrooms*, 76.

13. Susan Stryker and Aren Z. Aizura, "Introduction," in *The Transgender Studies Reader* 2, ed. Susan Stryker and Aren Z. Aizura (New York: Routledge, 2013), 8.

14. Thomas, "*In*human Rights," 320.

15. Ibid., 320.

16. Valentine, *Imagining Transgender*.

17. Sandy E. James, Jody L. Herman, Susan Rankin, Mara Keisling, Lisa Mottet, and Ma'ayan Anafi, *The Report of the 2015 U.S. Transgender Survey* (Washington, DC: National Center for Transgender Equality, 2016), 3.

18. Ibid.

19. Ibid., 4.

20. Ibid.

21. Daum, "The War on Solicitation"; Davis, "Sex Classification Policies as Transgender Discrimination"; Dean Spade, *Normal Life: Administrative Violence, Critical Trans Politics and the Limits of Law* (Durham: Duke University Press, 2015).

22. Minter, "Do Transsexuals Dream of Gay Rights?" 156.

23. Michael Warner, "Introduction: Fear of a Queer Planet," *Social Text* 29 (1991): 12.

24. Alexis Shotwell, *Against Purity: Living Ethically in Compromised Times* (Minneapolis: University of Minnesota Press, 2016), 147.

25. Paisley Currah and Shannon Minter, "Unprincipled Exclusions: The Struggle to Achieve Judicial and Legislative Equality for Transgender People," *William and Mary Journal of Women and the Law* 7, no. 1 (2000): 50.

26. Phyllis Randolph Frye, "The International Bill of Gender Rights vs. The Cider House Rules," *William and Mary Journal of Women and the Law* 7, no. 1 (2000): 136–37.

27. Ibid., 135–36.

28. Kylar W. Broadus, "The Evolution of Employment Discrimination Protections for Transgender People," in *Transgender Rights,* ed. Paisley Currah, Richard M. Juang, and Shannon Price Minter (Minneapolis: University of Minnesota Press, 2006), 95.

29. Holloway v. Arthur Andersen, 566 F.2d 659 (9th Cir. 1977), 664.

30. Ulane v. Eastern Airlines, Inc., 742 F.2d 1081 (7th Cir. 1984).

31. Currah and Minter, "Unprincipled Exclusions," 41–42.

32. Smith v. City of Salem, 378 F.3d 566 (6th Cir. 2004).

33. U.S. Equal Employment Opportunity Commission, "Examples of Court Decisions Supporting Coverage of LGBT-Related Discrimination Under Title VII," 2017, https://www.eeoc.gov/eeoc/newsroom/wysk/lgbt_examples_decisions.cfm.

34. Sharon M. McGowan, "Working with Clients to Develop Compatible Visions of What it Means to 'Win' a Case: Reflections on *Schroer v. Billington*," *Harvard Civil Rights-Civil Liberties Law Review* 45 (2010): 205.

35. Ibid., at 236.

36. Ann E. Marimow, "Two Years In, Trump's Appeals Court Confirmations at a Historic High Point," *The Washington Post*, Feb. 4, 2019; https://www.washingtonpost.com/local/legal-issues/two-years-in-trumps-appeals-court-confirmations-at-a-historic-high-point/2019/02/03/574226e6-1a90-11e9-9ebfc5fed1b7a081_story.html?utm_term=.08c2282d445f.

37. U.S. Equal Employment Opportunity Commission, "Facts about Discrimination in Federal Government Employment Based on Marital Status, Political Affiliation, Status as a Parent, Sexual Orientation, and Gender Identity," 2017; https://www.eeoc.gov/federal/otherprotections.cfm; *Macy v. Department of Justice*, EEOC Appeal No. 0120120821 (April 20, 2012).

38. G.G v. Gloucester County School Board (2015), U.S. District Court (E.D. Va.); G.G. v. Gloucester County School Board (2016), U.S. Court of Appeals, 4th Circuit; Gloucester County School Board v. G.G, No. 16-273, U.S. Supreme Court.

39. United States, "Statement of Interest of the United States," G.G v. Gloucester County School Board, U.S. District Court Eastern District of Virginia Newport News Division (2015), 1–2; https://www.aclu.org/legal-document/gg-v-gloucester-county-school-board-statement-interest-united-states.

40. Erica L. Green, Katie Benner, and Robert Pear, "'Transgender' Could Be Defined Out of Existence Under Trump Administration," *The New York Times*, Oct. 21, 2018; https://www.nytimes.com/2018/10/21/us/politics/transgender-trump-administration-sex-definition.html?rref=collection%2Ftimestopic%2FHealth%20and%20Human%20Services%20Department&action=click&contentCollection=timestopics®ion=stream&module=stream_unit&version=latest&contentPlacement=5&pgtype=collection.

41. Ibid.

42. Julie A. Greenberg, "The Roads Less Traveled: The Problem with Binary Sex Categories," in *Transgender Rights* ed. Paisley Currah, Richard M. Juang, and Shannon Price Minter (Minneapolis: University of Minnesota Press, 2006), 51–73.

43. James et al., *Transgender Survey*, 45.

44. Cavanagh, *Queering Bathrooms*, 59.

45. Davis, "Sex Classification Policies as Transgender Discrimination," 51.

46. Greenberg, 51–52.

47. Cavanagh, *Queering Bathrooms*, 8.

48. Currah, "Gender Pluralism," 14.

49. Ibid., 18.

50. Ibid.

51. Butler, *Gender Trouble*, 149.

52. Taylor Flynn, "The Ties that (Don't) Bind: Transgender Family Law and the Unmaking of Families," in *Transgender Rights* ed. Paisley Currah, Richard M. Juang, and Shannon Price Minter (Minneapolis: University of Minnesota Press, 2006), 46.

53. Enke, "The Education of Little Cis."

54. Ibid., 236.

55. Ibid., 236–37.

56. Serano, *Whipping Girl*.

57. Ibid., 174–75.

58. Warner, "Introduction: Fear of a Queer Planet," 12.

59. Flynn, "The Ties that (Don't) Bind," 46.

60. Butler, *Gender Trouble*, 23.

61. Jane Ward, *Respectably Queer: Diversity Culture in LGBT Activist Organizations* (Nashville: Vanderbilt University Press, 2008), 43.

62. Dan Irving, "Normalized Transgressions: Legitimizing the Transsexual Body as Productive," in *The Transgender Studies Reader* 2, ed. Susan Stryker and Aren Z. Aizura (New York and London: Routledge, 2016), 16.

63. Butler, *Gender Trouble*, 149.

64. Cavanagh, *Queering Bathrooms*, 8.

65. Angela Davis, *The Meaning of Freedom* (San Francisco: City Lights, 2012), 197.

66. Butler, *Gender Trouble*, 149.

67. Currah, "Gender Pluralism," 24.

68. Greenberg, "The Roads Less Traveled," 68.

69. Ibid., 63.

70. Stryker and Aizura, "Introduction," 9.

71. Paisley Currah and Lisa Jean Moore, "'We Won't Know Who You Are:' Contesting Sex Designations in New York City Birth Certificates," in *The Transgender Studies Reader* 2, ed. Susan Stryker and Aren Z. Aizura (New York and London: Routledge, 2013), 609.

72. Che Gossett, "Silhouettes of Defiance: Memorializing Historical Sites of Queer and Transgender Resistance in an Age of Neoliberal Inclusivity" in *The Transgender Studies Reader* 2, ed. Susan Stryker and Aren Z. Aizura (New York and London: Routledge, 2013), 581; Susan Stryker, "Transgender History, Homonormativity, and Disciplinarity," *Radical History Review* 100 (2008): 145–57.

73. Ben Golder, *Foucault and the Politics of Rights* (Stanford: Stanford University Press, 2015), 100.

Chapter 3

1. Dean Spade, "Compliance Is Gendered: Struggling for Gender Self-Determination in a Hostile Economy," in *Transgender Rights*, ed. Paisley Currah, Richard M. Juang, and Shannon Price Minter (Minneapolis: University of Minnesota Press, 2006), 217–41.

2. Joey L. Mogul, Andrea J. Ritchie, and Kay Whitlock, *Queer (In)Justice: The Criminalization of LGBT People in the United States* (Boston: Beacon Press, 2011), ch. 1.

3. Davis, *Beyond Trans*; Davis, "Sex Classification Policies as Transgender Discrimination," 26.

4. Butler, *Gender Trouble.*

5. Foucault, *Discipline and Punish*, 220.

6. Paisley Currah and Tara Mulqueen, "Securitizing Gender: Identity, Biometrics, and Transgender Bodies at the Airport," *Social Research* 78, no. 2 (2011): 558.

7. Davis, *Beyond Trans*; Davis, "Sex Classification Policies as Transgender Discrimination," 46.

8. Ibid.

9. Talia Mae Bettcher, "Evil Deceivers and Make-Believers: On Transphobic Violence and the Politics of Illusion," in *The Transgender Studies Reader* 2, ed. Susan Stryker and Aren Z. Aizura (New York and London: Routledge, 2013), 286.

10. Flynn, "The Ties that (Don't) Bind," 46.

11. Greenberg, "The Roads Less Traveled," 52.

12. Ibid.

13. Ibid.

14. Currah, "Gender Pluralism," 18.

15. Andrew R. Flores, Jody L. Herman, Gary J. Gates, and Taylor N. T. Brown, *How Many Adults Identify as Transgender in the United States* (Los Angeles: The Williams Institute, 2016); https://williamsinstitute.law.ucla.edu/wp-content/uploads/How-Many-Adults-Identify-as-Transgender-in-the-United-States.pdf, 3.

16. National Center for Transgender Equality, "ID Documents Center," 2017; http://www.transequality.org/documents.

17. National Center for Transgender Equality, "How Trans-Friendly Is the Driver's License Gender Change Policy in Your State?" 2019; https://transequality.org/documents.

18. Jami K. Taylor, Barry L. Tadlock, and Sarah J. Poggione, "Birth Certificate Amendment Laws and Morality Politics," in *Transgender Rights and Politics: Groups, Issue Framing, and Policy Adoption*, ed. Jami K. Taylor and Donald P. Haider-Markel (Ann Arbor: University of Michigan Press, 2015), 252–72.

19. James et al., *Transgender Survey*, 82.

20. Ibid., 87.

21. National Center for Transgender Equality, "ID Documents Center," 2019; https://transequality.org/documents.

22. Ibid.

23. James et al., *Transgender Survey*, 86.

24. Ibid., 9.

25. Ibid.

26. Davis, *Beyond Trans.*

27. James et al., *Transgender Survey*, 9.

28. Ibid., 84.

29. Ibid.

30. Ibid., 93.
31. Ibid., 100.
32. Ibid., 99.
33. Ibid.
34. Movement Advancement Project, *Mapping Transgender Equality in the United States* (Denver: Movement Advancement Project, 2017); http://lgbtqmap.org/file/mapping-trans-equality.pdf 2017, 16.
35. James et al., *Transgender Survey*, 94.
36. Ibid., 95.
37. Ibid., 96.
38. Ibid., 87.
39. Ibid., 89.
40. Ibid.
41. Paisley Currah, "The Transgender Rights Imaginary," in *Feminist and Queer Legal Theory: Intimate Encounters, Uncomfortable Conversations*, ed. Martha Albertson Fineman, Jack E. Jackson, Adam P. Romero (London: Ashgate Press, 2009), 254.
42. Davis, "Sex Classification Policies as Transgender Discrimination," 49.
43. Spade, "Compliance Is Gendered," 221.
44. Currah and Moore, " 'We Won't Know Who You Are,' " 618.
45. Spade, "Compliance Is Gendered," 226.
46. James et al., *Transgender Survey*, 9.
47. Ibid., 89.
48. Ibid., 90.
49. Ibid.
50. Ibid.
51. Dean Spade, *Normal Life: Administrative Violence, Critical Trans Politics, and the Limits of Law* (Durham: Duke University Press, 2011), 12.
52. Davis, *Beyond Trans*; Davis, "Sex Classification Policies as Transgender Discrimination," 45.
53. Ibid., 45.
54. Ibid., 48.
55. James et al., *Transgender Survey*, 85.
56. Currah and Mulqueen, "Securitizing Gender," 558–59.
57. Ibid., 559.
58. Ibid., 600.
59. Ibid.
60. James et al., *Transgender Survey*, 213, 222.
61. Ibid., 222.
62. Alissa Bohling, "Transgender Travelers Singled Out in TSA Screenings, Docs Show," *Aljazeera.com*, May 26, 2014; http://america.aljazeera.com/articles/2014/5/26/groin-anomalies-andpatdownstravelingwhiletrans.html.
63. Mogul et al., *Queer (In)Justice*, 36–37.

64. See Beauchamp, "Artful Concealment"; Pooja Gehi, "Gender (In)security: Migration and Criminalization in the Security State," *Harvard Journal of Law and Gender* 35 (2012).

65. Dean Spade, "Documenting Gender" *Hastings Law Journal* 59 (2008): 731.

66. REAL ID Act of 2005, Pub.L. 109–13, 119 Stat. 302; Beauchamp, "Artful Concealment," 50.

67. James et al., *Transgender Survey*, 85.

68. Spade, "Documenting Gender," 799.

69. Currah and Mulqueen, "Securitizing Gender," 576.

70. Ibid., 571, 576.

71. Mogul et al., *Queer (In)Justice*, 36–37.

72. Currah and Moore, " 'We Won't Know Who You Are,' " 615.

73. Davis, "Sex Classification Policies as Transgender Discrimination," 51.

74. Spade, "Compliance Is Gendered," 227.

75. James et al., *Transgender Survey*, 89.

76. Davis, "Sex Classification Policies as Transgender Discrimination," 48.

77. Michel Foucault, *Power/Knowledge: Selected Interviews and Other Writings, 1972–1977*, ed. Colin Gordon (New York: Pantheon Books, 1980), 102.

78. Davis, "Sex Classification Policies as Transgender Discrimination," 45.

79. Bettcher, "Evil Deceivers and Make-Believers," 286.

80. Currah and Moore, " 'We Won't Know Who You Are.' "

81. Alexander, *The New Jim Crow*; Kelley, "Thug Nation."

82. Davis, "Sex Classification Policies as Transgender Discrimination," 54.

83. Currah and Moore, " 'We Won't Know Who You Are,' " 609.

84. Ibid., 608.

85. Ibid.

86. Ibid., 613.

87. Ibid., 619.

88. Ibid.

89. Davis, "Sex Classification Policies as Transgender Discrimination," 54.

90. Brown, *States of Injury*, 193.

91. Ibid.

92. Currah and Moore, " 'We Won't Know Who You Are,' " 618.

93. James et al., *Transgender Survey*, 85.

94. Davis, "Sex Classification Policies as Transgender Discrimination," 54.

Chapter 4

The chapter title was the campaign slogan of the opponents of a Houston, Texas, ordinance known as Proposition 1 that would have prohibited discrimination against individuals for a variety of factors, including gender identity.

1. Harvey Molotch, "Introduction: Learning from the Loo," in *Toilet: Public Restrooms and the Politics of Sharing*, ed. Harvey Molotch and Laura Norén (New York and London: New York University Press, 2010), 2.

2. Halberstam, *Female Masculinity*, 23.

3. Gillian Frank, "The Anti-Trans Bathroom Nightmare Has Its Roots in Segregation," *Slate*, Nov. 10, 2015; http://www.slate.com/blogs/outward/2015/11/10/anti_trans_bathroom_propaganda_has_roots_in_racial_segregation.html.

4. Ibid.

5. Ibid.; Mary Anne Case, "Why Not Abolish Laws of Urinary Segregation?" in *Toilet: Public Restrooms and the Politics of Sharing*, ed. Harvey Molotch and Laura Norén (New York and London: New York University Press, 2010), 211–25.

6. Frank, "The Anti-Trans Bathroom Nightmare."

7. Richard Juang, "Transgendering the Politics of Recognition," in *Transgender Rights*, ed. Paisley Currah, Richard M. Juang, and Shannon Price Minter (Minneapolis: University of Minnesota Press, 2006), 257.

8. Cavanagh, *Queering Bathrooms*, 7.

9. Frank, "The Anti-Trans Bathroom Nightmare."

10. Ibid.

11. National Conference of State Legislatures, " 'Bathroom Bill' Legislative Tracking," 2017; http://www.ncsl.org/research/education/-bathroom-bill-legislative-tracking635951130.aspx.

12. Ibid.; Rob Schofield, "Bathroom Law Victory: Federal Court Allows Challenge to HB2 Replacement to Proceed," *The Progressive Pulse*, Oct. 1, 2018; http://pulse.ncpolicywatch.org/2018/10/01/bathroom-law-victory-federal-court-allows-challenge-to-hb2-replacement-to-proceed/.

13. National Conference of State Legislatures, " 'Bathroom Bill' Legislative Tracking."

14. Golder, *Foucault and the Politics of Rights*, 45.

15. Halberstam, *Female Masculinity*, 25.

16. Jeffrey R. Dudas, "In the Name of Equal Right: 'Special' Rights and the Politics of Resentment in Post–Civil Rights America," *Law and Society Review* 39, no. 4 (2005): 723–58; Jeffrey R. Dudas, *The Cultivation of Resentment: Treaty Rights and the New Right* (Stanford: Stanford University Press, 2008).

17. Foucault, *Power/Knowledge*, 102.

18. Butler, *Precarious Life*, 60.

19. Monica Hesse, "How the Bathroom Becomes a Political Battleground for Civil Rights," *The Washington Post*, April 1, 2016; https://www.washingtonpost.com/lifestyle/style/why-america-cant-stop-fighting-over-the-politics-of-public-restrooms/2016/04/01/16af2f94-f6b6-11e5-a3ce-f06b5ba21f33_story.html?utm_term=.a47bbc5a4a4c.

20. Ibid.

21. Maya Rhodan, "Why Do We Have Men's and Women's Bathrooms Anyway?" *Time.com*, May 16, 2016; http://time.com/4337761/history-sex-segregated-bathrooms/.

22. Ibid.

23. Hesse, "How the Bathroom Becomes a Political Battleground for Civil Rights."

24. Molotch, "Learning from the Loo," 5.

25. Case, "Why Not Abolish Laws of Urinary Segregation?" 223–24.

26. Ibid., 224.

27. Barbara Penner, *Bathroom* (London: Reaktion Books, 2013), 9.

28. Cavanagh, *Queering Bathrooms*, 43.

29. Juang, "Transgendering the Politics of Recognition," 249.

30. Cavanagh, *Queering Bathrooms*, 49.

31. Colin Campbell, "NC's New LGBT Law Finds Support from Many in Rural Communities," *The Charlotte Observer*, April 11, 2016; http://www.charlotteobserver.com/news/politics-government/article71140652.html#storylink=cpy.

32. Brian S. Barnett, Ariana E. Nesbit, and Renée M. Sorrentino, "The Transgender Bathroom Debate at the Intersection of Politics, Law, Ethics, and Science," *Journal of the American Academy of Psychiatry and the Law Online* 46, no. 2 (June 2018): 232–41; http://jaapl.org/content/46/2/232.

33. James et al., *Transgender Survey*, 16.

34. Butler, *Precarious Life*, 98.

35. Flynn, "The Ties that (Don't) Bind," 37.

36. Serano, "Skirt Chasers."

37. Elena Boffetta, "Supporters and Opponents Hold HB2 Rallies in Raleigh," *The Charlotte Observer*, April 11, 2016; http://www.charlotteobserver.com/news/politics-government/article71240977.html.

38. Bettcher, "Evil Deceivers and Make-Believers," 280.

39. Serano, "Skirt Chasers."

40. Cavanagh, *Queering Bathrooms*, 69.

41. Ibid., 69.

42. Alexander, *The New Jim Crow*; Kelley, "Thug Nation."

43. Patrick R, Miller, Andrew R. Flores, Donald P. Haider-Markel, Daniel C. Lewis, Barry L. Tadlock, and Jami K. Taylor, "Transgender Politics as Body Politics: Effects of Disgust Sensitivity and Authoritarianism on Transgender Rights Attitudes," *Politics, Groups, and Identities* 5, no. 1 (2017): 4–24.

44. Campbell, "NC's New LGBT Law Finds Support from Many in Rural Communities."

45. James et al., *Transgender Survey*, 16.

46. Ibid., 225.

47. Ibid., 227.

48. Jody L. Herman, "Gendered Restrooms and Minority Stress: The Public Regulation of Gender and its Impact on Transgender People's Lives," *Journal of Public Management and Social Policy* 19, 1 (2013): 65–80.

49. James et al., *Transgender Survey*, 227.

50. Golder, *Foucault and the Politics of Rights*, 54.

51. James et al., *Transgender Survey*, 213.

52. Ibid., 17.

53. Herman 2013, 77.

54. Ibid., 77.

55. James et al., *Transgender Survey*, 229.

56. Ibid., 228.

57. Herman 2013.

58. James et al., *Transgender Survey*, 228.

59. Ibid., 228.

60. Ibid., 228.

61. National Center for Transgender Equality, *2015 U.S. Transgender Survey: North Carolina State Report* (Washington, DC, 2017); http://www.transequality.org/sites/default/files/docs/usts/USTS_NC_state_report.pdf.

62. Cavanagh, *Queering Bathrooms*, 71.

63. James et al., *Transgender Survey*, 17.

64. Ibid., 229.

65. Ibid., 228.

66. Molotch, "Learning from the Loo," 3–4.

67. Grace Dolan-Sandrino, "Gavin Grimm Talks Bringing Transgender Rights to the Supreme Court," *Teenvogue*.com, Feb. 22, 2017; http://www.teenvogue.com/story/gavin-grimm-supreme-court-case-interview.

68. Gavin Grimm, "Gavin Grimm at Gloucester County School Board Meeting," www.youtube.com, Sept. 1, 2016; https://www.youtube.com/watch?v=My0GYq_Wydw&feature=youtu.be.

69. Ibid.

70. James et al., *Transgender Survey*, 228.

71. Ibid., 11.

72. Ibid.

73. Ibid., 134.

74. Ibid., 225–26.

75. Ibid., 227.

76. Cavanagh, *Queering Bathrooms*, 6.

77. Halberstam, *Female Masculinity*, 23.

78. Molotch, "Learning from the Loo," 4.

79. James et al., *Transgender Survey*, 228.

80. Cavanagh, *Queering Bathrooms*, 6.

81. James et al., *Transgender Survey*, 228.

82. Golder, *Foucault and the Politics of Rights*, 46.

83. Halberstam, *Female Masculinity*, 22.

84. Golder, *Foucault and the Politics of Rights*, 46.

85. Michael Walsh, "N.C. Gov. Pat McCrory Defends HB2: I Can't Believe We're Talking About This," *Yahoo! News*, April 29, 2016; https://www.yahoo.com/news/nc-gov-pat-mccrory-defends-hb2-i-cant-believe-161442832.html.

86. Cavanagh, *Queering Bathrooms*, 56.

87. James et al., *Transgender Survey*, 134.

88. Dave Solomon, "NH House Speaker Leads Opposition to Transgender Bill," *New Hampshire Union Leader*, March 6, 2017; http://www.unionleader.com/state-government/House-Speaker-leads-opposition-to-transgender-bill-03062017.

89. Dudas, "In the Name of Equal Rights."

90. Mark Joseph Stern, "Professional Victim Pat McCrory Has Slid into Delusions of Grandeur," *Slate.com*, March 14, 2017; http://www.slate.com/blogs/outward/2017/03/14/pat_mccrory_a_paranoid_delusional_professional_victim.html.

91. Boffetta, "Supporters and Opponents Hold HB2 Rallies in Raleigh."

92. Campbell, "NC's New LGBT Law Finds Support from Many in Rural Communities."

93. Pat McCrory, "@PatMcCroryNC," Twitter, March 23, 2016.

94. Cavanagh, *Queering Bathrooms*, 53.

95. Juang, "Transgendering the Politics of Recognition," 247.

Chapter 5

This chapter was previously published in *New Political Science: A Journal of Politics and Culture* as Courtenay W. Daum, "The War on Solicitation and Intersectional Subjection: Quality-of-Life Policing as a Tool to Control Transgender Populations," *New Political Science* 37, no. 4 (2015): 562–81.

1. Make the Road New York, *Transgressive Policing: Police Abuse of LGBTQ Communities of Color in Jackson Heights* (New York, 2012), 20; http://www.maketheroad.org/pix_reports/MRNY_Transgressive_Policing_Full_Report_10.23.12B.pdf.

2. Ibid., 4; Human Rights Watch, *Sex Workers at Risk: Condoms as Evidence of Prostitution in Four U.S. Cities* (Washington, DC: Human Rights Watch, 2012), 19; http://www.hrw.org/sites/default/files/reports/us0712ForUpload_1.pdf; PROS Network and the Sex Workers Project, *Public Health Crisis: The Impact of Using Condoms as Evidence of Prostitution in New York City* (New York: Urban Justice Center, 2012); http://sexworkersproject.org/downloads/2012/20120417-public-health-crisis.pdf.

3. Alexander, *The New Jim Crow*.

4. Foucault, *Security, Territory, Population*.

5. Butler, *Precarious Life*, 94.

6. The use of the term *subjection* as opposed to *oppression* is inspired by Dean Spade's argument that subjection may be more useful in getting at systemic discrimination in ways that oppression is not because the former accounts for the ways in which power is decentralized, multifaceted, and diffuse. Spade, *Normal Life*.

7. See Amnesty International, *Stonewalled—Still Demanding Respect: Police Abuses against Lesbian, Gay, Bisexual, and Transgender People in the USA* (London: Amnesty International Publications, 2006); Human Rights Watch, *Sex Workers at Risk*; Make the Road New York, *Transgressive Policing*.

8. Human Rights Watch, *Sex Workers at Risk*.

9. See Elijah Adiv Edelman, "'Walking While Transgender': Necropolitical Regulations of Trans Feminine Bodies of Colour in the US Nation's Capital," in *Queer Necropolitics*, ed. Jin Haritaworn, Adi Kuntsman, and Silvia Posocco (New York: Routledge, 2014), 172–90; Human Rights Watch, *Sex Workers at Risk*.

10. See Amnesty International, *Stonewalled*; Frank H. Galvan and Mohsen Bazargan, *Interactions of Latina Transgender Women with Law Enforcement* (Los Angeles: Bienestar Human Services, 2012); http://williamsinstitute.law.ucla.edu/wp-content/uploads/Galvan-Bazargan-Interactions-April-2012.pdf.; Human Rights Watch, *Sex Workers at Risk*; Jordan Blair Woods, Frank H. Galvan, Mohsen Bazargan, Jody L. Herman, and Ying-Tung Chen, "Latina Transgender Women's Interactions with Law Enforcement in Los Angeles County," *Policing* 7, no. 4 (2013): 379–91.

11. Human Rights Watch, *Sex Workers at Risk*; Andrea J. Ritchie, "Crimes against Nature: Challenging Criminalization of Queerness and Black Women's Sexuality," *Loyola Journal of Public Interest Law* 14 (2013): 355.

12. Amnesty International, *Stonewalled*.

13. Ibid.

14. Make the Road New York, *Transgressive Policing*, 4.

15. James et al., *Transgender Survey*, 186.

16. Ibid., 187.

17. Human Rights Watch, *Sex Workers at Risk*, 2, 24.

18. Ibid., 20.

19. Make the Road New York, *Transgressive Policing*, 21.

20. Human Rights Watch, *Sex Workers at Risk*, 19.

21. Jaime M. Grant, Lisa A. Mottet, Justin Tanis, Jack Harrison, Jody L. Herman, and Mara Keisling, *Injustice at Every Turn: A Report of the National Transgender Discrimination Survey* (Washington, DC: National Center for Transgender Equality and National Gay and Lesbian Task Force, 2011), 163; http://www.thetaskforce.org/static_html/downloads/reports/reports/ntds_full.pdf.

22. Make the Road New York, *Transgressive Policing*, 20.

23. PROS Network and the Sex Workers Project, *Public Health Crisis*.

24. Make the Road New York, *Transgressive Policing*, 4.

25. Mike Ludwig, "'Walking While Woman' and the Fight to Stop Violent Policing of Gender Identity," *Truthout*, May 7, 2014; www.truth-out.org.

26. Amnesty International, *Stonewalled*, 58.

27. Butler, *Precarious Life*, 54.

28. Alexander, *The New Jim Crow*.

29. Ibid., 185.

30. Ibid., 197.

31. Butler, *Precarious Life*, xx–xxi.

32. Mogul et al., *Queer (In)Justice*, ch. 1.

33. James et al., *Transgender Survey*, 14.

34. Grant et al., *Injustice at Every Turn*, 2.

35. Ibid., 65.

36. Ibid., 64.

37. Human Rights Watch, *Sex Workers at Risk*, 16–17; PROS Network and the Sex Workers Project, *Public Health Crisis*, 12.

38. Human Rights Watch, *Sex Workers at Risk*, 20; emphasis added.

39. Make the Road New York, *Transgressive Policing*, 10–11.

40. Ritchie, "Crimes against Nature," 369.

41. Gehi, "Gender (In)security," 385.

42. Human Rights Watch, *Sex Workers at Risk*, 19.

43. Ibid., 22.

44. Ibid., 50–51.

45. J. Jeanty and H. J. Tobin, *Our Moment for Reform: Immigration and Transgender People* (Washington, DC: National Center for Transgender Equality, 2013), 6; http://transequality.org/sites/default/files/docs/resources/OurMoment_CIR_en.pdf.

46. Ibid., 7.

47. Ibid., 6.

48. See Edelman, "Walking While Transgender."

49. Butler, *Precarious Life*, 98.

50. Sarah Lamble, "Queer Investments in Punitiveness: Sexual Citizenship, Social Movements, and the Expanding Carceral State," in *Queer Necropolitics*, ed. Jin Haritaworn, Adi Kuntsman, and Silvia Posocco (New York: Routledge, 2014), 159–60.

51. Ibid., 159.

52. Spade, *Normal Life*, 53–54.

53. Grant et al., *Injustice at Every Turn*, 163.

54. Galvan and Bazargan, *Interactions of Latina Transgender Women*, 1.

55. Butler, *Precarious Life*, 98.

56. Human Rights Watch, *Sex Workers at Risk*, 24–25; emphasis added.

57. Ibid., 19.

58. Edelman, "Walking While Transgender," 178.

59. Ibid., 179.
60. Dean Spade, *Normal Life*, 53–54.
61. Beauchamp, "Artful Concealment."
62. Make the Road New York, *Transgressive Policing*, 23.
63. Illegal Immigration Reform and Immigrant Responsibility Act of 1996, PUBLIC LAW 104–208, 110 STAT. 3009, 546.
64. Gehi, "Gender (In)security," 380.
65. Jeanty and Tobin, *Our Moment for Reform*, 21.
66. Dean Spade, *Normal Life*, 27.
67. Edelman, " 'Walking While Transgender,' " 176.
68. Butler, *Bodies that Matter*, 1.
69. Currah and Moore, " 'We Won't Know Who You Are,' " 608.
70. Ibid.
71. Ibid., 610; Beauchamp, "Artful Concealment."
72. Butler, *Precarious Life*, 26.
73. Ibid., 27.
74. Butler, *Gender Trouble*.
75. Butler, *Bodies that Matter*, 2.
76. Human Rights Watch, *Sex Workers at Risk*, 23.
77. Butler, *Bodies that Matter*, 3.
78. PROS Network and the Sex Workers Project, *Public Health Crisis*, 21.
79. Butler, *Bodies that Matter*, 16.
80. Ibid., 4.
81. Ibid., 95.
82. Beauchamp, "Artful Concealment," 50.
83. Make the Road New York, *Transgressive Policing*, 11.
84. James et al., *Transgender Survey*, 14.
85. Ibid., 186.
86. Ibid.
87. Mogul et al., *Queer (In)Justice*, 50.
88. Amnesty International, *Stonewalled*; Human Rights Watch, *Sex Workers at Risk*, 25–26; Make the Road New York, *Transgressive Policing*, 5.
89. James et al., *Transgender Survey*, 187–88.
90. Make the Road New York, *Transgressive Policing*, 23.
91. Amnesty International, *Stonewalled*, 22.
92. James et al., *Transgender Survey*, 14.
93. See, for example, Grant et al., *Injustice at Every Turn*, 162; James et al., *Transgender Survey*, 12; Kae Greenberg, "Still Hidden in the Closet: Trans Women and Domestic Violence," *Berkeley Journal of Gender, Law and Justice* 27, no. 2 (2012): 198–251.
94. Gehi, "Gender (In)security," 388.
95. Greenberg, "Still Hidden in the Closet," 233.

96. Grant et al., *Injustice at Every Turn*, 158.
97. Ibid., 159.
98. Mogul et al., *Queer (In)Justice*, 130.
99. Bettcher, "Evil Deceivers and Make-Believers."
100. Butler, *Bodies that Matter.*

Chapter 6

1. Ochoa, "Perverse Citizenship," 447.

2. See, e.g., Epp, *The Rights Revolution*; McCann, *Rights at Work*; Scheingold, *The Politics of Rights*.

3. Nownes, *Organizing for Transgender Rights*.

4. Dean Spade, "Trans Law Reform Strategies, Co-Optation, and the Potential for Transformative Change," *Women's Rights Law Reporter* 30 (2009): 306–307.

5. See Spade, *Normal Life*.

6. Scheingold, *The Politics of Rights*, 131.

7. Ibid., 148.

8. Dean Spade, "Fighting to Win!," in *That's Revolting! Queer Strategies for Resisting Assimilation*, ed. Mattilda Bernstein Sycamore (Berkeley: Soft Skull, 2004), 53.

9. See, e.g., Zein Murib, "Transgender: Examining an Emerging Political Identity Using Three Political Processes," *Politics, Groups, and Identities* 3, no. 3 (2015): 381–97; Spade, "Fighting to win!"; Stryker, "Transgender History, Homonormativity, and Disciplinarity."

10. Robert Hill, "Before Transgender: *Transvestia's* Spectrum of Gender Variance, 1960–1980," in *The Transgender Studies Reader* 2, ed. Susan Stryker and Aren Z. Aizura (New York and London: Routledge, 2013), 366.

11. Jessi Gan, "'Still at the Back of the Bus,'" 296.

12. Gossett, "Silhouettes of Defiance," 583.

13. Minter, "Do Transsexuals Dream of Gay Rights?" 150.

14. Daum, "Marriage Equality."

15. Gossett, "Silhouettes of Defiance," 585.

16. Courtenay W. Daum, "Putting the T back in LGBTQ? Transgender Activism and Interests After Marriage Equality," in *Queer Activism after Marriage Equality*, ed. Joseph DeFilippis, Angela Jones, and Michael Yarbrough (New York: Routledge Press, 2018).

17. McCann, *Rights at Work*, 136.

18. Keegan O'Brien, "Tearing Down the Walls: The Story of the Stonewall Rebellion and the Rise of the Gay Liberation Movement," *Jacobin*, Aug. 20, 2015; https://www.jacobinmag.com/2015/08/lgbtq-stonewall-marriage-equality-mattachine-sylvia-rivera/; Deborah Sontag, "Once a Pariah, Now a Judge: The Early Transgender Journey of Phyllis Frye," *The New York Times*, Aug. 29, 2015; http://www.

nytimes.com/2015/08/30/us/transgender-judge-phyllis-fryes-early-transformative-journey.html.

19. Ibid.

20. Dallas Denny, "Transgender Communities of the United States in the Late Twentieth Century," in *Transgender Rights*, ed. Paisley Currah, Richard M. Juang, and Shannon Price Minter (Minneapolis: University of Minnesota Press, 2006), 174.

21. Evan Wolfson, "What's Next in the Fight for Gay Equality?" *The New York Times*, June 26, 2015; http://www.nytimes.com/2015/06/27/opinion/evan-wolfson-whats-next-in-the-fight-for-gay-equality.html.

22. Chad Griffin, "Transcript: HRC President Chad Griffin Apologizes to Trans People at Southern Comfort"; Daum, "Putting the T back in LGBTQ?"

23. Gloucester County School Board v. Grimm 579 U.S.___ (2016).

24. Daum, "Putting the T back in LGBTQ?"

25. Gossett, "Silhouettes of Defiance," 585.

26. Denny, "Transgender Communities of the United States in the Late Twentieth Century," 174.

27. Minter, "Do Transsexuals Dream of Gay Rights?" 146.

28. Jami K. Taylor and Daniel C. Lewis, "The Advocacy Coalition Framework and Transgender Inclusion in LGBT Rights Activism," in *Transgender Rights and Politics: Groups, Issue Framing, and Policy Adoption*, ed. Jami K. Taylor and Donald P. Haider-Markel (Ann Arbor: University of Michigan Press), 122.

29. Spade, "Compliance Is Gendered," 218.

30. Ibid., 229; Daum, "Marriage Equality."

31. Irving, "Normalized Transgressions," 27.

32. Gossett, "Silhouettes of Defiance," 581.

33. Ibid., 586.

34. Mucciaroni, "Will Victory Bring Change?" 21.

35. Morgan Bassichis, Alexander Lee, and Dean Spade, "Building an Abolitionist Trans Queer Movement with Everything We've Got," in *The Transgender Studies Reader* 2, ed. Susan Stryker and Aren Z. Aizura (New York: Routledge, 2013), 661.

36. Currah, "Gender Pluralism," 14.

37. Mucciaroni, "Will Victory Bring Change?" 22.

38. Minter, "Do Transsexuals Dream of Gay Rights?" 153.

39. Mucciaroni, "Will Victory Bring Change?" 25.

40. Anthony J. Nownes, *Organizing for Transgender Rights*.

41. Gossett, "Silhouettes of Defiance," 588.

42. Denny, "Transgender Communities of the United States in the Late Twentieth Century," 183.

43. Nownes, *Organizing for Transgender Rights*.

44. Scheingold, *The Politics of Rights*, 131.

45. Spade, *Normal Life*.

46. Nownes, *Organizing for Transgender Rights*, 10–11.

47. Minter, "Do Transsexuals Dream of Gay Rights?" 159.

48. Scheingold, *The Politics of Rights*, 132.

49. Broadus, "The Evolution of Employment Discrimination Protections for Transgender People," 99.

50. Scheingold, *The Politics of Rights*, 148.

51. Fuss, *Essentially Speaking*, 104.

52. Currah and Minter, "Unprincipled Exclusions," 50. That being said, one of the pros of interpreting prohibitions on sex discrimination in existing civil rights statutes to include gender identity is that this situates transgender people in existing privileged categories, whereas "identifying gender identity as a distinct classification may enforce the perception, which is already so pervasive and damaging in the case law, that transgender people are somehow fundamentally distinct from—and by implication inferior to—non-transgender people, i.e., that transgender people are not men or women, but something other or in-between" (Currah and Minter, "Unprincipled Exclusions," 50). Yet, as argued throughout this book, this approach problematically dislocates those who either do not identity as male or female or are unable to meet the legal and/or sociocultural requirements for recognition as male or female.

53. Ibid., 51–54.

54. Ibid., 51.

55. Dean Spade, "Keynote Address: Trans Law and Politics on a Neoliberal Landscape," *Temple Political and Civil Rights Law Review* 18, no. 2 (2009): 356.

56. The Matthew Shepard and James Byrd Jr. Hate Crimes Prevention Act of 2009, 18 U.S.C. § 249. Many trans and queer activists and scholars have been critical of hate crimes statutes and other legislation that increases the scope of the prison industrial complex. See, e.g., Reddy, *Freedom with Violence*; Spade, *Normal Life*.

57. H.R.4636 and S.2238 Employment Non-Discrimination Act of 1994.

58. H.R.2015—Employment Non-Discrimination Act of 2007.

59. Ibid.

60. Ibid.

61. Movement Advancement Project, *Mapping Transgender Equality*, 13.

62. Currah and Minter, "Unprincipled Exclusions," 46; Movement Advancement Project, *Mapping Transgender Equality*.

63. Mucciaroni, "Will Victory Bring Change?" 27.

64. Movement Advancement Project, *Mapping Transgender Equality*, 14; Movement Advancement Project, *State Religious Exemption Laws* (Denver: Movement Advancement Project, 2017); http://www.lgbtmap.org/equality-maps/religious_exemption_laws.

65. Movement Advancement Project, *Mapping Transgender Equality*, 15.

66. Ibid., 1.
67. Ibid.
68. Ibid.
69. Ibid., 7.
70. Ibid., 19.
71. Ibid., 11.
72. Ibid., 17.
73. Spade, "Keynote Address: Trans Law and Politics on a Neoliberal Landscape," 356.
74. Scheingold, *The Politics of Rights*, 23.
75. Ibid., 130.
76. Ibid., 123.
77. Richard Delgado and Jean Stefancic, *Critical Race Theory* (New York: New York University Press, 2012), 37.
78. Spade, "Keynote Address: Trans Law and Politics on a Neoliberal Landscape," 359.
79. Reddy, *Freedom with Violence*, 9.
80. Ibid., 7.
81. Ibid., 8.
82. Ibid.
83. Spade, "Keynote Address: Trans Law and Politics on a Neoliberal Landscape," 356.
84. Ibid., 357.
85. Bassichis, Lee, and Spade, "Building an Abolitionist Trans Queer Movement," 661.
86. Ibid.
87. Ibid., 660.

Chapter 7

1. Warner, "Introduction: Fear of a Queer Planet," 12.
2. Ibid.
3. Brown, *States of Injury*, 121, note 41.
4. Courtenay W. Daum, "Counterpublics and Intersectional Radical Resistance: Agitation as a Mechanism for Transforming the Dominant Discourse," *New Political Science* 39, no. 4 (2017): 523–37.
5. Nancy Fraser, "Rethinking the Public Sphere: A Contribution to the Critique of Actually Existing Democracy," *Social Text* 25/26 (1990): 56–80; Michael Warner, "Publics and Counterpublics," *Public Culture* 14, no. 1 (2002): 49–90; Warner, *Publics and Counterpublics*.
6. Warner, *Publics and Counterpublics*, 89.

7. Andrew Reynolds, "Representation and Rights: The Impact of LGBT Legislators in Comparative Perspective," *American Political Science Review* 107, no. 2 (2013): 259–74; Andrew Reynolds, *Out in Office: LGBT Legislators and LGBT Rights around the World* (Chapel Hill: University of North Carolina LGBT Representation and Rights Initiative, 2013).

8. Jeremiah J. Garretson, "Exposure to the Lives of Lesbians and Gays and the Origin of Young People's Greater Support for Gay Rights," *International Journal of Public Opinion Research* 27, no. 2 (2015): 277–88; Gregory B. Lewis, "The Friends and Family Plan: Contact with Gays and Support for Gay Rights," *Policy Studies Journal* 39, no. 2 (2011): 217–38; Leslia A. Zebrowitz, Benjamin White, and Kristin Wieneke, "Mere Exposure and Racial Prejudice: Exposure to Other-Race Faces Increases Liking For Strangers of That Race," *Social Cognition* 26, no. 3 (2008): 259–75.

9. Andrew R. Flores, "Attitudes toward Transgender Rights: Perceived Knowledge and Secondary Interpersonal Contact," *Politics, Groups, and Identities* 3, no. 3 (2015): 398–416; Barry L. Tadlock, Andrew R. Flores, Donald P. Haider-Markel, Daniel C. Lewis, Patrick R. Miller, and Jami K Taylor, "Testing Contact Theory and Attitudes on Transgender Rights," *Public Opinion Quarterly* 81, no. 4 (2017): 956–72.

10. David Broockman and Joshua Kalla, "Durably Reducing Transphobia: A Field Experiment on Door-to-Door Canvassing," *Science* 352, no. 6282 (2016): 220–24; Brian F. Harrison and Melissa R. Michelson, "Using Experiments to Understand Public Attitudes towards Transgender Rights," *Politics, Groups, and Identities* 5, no. 1 (2017): 152–60; Andrew R. Flores, Donald P. Haider-Markel, Daniel C. Lewis, Patrick R. Miller, Barry L. Tadlock, and Jami K, Taylor, "Transgender Prejudice Reduction and Opinions on Transgender Rights? Results from a Mediation Analysis on Experimental Data," *Research and Politics* (Jan.-March 2018): 5.

11. Flores et al., *How Many Adults Identify as Transgender in the United States?*

12. Davis, *Does Gender Matter?*, 7.

13. Morehouse College, "Gender Identity Policy," http://www.morehouse.edu/genderidentity/.

14. Gina Kolata, "Does Testosterone Really Give Caster Semenya an Edge on the Track?" *The New York Times*, May 1, 2019; https://www.nytimes.com/2019/05/01/health/caster-semenya-testosterone.html.

15. Golder, *Foucault and the Politics of Rights*, 112.

16. Judith Butler, "Restaging the Universal: Hegemony and the Limits of Formalism," in *Contingency, Hegemony, Universality: Contemporary Dialogues on the Left*, ed. Judith Butler, Ernesto Laclau, and Slavoj Žižek (London and New York: Verso, 2000), 14.

17. Golder, *Foucault and the Politics of Rights*, 112.

18. Nancy Fraser, "Abnormal Justice," *Critical Inquiry* 34, no. 3 (2008): 422.

19. Springer, *The Anarchist Roots of Geography*, 129.

20. Warner, "Publics and Counterpublics," 89.

21. Brown, *States of Injury*, 121, note 41.

22. Reddy, *Freedom with Violence*, 218.

23. Fraser, "Rethinking the Public Sphere," 67.

24. Ibid.

25. Ibid.

26. Warner, "Publics and Counterpublics," 86.

27. Ibid., 87.

28. Ibid., 86.

29. Butler, "Restaging the Universal"; Alexandra Chasin, *Selling Out: The Gay and Lesbian Movement Goes to Market* (New York: St. Martin's Press, 2000); Daum, "Marriage Equality;" Duggan, *The Twilight of Equality?*

30. Southerners on New Ground, "About." *Southernersonnewground.org*; http://southernersonnewground.org/about/.

31. Black Girl Dangerous, "About BGD: Amplifying the Voices of Queer and Trans People of Color"; https://www.bgdblog.org/about-bgd/.

32. Springer, *The Anarchist Roots of Geography*, 128.

33. allgo, "What We Do," *allgo.org*, http://allgo.org/what-we-do/social-justice/; emphasis added.

34. FIERCE, "What We Do," *Fiercenyc*.org; http://fiercenyc.org/what-we-do.

35. Audre Lorde Project, "TransJustice Community School 2017 Application Open!" *alp.org*; http://alp.org/transjustice-community-school-2017-application-open-deadline-extended.

36. FIERCE, "Leadership Development." *Fiercenyc.org*; http://fiercenyc.org/leadership-development.

37. FIERCE, "What We Do."

38. Familia, "Mission," *Familiatglqm.org*; http://familiatqlm.org/mission-3/; emphasis added.

39. Fraser, "Rethinking the Public Sphere," 67.

40. Dana R. Villa, "Postmodernism and the Public Sphere," *American Political Science Review* 86, no. 3 (1992): 714.

41. Alexander Livingston, "Avoiding Deliberative Democracy? Micropolitics, Manipulation, and the Public Sphere," *Philosophy & Rhetoric* 45, no. 3 (2012): 269–94.

42. Ibid.

43. Ibid.

44. Fraser, "Rethinking the Public Sphere," 63.

45. Ibid.

46. Ibid., 65.

47. Livingston, "Avoiding Deliberative Democracy?"

48. Holly Boux and Courtenay W. Daum, "At the Intersection of Social Media and Rape Culture: How Facebook, Texting and Other Personal Communications Challenge the 'Real' Rape Myth in the Criminal Justice System," *Journal of Law, Technology and Policy* 1 (2015): 149–86; Susan Estrich, *Real Rape: How the Legal System Victimizes Women Who Say No* (Cambridge: Harvard University Press, 1988).

49. Lincoln Dahlberg, "The Habermasian Public Sphere: Taking Difference Seriously?" *Theory and Society* 34, no. 2 (April 2005): 121.

50. Wolfson, "What's Next in the Fight for Gay Equality?"

51. Warner, "Publics and Counterpublics," 89.

52. See, e.g., Beyond Marriage, "Beyond Same-Sex Marriage," July 26, 2006; *Beyondmarriage.org.*; Daum, "Marriage Equality."

53. Warner, "Publics and Counterpublics," 88.

54. Wolfson, "What's Next in the Fight for Gay Equality?"

55. Beyond Marriage, "Beyond Same-Sex Marriage"; Nancy D. Polikoff, *Beyond (Straight and Gay) Marriage: Valuing All Families Under the Law* (Boston: Beacon Press, 2008).

56. Daum, "Marriage Equality"; Urvashi Vaid, *Virtual Equality: The Mainstreaming of Gay and Lesbian Liberation* (New York: Anchor Books, 1995).

57. Golder, *Foucault and the Politics of Rights*, 102.

58. Ibram X. Kendi, *Stamped from the Beginning: The Definitive History of Racist Ideas in America* (New York: Nation Books, 2016), 105.

59. Springer, *The Anarchist Roots of Geography*, 128.

60. Warner, "Publics and Counterpublics," 86.

61. Lauren Berlant and Elizabeth Freeman, "Queer Nationality," in *Fear of a Queer Planet: Queer Politics and Social Theory*, ed. Michael Warner (Minneapolis: University of Minneapolis Press, 1993), 200.

62. Ibid., 200–201.

63. Democracy Now! "Undocumented Trans Activist Jennicet Gutiérrez Challenges Obama on Deportations at White House Event," *Democracy Now!* June 25, 2015; https://www.youtube.com/watch?v=ER9_M002aQY.

64. Kevin Liptak, "Obama Shuts Down Heckler: 'You're in My House!' " cnn.com, 2015; www.cnn.com/2015/06/24/politics/obama-heckler-white-house-lgbt/index.html.

65. Democracy Now! "Undocumented Trans Activist Jennicet Gutiérrez Challenges Obama."

66. Liptak, "Obama Shuts Down Heckler."

67. Fraser, "Rethinking the Public Sphere," 61.

68. Fraser, "Abnormal Justice," 422; Warner, "Publics and Counterpublics," 89.

69. Fraser, "Abnormal Justice," 417.

70. Southerners on New Ground, "2016 End of Year Report," Southernersonnewground.org; http://southernersonnewground.org/2016/12/16endofyearreport/.

71. Ibid.

72. Ibid.

73. Ochoa, "Perverse Citizenship," 449.

74. See, e.g., Cain, *Rainbow Rights*; Engel and Munger, *Rights of Inclusion*; Epp, *The Rights Revolution*; McCann, *Rights at Work*; Tushnet, *The NAACP's Legal Strategy against Segregated Education*; Olson, *Clients and Lawyers*.

75. Scheingold, *The Politics of Rights*.

76. Hall, *The Nature of Supreme Court Power*; Rosenberg, "Hollow Hopes and Other Aspirations"; Rosenberg, *The Hollow Hope*.

Works Cited

Alexander, Michelle. *The New Jim Crow: Mass Incarceration in the Age of Colorblindess*. New York: The New Press, 2012.

Allgo. "What We Do." *allgo.org*, allgo.org/what-we-do/social-justice/.

Amnesty International. *Stonewalled—Still Demanding Respect: Police Abuses against Lesbian, Gay, Bisexual, and Transgender People in the USA*. London: Amnesty International Publications, 2006.

Arnold, Lisa, and Christina Campbell. "The High Price of Being Single in America." *The Atlantic*, January 24, 2013; www.theatlantic.com/sexes/archive/2013/01/the-highprice-of-being-single-in-america/267043/.

Audre Lorde Project. "TransJustice Community School 2017 Application Open!" *alp.org*; alp.org/transjustice-community-school-2017-application-open-deadline-extended.

Barclay, Scott, Mary Bernstein, and Anna-Maria Marshall. *Queer Mobilizations: LGBT Activists Confront the Law*. New York: New York University Press, 2009.

Barnett, Brian S., Ariana E. Nesbit, and Renée M. Sorrentino. "The Transgender Bathroom Debate at the Intersection of Politics, Law, Ethics, and Science." *Journal of the American Academy of Psychiatry and the Law Online* 46, no. 2 (June 2018): 232–41; jaapl.org/content/46/2/232.

Bassichis, Morgan, Alexander Lee, and Dean Spade. "Building an Abolitionist Trans Queer Movement with Everything We've Got." In *The Transgender Studies Reader* 2, edited by Susan Stryker and Aren Z. Aizura, 653–67. New York: Routledge, 2013.

Beauchamp, Toby. "Artful Concealment and Strategic Visibility: Transgender Bodies and U.S. State Surveillance after 9/11." In *The Transgender Studies Reader* 2, edited by Susan Stryker and Aren Z. Aizura, 46–55. New York: Routledge, 2013.

Berlant, Lauren, and Elizabeth Freeman. "Queer Nationality." In *Fear of a Queer Planet: Queer Politics and Social Theory*, edited by Michael Warner, 193–229. Minneapolis: University of Minneapolis Press, 1993.

Bettcher, Talia Mae. "Evil Deceivers and Make-Believers: On Transphobic Violence and the Politics of Illusion." In *The Transgender Studies Reader* 2, edited by Susan Stryker and Aren Z. Aizura, 278–90. New York and London: Routledge, 2013.

Beyond Marriage. "Beyond Same-Sex Marriage." *Beyondmarriage.org*, July 26, 2006.

Black Girl Dangerous. "About BGD: Amplifying the Voices of Queer and Trans People of Color"; www.bgdblog.org/about-bgd/.

Boffetta, Elena. "Supporters and Opponents Hold HB2 Rallies in Raleigh." *The Charlotte Observer*, April 11, 2016; www.charlotteobserver.com/news/politics-government/article71240977.html.

Bohling, Alissa. "Transgender Travelers Singled Out in TSA Screenings, Docs Show." *Aljazeera.com*, May 26, 2014; america.aljazeera.com/articles/2014/5/26/groin-anomalies-andpatdownstravelingwhiletrans.html.

Boux, Holly, and Courtenay W. Daum. "At the Intersection of Social Media and Rape Culture: How Facebook, Texting, and Other Personal Communications Challenge the 'Real' Rape Myth in the Criminal Justice System." *Journal of Law, Technology and Policy* 1 (2015): 149–86.

Bowman, Cynthia, Laura Rosenbury, Deborah Tuerkheimer, and Kimberly Yuracko. *Feminist Jurisprudence: Cases and Materials*, 4th ed. Saint Paul, MN: West, 2010.

Boyd, Nan Alamilla. *Wide-Open Town: A History of Queer San Francisco to 1965*. Berkeley: University of California Press, 2003.

Broadus, Kylar W. "The Evolution of Employment Discrimination Protections for Transgender People." In *Transgender Rights*, edited by Paisley Currah, Richard M. Juang, and Shannon Price Minter, 93–101. Minneapolis: University of Minnesota Press, 2006.

Broockman, David, and Joshua Kalla. "Durably Reducing Transphobia: A Field Experiment on Door-to-Door Canvassing." *Science* 352, no. 6282 (2016): 220–24.

Brown, Wendy. *States of Injury: Power and Freedom in Late Modernity*. Princeton: Princeton University Press, 1995.

Butler, Judith. *Gender Trouble: Feminism and the Subversion of Identity*. New York: Routledge, 1990.

———. *Bodies that Matter: On the Discursive Limits of "Sex."* New York: Routledge, 1993.

———. "Restaging the Universal: Hegemony and the Limits of Formalism." In *Contingency, Hegemony, Universality: Contemporary Dialogues on the Left*, edited by Judith Butler, Ernesto Laclau, and Slavoj Žižek, 11–43. London and New York: Verso, 2000.

———. *Precarious Life: The Powers of Mourning and Violence*. New York: Verso, 2006.

Cain, Patricia. *Rainbow Rights: The Role of Lawyers and Courts in the Lesbian and Gay Civil Rights Movement*. Boulder: Westview Press, 2000.

Calavita, Kitty. *Invitation to Law and Society*. Chicago: University of Chicago Press, 2010.

Camp, Jordan T., and Christina Heatherton. "How Liberals Legitimate Broken Windows: An Interview with Naomi Murakawa." In *Policing the Planet: Why the Policing Crisis Led to Black Lives Matter*, edited by Jordan T. Camp and Christina Heatherton, 228–35. New York: Verso, 2016.

Campbell, Colin. "NC's New LGBT Law Finds Support from Many in Rural Communities." *The Charlotte Observer*, April 11, 2016; www.charlotte observer.com/news/politics-government/article71140652.html#storylink=cpy.

Case, Mary Anne. "Why Not Abolish Laws of Urinary Segregation?" In *Toilet: Public Restrooms and the Politics of Sharing*, edited by Harvey Molotch and Laura Norén, 211–25. New York and London: New York University Press, 2010.

Cavanagh, Sheila L. *Queering Bathrooms: Gender, Sexuality, and the Hygienic Imagination*. Toronto: University of Toronto Press, 2010.

Chasin, Alexandra. *Selling Out: The Gay and Lesbian Movement Goes to Market*. New York: St. Martin's Press, 2000.

Crenshaw, Kimberlé. "Demarginalizing the Intersection of Race and Sex: A Black Feminist Critique of Antidiscrimination Doctrine, Feminist Theory, and Antiracist Politics," *The University of Chicago Legal Forum* (1989).

Critchley, Mark. "Rio 2016: Fifth-placed Joanna Jozwik 'Feels Like Silver Medallist' after 800m Defeat to Caster Semenya." *Independent*, 2016; www.independent.co.uk/sport/olympics/rio-2016-joanna-jozwik-caster-semenya-800m-hyper androgenism-a7203731.html.

Currah, Paisley. "Gender Pluralism: Under the Transgender Umbrella." In *Transgender Rights*, edited by Paisley Currah, Richard M. Juang, and Shannon Price Minter, 3–31. Minneapolis: University of Minnesota Press, 2006.

———. "The Transgender Rights Imaginary." In *Feminist and Queer Legal Theory: Intimate Encounters, Uncomfortable Conversations*, edited by Martha Albertson Fineman, Jack E. Jackson, and Adam P. Romero, 245–58. London: Ashgate Press, 2009.

Currah, Paisley, and Shannon Minter. "Unprincipled Exclusions: The Struggle to Achieve Judicial and Legislative Equality for Transgender People." *William and Mary Journal of Women and the Law* 7, no. 1 (2000): 37–66.

Currah, Paisley, and Lisa Jean Moore. " 'We Won't Know Who You Are:' Contesting Sex Designations in New York City Birth Certificates." In *The Transgender Studies Reader* 2, edited by Susan Stryker and Aren Z. Aizura, 607–22. New York and London: Routledge, 2013.

Currah, Paisley, and Tara Mulqueen. "Securitizing Gender: Identity, Biometrics, and Transgender Bodies at the Airport." *Social Research* 78, no. 2 (2011): 557–82.

Currah, Paisley, Richard M. Juang, and Shannon Price Minter. "Introduction." In *Transgender Rights*, edited by Paisley Currah, Richard M. Juang, and Shannon Price Minter, xiii–xxiv. Minneapolis: University of Minnesota Press 2006.

Dahlberg, Lincoln. "The Habermasian Public Sphere: Taking Difference Seriously?" *Theory and Society* 34, no. 2 (April 2005): 111–36.

Daum, Courtenay W. "The War on Solicitation and Intersectional Subjection: Quality-of-life Policing as a Tool to Control Transgender Populations." *New Political Science* 37, no. 4 (2015): 562–81.

———. "Counterpublics and Intersectional Radical Resistance: Agitation as a Mechanism for Transforming the Dominant Discourse." *New Political Science* 39, no. 4 (2017): 523–37.

———. "Marriage Equality: Assimilationist Victory or Pluralist Defeat? What the Struggle for Marriage Equality Tells Us about the History and the Future of LGBTQ Politics." In *LGBTQ Politics: A Critical Reader*, edited by Susan Burgess, Marla Brettschneider, and Cricket Keating, 353–73. New York: New York University Press, 2017.

———. "Putting the T back in LGBTQ? Transgender Activism and Interests after Marriage Equality." In *Queer Activism after Marriage Equality*, edited by Joseph DeFilippis, Angela Jones, and Michael Yarbrough. New York: Routledge Press, 2018.

———, forthcoming, "Social Equity, Homonormativity, and Equality: An Intersectional Critique of the Administration of Marriage Equality and Opportunities for LGBTQ Social Justice." *Administrative Theory & Praxis.*

Davis, Angela Y. *Women, Race, and Class.* New York: Vintage, 1983.

———. *The Meaning of Freedom.* San Francisco: City Lights, 2012.

Davis, Heath Fogg. "Sex Classification Policies as Transgender Discrimination: An Intersectional Critique." *Perspectives on Politics* 12, no. 1 (2014): 45–60.

———. *Beyond Trans Does Gender Matter?* New York: New York University Press, 2017.

Decker, Jefferson. *The Other Rights Revolution: Conservative Lawyers and the Remaking of American Government.* New York: Oxford University Press, 2016.

Delgado, Richard, and Jean Stefancic. *Critical Race Theory.* New York: New York University Press, 2012.

D'Emilio, John. *Sexual Politics, Sexual Communities: The Making of a Homosexual Minority in the United States 1940–1970.* Chicago: The University of Chicago Press, 1998.

Democracy Now! "Undocumented Trans Activist Jennicet Gutiérrez Challenges Obama on Deportations at White House Event." *Democracy Now!* June 25, 2015; www.youtube.com/watch?v=ER9_M002aQY.

Denny, Dallas. "Transgender Communities of the United States in the Late Twentieth Century." In *Transgender Rights*, edited by Paisley Currah, Richard M. Juang, and Shannon Price Minter, 171–91. Minneapolis: University of Minnesota Press, 2006.

Dolan-Sandrino, Grace. "Gavin Grimm Talks Bringing Transgender Rights to the Supreme Court." *Teenvogue*.com, February 22, 2017; www.teenvogue.com/story/gavin-grimm-supreme-court-case-interview.

Duberman, Martin, and Andrew Kopkind. "The Night They Raided Stonewall." *Grand Street* 44 (1993): 120–47.

Dudas, Jeffrey. "In the Name of Equal Rights: 'Special' Rights and the Politics of Resentment in Post-Civil Rights America." *Law & Society Review* 39, no. 4 (December 2005): 723–57.

———. *The Cultivation of Resentment: Treaty Rights and the New Right*. Stanford: Stanford University Press, 2007.

Duggan, Lisa. *The Twilight of Equality? Neoliberalism, Cultural Politics, and the Attack on Democracy*. Boston: Beacon Press, 2003.

Edelman, Elijah Adiv. " 'Walking While Transgender': Necropolitical Regulations of Trans Feminine Bodies of Colour in the US Nation's Capital." In *Queer Necropolitics*, edited by Jin Haritaworn, Adi Kuntsman, and Silvia Posocco, 172–90. New York: Routledge, 2014.

Engel, David M., and Frank W. Munger. *Rights of Inclusion: Law and Identity in the Life Stories of Americans with Disabilities*. Chicago: University of Chicago Press, 2003.

Engel, Stephen M. *Fragmented Citizens: The Changing Landscape of Gay and Lesbian Lives*. New York: New York University Press, 2016.

Enke, A. Finn. "The Education of Little Cis: Cisgender and the Discipline of Opposing Bodies." In *The Transgender Studies Reader* 2, edited by Susan Stryker and Aren Z. Aizura, 234–47. New York and London: Routledge, 2013.

Ennis, Dawn. "Why Is *The New York Times* Suddenly Focused on Transgender People?" *The Advocate*, June 9, 2015; www.advocate.com/politics/media/2015/06/09/why-new-york-times-suddenly-focused-transgender-people.

Epp, Charles R. *The Rights Revolution: Lawyers, Activists, and Supreme Courts in Comparative Perspective*. Chicago: University of Chicago Press, 1998.

Estrich, Susan. *Real Rape: How the Legal System Victimizes Women Who Say No*. Cambridge: Harvard University Press, 1988.

Familia. "Mission." *Familiatglqm.org*; familiatqlm.org/mission-3/.

Fanon, Frantz. *Black Skin, White Masks*. Translated by Richard Philcox. New York: Grove Press, 2008.

Feeley, Malcolm M. "Review: Hollow Hopes, Flypaper, and Metaphors." *Law and Social Inquiry* 17, no. 4 (1992): 745–60.

FIERCE. "Leadership Development." *Fiercenyc.org*; fiercenyc.org/leadership development.

———. "What We Do." *Fiercenyc.org*; fiercenyc.org/what-we-do.

Flores, Andrew R. "Attitudes toward Transgender Rights: Perceived Knowledge and Secondary Interpersonal Contact." *Politics, Groups, and Identities* 3, no. 3 (2015): 398–416.

Flores, Andrew R., Donald P. Haider-Markel, Daniel C. Lewis, Patrick R. Miller, Barry L. Tadlock, and Jami K, Taylor, "Transgender Prejudice Reduction and Opinions on Transgender Rights? Results from a Mediation Analysis on Experimental Data." *Research and Politics* (January-March 2018): 1–7.

Flores, Andrew R., Jody L. Herman, Gary J. Gates, and Taylor N. T. Brown. *How Many Adults Identify as Transgender in the United States*. Los Angeles: The Williams Institute, 2016; williamsinstitute.law.ucla.edu/wp-content/uploads/How-Many-Adults-Identify-as-Transgender-in-the-United-States.pdf.

Flynn, Taylor. "The Ties that (Don't) Bind: Transgender Family Law and the Unmaking of Families." In *Transgender Rights*, edited by Paisley Currah, Richard M. Juang, and Shannon Price Minter, 32–50. Minneapolis: University of Minnesota Press, 2006.

Foucault, Michel. *Power/Knowledge: Selected Interviews and Other Writings, 1972–1977*. Edited by Colin Gordon. New York: Pantheon Books, 1980.

———. *Discipline and Punish: The Birth of the Prison*. Translated by Alan Sheridan. New York: Vintage Books, 1995.

———. *Security, Territory, Population: Lectures at the College de France 1977–78*. London: Palgrave Macmillan, 2007.

Frank, Gillian. "The Anti-Trans Bathroom Nightmare Has Its Roots in Segregation." *Slate*, November 10, 2015; www.slate.com/blogs/outward/2015/11/10/anti_trans_bathroom_propaganda_has_roots_in_racial_segregation.html.

Fraser, Nancy. "Rethinking the Public Sphere: A Contribution to the Critique of Actually Existing Democracy." *Social Text* 25/26 (1990): 56–80.

———. "Abnormal Justice." *Critical Inquiry* 34, no. 3 (2008): 393–422.

Freire, Paulo. *Pedagogy of the Oppressed*. New York: Bloomsbury Academic 2000.

Frye, Phyllis Randolph. "The International Bill of Gender Rights vs. The Cider House Rules." *William and Mary Journal of Women and the Law* 7, no. 1 (2000): 133–216.

———. "History of the International Conference on Transgender Law and Employment Policy, Inc." *Transgenderlegal.com*, 2001; www.transgenderlegal.com/ictlephis1.htm.

Fuss, Diana. *Essentially Speaking: Feminism, Nature, and Difference*. New York and London: Routledge, 1989.

Galanter, Marc. "Why the 'Haves' Come out Ahead: Speculations on the Limits of Legal Change." *Law and Society Review* 9, no. 1 (1974): 95–160.

Galvan, Frank H., and Mohsen Bazargan. *Interactions of Latina Transgender Women with Law Enforcement*. Los Angeles: Bienestar Human Services, 2012; williamsinstitute.law.ucla.edu/wp-content/uploads/Galvan-Bazargan-Interactions-April-2012.pdf.

Gan, Jessi. "'Still at the Back of the Bus': Sylvia Rivera's Struggle." In *The Transgender Studies Reader 2*, edited by Susan Stryker and Aren Z. Aizura, 291–301. New York: Routledge, 2013.

Garretson, Jeremiah J. "Exposure to the Lives of Lesbians and Gays and the Origin of Young People's Greater Support for Gay Rights." *International Journal of Public Opinion Research* 27, no. 2 (2015): 277–88.

Gehi, Pooja. "Gender (In)security: Migration and Criminalization in the Security State." *Harvard Journal of Law and Gender* 35 (2012).

Ghaziani, Amin. *The Dividends of Dissent: How Conflict and Culture Work in Lesbian and Gay Marches on Washington*. Chicago: University of Chicago Press, 2008.

Gilmore, Ruth Wilson, and Craig Gilmore. "Beyond Bratton." In *Policing the Planet: Why the Policing Crisis Led to Black Lives Matter*, edited by Jordan T. Camp and Christina Heatherton, 173–99. New York: Verso, 2016.

Goldberg-Hiller, Jonathan. *The Limits to Union: Same-Sex Marriage and the Politics of Civil Rights*. Ann Arbor: University of Michigan Press, 2002.

Golder, Ben. *Foucault and the Politics of Rights*. Stanford: Stanford University Press, 2015.

Gossett, Che. "Silhouettes of Defiance: Memorializing Historical Sites of Queer and Transgender Resistance in an Age of Neoliberal Inclusivity." In *The Transgender Studies Reader* 2, edited by Susan Stryker and Aren Z. Aizura, 580–90. New York and London: Routledge, 2013.

Grant, Jaime M., Lisa A. Mottet, Justin Tanis, Jack Harrison, Jody L. Herman, and Mara Keisling. *Injustice at Every Turn: A Report of the National Transgender Discrimination Survey*. Washington, DC: National Center for Transgender Equality and National Gay and Lesbian Task Force, 2011; www.thetaskforce.org/static_html/downloads/reports/reports/ntds_full.pdf.

Green, Erica L., Katie Benner, and Robert Pear. " 'Transgender' Could be Defined Out of Existence Under Trump Administration." *The New York Times*, October 21, 2018; www.nytimes.com/2018/10/21/us/politics/transgender-trump-administration-sex-definition.html?rref=collection%2Ftimestopic%2FHealth%20and%20Human%20Services%20Department&action=click&contentCollection=timestopics®ion=stream&module=stream_unit&version=latest&contentPlacement=5&pgtype=collection.

Greenberg, Julie A. "The Roads Less Traveled: The Problem with Binary Sex Categories." In *Transgender Rights*, edited by Paisley Currah, Richard M. Juang, and Shannon Price Minter, 51–73. Minneapolis: University of Minnesota Press, 2006.

Greenberg, Kae. "Still Hidden in the Closet: Trans Women and Domestic Violence." *Berkeley Journal of Gender, Law and Justice* 27, no. 2 (2012): 198–251.

Greer, Evan. "Powerful Gay Rights Groups Excluded Trans People for Decades—Leaving Them Vulnerable to Trump's Attack." *The Washington* Post, October 29, 2018; www.washingtonpost.com/outlook/2018/10/29/trumps-attack-trans-people-should-be-wake-up-call-mainstream-gay-rights-movement/?utm_term=.34f1fda516b3.

Gregory, Alice. "Has the Fashion Industry Reached a Transgender Turning Point?" *Vogue*, April 21, 2015; www.vogue.com/13253741/andreja-pejic-transgender-model/.

Griggs, Brandon. "America's Transgender Moment." *CNN.com*, June 1, 2015; www.cnn.com/2015/04/23/living/transgender-moment-jenner-feat/.

Grimm, Gavin. "Gavin Grimm at Gloucester County School Board Meeting," September 1, 2016; www.youtube.com/watch?v=My0GYq_Wydw&feature=youtu.be.

Habermas, Jürgen. *The Structural Transformation of the Public Sphere*. Cambridge: MIT Press, 1989.

Halberstam, Judith. *Female Masculinity*. Durham: Duke University Press, 1998.

Hale, Jacob. "Suggested Rules for Non-Transsexuals Writing about Transsexuals, Transsexuality, Transsexualism, or Trans_____," November 18, 2008; sandystone.com/hale.rules.html.

Hall, Matthew E. K. *The Nature of Supreme Court Power*. Cambridge: Cambridge University Press, 2011.

Harrison, Brian F., and Melissa R. Michelson. "Using Experiments to Understand Public Attitudes towards Transgender Rights." *Politics, Groups, and Identities* 5, no. 1 (2017): 152–60.

Harris-Perry, Melissa V. *Sister Citizen: Shame, Stereotypes, and Black Women in America*. New Haven: Yale University Press, 2011.

Herman, Jody L. "Gendered Restrooms and Minority Stress: The Public Regulation of Gender and its Impact on Transgender People's Lives." *Journal of Public Management and Social Policy* 19, 1 (2013): 65–80.

Hesse, Monica. "How the Bathroom Becomes a Political Battleground for Civil Rights." *The Washington Post*, April 1, 2016; www.washingtonpost.com/lifestyle/style/whyamerica-cant-stop-fighting-over-the-politics-of-public-restrooms/2016/04/01/16af2f94-f6b6-11e5-a3ce-f06b5ba21f33_story.html?utm_term=.a47bbc5a4a4c.

Hill, Robert. "Before Transgender: *Transvestia's* Spectrum of Gender Variance, 1960–1980." In *The Transgender Studies Reader* 2, edited by Susan Stryker and Aren Z. Aizura, 364–79. New York and London: Routledge, 2013.

Hollis-Brusky, Amanda. *Ideas with Consequences: The Federalist Society and the Conservative Counterrevolution*. New York: Oxford University Press, 2014.

Human Rights Watch. *Sex Workers at Risk: Condoms as Evidence of Prostitution in Four U.S. Cities*. Washington, DC: Human Rights Watch, 2012; www.hrw.org/sites/default/files/reports/us0712ForUpload_1.pdf.

Irving, Dan. "Normalized Transgressions: Legitimizing the Transsexual Body as Productive." In *The Transgender Studies Reader* 2, edited by Susan Stryker and Aren Z. Aizura, 15–29. New York and London: Routledge, 2016.

James, Sandy E., Jody L. Herman, Susuan Rankin, Mara Keisling, Lisa Mottet, and Ma'ayan Anafi. *The Report of the 2015 U.S. Transgender Survey*. Washington, DC: National Center for Transgender Equality, 2016.

Jeanty, J., and H. J. Tobin. *Our Moment for Reform: Immigration and Transgender People*. Washington, DC: National Center for Transgender Equality, 2013; transequality.org/sites/default/files/docs/resources/OurMoment_CIR_en.pdf.

Juang, Richard. "Transgendering the Politics of Recognition." In *Transgender Rights*, edited by Paisley Currah, Richard M. Juang, and Shannon Price Minter, 242–61. Minneapolis: University of Minnesota Press, 2006.

Keen, Lisa, and Suzanne B. Goldberg. *Strangers to the Law: Gay People on Trial.* Ann Arbor: The University of Michigan Press, 1998.

Kelley, Robin D. G. "Thug Nation: On State Violence and Disposability." In *Policing the Planet: Why the Policing Crisis Led to Black Lives Matter*, edited by Jordan T. Camp and Christina Heatherton, 15–33. New York: Verso, 2016.

Kendi, Ibram X. *Stamped from the Beginning: The Definitive History of Racist Ideas in America.* New York: Nation Books, 2016.

Kolata, Gina. "Does Testosterone Really Give Caster Semenya an Edge on the Track?" *The New York Times,* May 1, 2019; www.nytimes.com/2019/05/01/health/caster-semenya-testosterone.html.

Lamble, Sarah. "Queer Investments in Punitiveness: Sexual Citizenship, Social Movements, and the Expanding Carceral State." In *Queer Necropolitics*, edited by Jin Haritaworn, Adi Kuntsman, and Silvia Posocco, 159–60. New York: Routledge, 2014.

Lewis, Gregory B. "The Friends and Family Plan: Contact with Gays and Support for Gay Rights." *Policy Studies Journal* 39, no. 2 (2011): 217–38.

Leyens, Jacques-Philippe, Paola M. Paladino, Ramon Rodriguez-Torres, Jeroen Vaes, Stéphanie Demoulin, Armando Rodriguez-Perez, and Ruth Gaunt. "The Emotional Side of Prejudice: The Attribution of Secondary Emotions to Ingroups and Outgroups." *Personality and Social Psychology Review* 4, no. 2 (2000): 186–97.

Liptak, Kevin. "Obama Shuts Down Heckler: 'You're in My House!'" *cnn.com,* 2015; www.cnn.com/2015/06/24/politics/obama-heckler-white-house-lgbt/index.html.

Livingston, Alexander. "Avoiding Deliberative Democracy? Micropolitics, Manipulation, and the Public Sphere." *Philosophy & Rhetoric* 45, no. 3 (2012): 269–94.

Longman, Jere. "Understanding the Controversy over Caster Semenya." *The New York Times*, August 18, 2016; www.nytimes.com/2016/08/20/sports/caster-semenya-800 meters.html.

López, Ian Haney. *White by Law: The Legal Construction of Race.* New York: New York University Press, 2006.

Lorde, Audre. "The Master's Tools Will Never Dismantle the Master's House." In *Sister Outsider: Essays and Speeches*, 110–14. Berkeley: Crossing Press, 2007.

Ludwig, Mike. "'Walking While Woman' and the Fight to Stop Violent Policing of Gender Identity." *Truthout*, May 7, 2014; www.truth-out.org.

Make the Road New York. *Transgressive Policing: Police Abuse of LGBTQ Communities of Color in Jackson Heights*. New York, 2012; www.maketheroad.org/pix_reports/MRNY_Transgressive_Policing_Full_Report_10.23.12B.pdf.

Marimow, Ann E. "Two Years In, Trump's Appeals Court Confirmations at a Historic High Point." *The Washington Post*, February 4, 2019; www.washingtonpost.com/local/legal-issues/two-years-in-trumps-appeals-court-confirmations-at-a-historic-high-point/2019/02/03/574226e6-1a90-11e9-9ebfc5fed1b7a081_story.html?utm_term=.08c2282d445f.

McCann, Michael W. "Review: Reform Litigation on Trial." *Law and Social Inquiry* 17, no. 4 (1992): 715–43.

———. *Rights at Work: Pay Equity Reform and the Politics of Legal Mobilization*. Chicago: The University of Chicago Press, 1994.

McGowan, Sharon M. "Working with Clients to Develop Compatible Visions of What It Means to 'Win' a Case: Reflections on *Schroer v. Billington*." *Harvard Civil Rights-Civil Liberties Law Review* 45 (2010): 205–45.

Miller, Patrick R., Andrew R. Flores, Donald P. Haider-Markel, Daniel C. Lewis, Barry L. Tadlock, and Jami K. Taylor. "Transgender Politics as Body Politics: Effects of Disgust Sensitivity and Authoritarianism on Transgender Rights Attitudes." *Politics, Groups, and Identities* 5, no. 1 (2017): 4–24.

Minter, Shannon Price. "Do Transsexuals Dream of Gay Rights? Getting Real about Transgender Inclusion." In *Transgender Rights*, edited by Paisley Currah, Richard M. Juang, and Shannon Price Minter, 141–70. Minneapolis: University of Minnesota Press, 2006.

Mogul, Joey L., Andrea J. Ritchie, and Kay Whitlock. *Queer (In)Justice: The Criminalization of LGBT People in the United States*. Boston: Beacon Press, 2011.

Molotch, Harvey. "Introduction: Learning from the Loo." In *Toilet: Public Restrooms and the Politics of Sharing*, edited by Harvey Molotch and Laura Norén, 1–21. New York and London: New York University Press, 2010.

Moraga, Cherríe, and Gloria Anzaldúa. *This Bridge Called My Back: Writings by Radical Women of Color*. 4th ed. Albany: State University of New York Press, 2015.

Morehouse College, "Gender Identity Policy"; www.morehouse.edu/genderidentity/.

Movement Advancement Project. *Mapping Transgender Equality in the United States*. Denver: Movement Advancement Project, 2017; lgbtqmap.org/file/mapping-trans-equality.pdf 2017.

Movement Advancement Project. *State Religious Exemption Laws*. Denver: Movement Advancement Project, 2017; www.lgbtmap.org/equalitymaps/religious_exemption_laws.

Mucciaroni, Gary. "Will Victory Bring Change? A Mature Social Movement Faces the Future." In *After Marriage Equality: The Future of LGBT Rights*, edited by Carlos Ball, 17–41. New York: New York University Press, 2016.

Murib, Zein. "Transgender: Examining an Emerging Political Identity Using Three Political Processes." *Politics, Groups, and Identities* 3, no. 3 (2015): 381–97.

National Center for Transgender Equality. *2015 U.S. Transgender Survey: North Carolina State Report*. Washington, DC, 2017; www.transequality.org/sites/default/files/docs/usts/USTS_NC_state_report.pdf.

National Center for Transgender Equality. "ID Documents Center," 2017; www.transequality.org/documents.

National Center for Transgender Equality. "ID Documents Center," 2019; www.transequality.org/documents.

National Center for Transgender Equality. "How Trans-Friendly Is the Driver's License Gender Change Policy in Your State?" 2019; www.transequality.org/documents.

National Conference of State Legislatures. "'Bathroom Bill' Legislative Tracking," 2017; www.ncsl.org/research/education/-bathroom-bill-legislative-tracking 635951130.aspx.

Nownes, Anthony J. "Interest Groups and Transgender Politics: Opportunities and Challenges." In *Transgender Rights and Politics: Groups, Issue Framing, and Policy Adoption*, edited by Jami K. Taylor and Donald P. Haider-Markel, 93–107. Ann Arbor: University of Michigan Press, 2014.

———. *Organizing for Transgender Rights: Collective Action, Group Development, and the Rise of a New Social Movement.* Albany: State University of New York Press, 2019.

O'Brien, Keegan. "Tearing Down the Walls: The Story of the Stonewall Rebellion and the Rise of the Gay Liberation Movement." *Jacobin*, August 20, 2015; www.jacobinmag.com/2015/08/lgbtq-stonewall-marriage-equality-mattachine-sylvia-rivera/.

Ochoa, Maria. "Perverse Citizenship: Divas, Marginality, and Participation in 'Loca-lization.'" In *The Transgender Studies Reader* 2, edited by Susan Stryker and Aren Z. Aizura, 443–56. New York and London: Routledge, 2013.

Olson, Susan. *Clients and Lawyers: Securing the Rights of Disabled Persons*. New York: Praeger, 1984.

Penner, Barbara. *Bathroom*. London: Reaktion Books, 2013.

Polikoff, Nancy D. *Beyond (Straight and Gay) Marriage: Valuing All Families Under the Law.* Boston: Beacon Press, 2008.

PROS Network and the Sex Workers Project. *Public Health Crisis: The Impact of Using Condoms as Evidence of Prostitution in New York City*. New York: Urban Justice Center, 2012; sexworkersproject.org/downloads/2012/20120417-public-health-crisis.pdf.

Reddy, Chandan. *Freedom with Violence: Race, Sexuality, and the US State*. Durham and London: Duke University Press, 2011.

Reynolds, Andrew. *Out in Office: LGBT Legislators and LGBT Rights Around the World*. Chapel Hill: University of North Carolina LGBT Representation and Rights Initiative, 2013.

———. "Representation and Rights: The Impact of LGBT Legislators in Comparative Perspective." *American Political Science Review* 107, no. 2 (2013): 259–74.

Rhodan, Maya. "Why Do We Have Men's and Women's Bathrooms Anyway?" *Time.com*, May 16, 2016; time.com/4337761/history-sex-segregated-bathrooms/.

Rimmerman, Craig A., Kenneth D. Wald, and Clyde Wilcox, eds. *The Politics of Gay Rights*. Chicago: University of Chicago Press, 2000.

Ritchie, Andrea J. "Crimes against Nature: Challenging Criminalization of Queerness and Black Women's Sexuality." *Loyola Journal of Public Interest Law* 14 (2013): 355.

Rosenberg, Gerald N. "Hollow Hopes and Other Aspirations: A Reply to Feeley and McCann." *Law and Social Inquiry* 17, no. 4 (1992): 761–78.

———. *The Hollow Hope*. 2nd ed. Chicago: University of Chicago Press, 2008.

Scheingold, Stuart A. *The Politics of Rights: Lawyers, Public Policy, and Political Change*. Ann Arbor: University of Michigan Press, 2004.

Schofield, Rob. "Bathroom Law Victory: Federal Court Allows Challenge to HB2 Replacement to Proceed." *The Progressive Pulse*, October 1, 2018; pulse.ncpolicywatch.org/2018/10/01/bathroom-law-victory-federal-court-allows-challenge-to-hb2-replacement-to-proceed/.

Sears, Clare. "Electric Brilliancy: Cross-dressing Law and Freak Show Displays in Nineteenth century San Francisco." In *The Transgender Studies Reader 2*, edited by Susan Stryker and Aren Z. Aizura, 554–65. New York and London: Routledge, 2013.

Sellers, Mitchell D. "Executive Expansion of Transgender Rights: Electoral Incentives to Issue or Revoke Executive Orders." In *Transgender Rights and Politics: Groups, Issue Framing, and Policy Adoption*, edited by Jami K. Taylor and Donald P. Haider-Markel, 189–207. Ann Arbor: University of Michigan Press, 2014.

Serano, Julia. *Whipping Girl: A Transsexual Woman on Sexism and the Scapegoating of Femininity*. Emeryville, CA: Seal Press, 2007.

———. "Skirt Chasers: Why the Media Depicts the Trans Revolution in Lipstick and Heels." In *The Transgender Studies Reader 2*, edited by Susan Stryker and Aren Z. Aizura, 226–33. New York and London: Routledge, 2013.

Shotwell, Alexis. *Against Purity: Living Ethically in Compromised Times*. Minneapolis: University of Minnesota Press, 2016.

Silverstein, Helena. *Unleashing Rights: Law, Meaning, and the Animal Rights Movement*. Ann Arbor: University of Michigan Press, 1996.

Sitton, Jane Allison. "Introduction to the Symposium, (De)Constructing Sex: Transgenderism, Intersexuality, Gender Identity, and the Law." *William and Mary Journal of Women and the Law* 7, no. 1 (2000): 1–4.

Solomon, Dave. "NH House Speaker Leads Opposition to Transgender Bill." *New Hampshire Union Leader*, March 6, 2017; www.unionleader.com/state-government/House-Speaker-leads-opposition-to-transgender-bill-03062017.

Sontag, Deborah. "Once a Pariah, Now a Judge: The Early Transgender Journey of Phyllis Frye." *The New York Times*, August 29, 2015; www.nytimes.com/2015/08/30/us/transgender-judge-phyllis-fryes-early-transformative-journey.html.

Southerners on New Ground. "About." *Southernersonnewground.org*; southerners onnewground.org/about/.

———. "2016 End of Year Report." *Southernersonnewground.org*; southernerson newground.org/2016/12/16endofyearreport/.

Spade, Dean. "Fighting to Win!" In *That's Revolting! Queer Strategies for Resisting Assimilation*, edited by Mattilda Bernstein Sycamore, 47–53. Berkeley: Soft Skull, 2004.

———. "Compliance Is Gendered: Struggling for Gender Self-Determination in a Hostile Economy." In *Transgender Rights*, edited by Paisley Currah, Richard M. Juang, and Shannon Price Minter, 217–41. Minneapolis: University of Minnesota Press, 2006.

———. "Documenting Gender." *Hastings Law Journal* 59 (2008): 731.

———. "Keynote Address: Trans Law and Politics on a Neoliberal Landscape." *Temple Political and Civil Rights Law Review* 18, no. 2 (2009): 353–73.

———. "Trans Law Reform Strategies, Co-Optation, and the Potential for Transformative Change." *Women's Rights Law Reporter* 30 (2009): 306–307.

———. *Normal Life: Administrative Violence, Critical Trans Politics, and the Limits of Law.* Durham: Duke University Press, 2011.

———. *Normal Life: Administrative Violence, Critical Trans Politics, and the Limits of Law.* Durham: Duke University Press, 2015.

Springer, Simon. *The Anarchist Roots of Geography: Toward Spacial Emancipation.* Minneapolis: University of Minnesota Press, 2016.

Stein, Marc. *City of Sisterly and Brotherly Loves: Lesbian and Gay Philadelphia: 1945–1972.* Chicago: University of Chicago Press, 2000.

Steinmetz, Katy. "The Transgender Tipping Point." *Time Magazine*, May 29, 2014; search.time.com/results.html?Ntt=laverne+cox.

Stern, Mark Joseph. "Professional Victim Pat McCrory Has Slid into Delusions of Grandeur." *Slate.com*, March 14, 2017; www.slate.com/blogs/outward/2017/03/14/pat_mccrory_a_paranoid_delusional_professional_victim.html.

Stone, Sandy. "The *Empire* Strikes Back: A Posttranssexual Manifesto." In *Body Guards: The Cultural Politics of Gender Ambiguity*, edited by Kristina Straub and Julia Epstein. New York: Routledge, 1991.

Stryker, Susan. "My Words to Victor Frankenstein above the Village of Chamounix: Performing Transgender Rage." *GLQ* 1, no. 3 (1994).

———. "(De)Subjugated Knowledges: An Introduction to Transgender Studies," In *The Transgender Studies Reader*, edited by Susan Stryker and Stephen Whittle. New York: Routledge, 2006.

———. "Transgender History, Homonormativity, and Disciplinarity." *Radical History Review* 100 (2008): 145–57.

———. "Kaming Mga Talyada (We Who Are Sexy): The Transsexual Whiteness of Christine Jorgensen in the (Post)colonial Philippines." In *The Transgender*

Studies Reader 2, edited by Susan Stryker and Aren Z. Aizura, 543–53. New York and London: Routledge, 2013.

———. *Transgender History: The Roots of Today's Revolution.* 2nd ed. New York: Seal Press, 2017.

———, and Aren Z. Aizura. "Introduction." In *The Transgender Studies Reader* 2, edited by Susan Stryker and Aren Z. Aizura, 1–12. New York: Routledge, 2013.

"Sylvia Rivera Law Project"; srlp.org.

Tadlock, Barry L., Andrew R. Flores, Donald P. Haider-Markel, Daniel C. Lewis, Patrick R. Miller, and Jami K Taylor. "Testing Contact Theory and Attitudes on Transgender Rights." *Public Opinion Quarterly* 81, no. 4 (2017): 956–72.

Taylor, Jami K., and Daniel C. Lewis. "The Advocacy Coalition Framework and Transgender Inclusion in LGBT Rights Activism." In *Transgender Rights and Politics: Groups, Issue Framing, and Policy Adoption*, edited by Jami K. Taylor and Donald P. Haider-Markel, 108–32. Ann Arbor: University of Michigan Press, 2014.

Taylor, Jami K., Daniel C. Lewis, and Donald P. Haider-Markel. *The Remarkable Rise of Transgender Rights.* Ann Arbor: University of Michigan Press, 2018.

Taylor, Jami K., Barry L. Tadlock, and Sarah J. Poggione. "Birth Certificate Amendment Laws and Morality Politics." In *Transgender Rights and Politics: Groups, Issue Framing, and Policy Adoption*, edited by Jami K. Taylor and Donald P. Haider-Markel, 252–72. Ann Arbor: University of Michigan Press, 2015.

Teles, Steven M. *The Rise of the Conservative Legal Movement: The Battle for Control of the Law.* Princeton: Princeton University Press, 2010.

Thomas, Kendall. "Afterword: Are Transgender Rights *In*human Rights?" In *Transgender Rights*, edited by Paisley Currah, Richard M. Juang, and Shannon Price Minter, 310–26. Minneapolis: University of Minnesota Press, 2006.

"Transcript: HRC President Chad Griffin Apologizes to Trans People at Southern Comfort," *The Advocate*, September 5, 2014; www.advocate.com/politics/transgender/2014/09/05/transcript-hrc-president-chad-griffin-apologizes-trans-people-speech.

Tushnet, Mark. *The NAACP's Legal Strategy against Segregated Education.* Chapel Hill: The University of North Carolina Press, 1987.

———. *Making Civil Rights Law: Thurgood Marshall and the Supreme Court.* New York: Oxford University Press, 1994.

U.S. Equal Employment Opportunity Commission. "Examples of Court Decisions Supporting Coverage of LGBT-Related Discrimination under Title VII," 2017; www.eeoc.gov/eeoc/newsroom/wysk/lgbt_examples_decisions.cfm.

———. "Facts about Discrimination in Federal Government Employment Based on Marital Status, Political Affiliation, Status as a Parent, Sexual Orientation, and Gender Identity," 2017; www.eeoc.gov/federal/otherprotections.cfm.

United States. "Statement of Interest of the United States," in *G.G v. Gloucester County School Board*, U.S. District Court Eastern District of Virginia

Newport News Division (2015), 1–2; https://www.aclu.org/legal-document/gg-v-gloucester-county-school-board-statement-interest-united-states.

Vaid, Urvashi. *Virtual Equality: The Mainstreaming of Gay and Lesbian Liberation.* New York: Anchor Books, 1995.

Valentine, David. *Imagining Transgender: An Ethnography of a Category.* Durham: Duke University Press, 2007.

Villa, Dana R. "Postmodernism and the Public Sphere." *American Political Science Review* 86, no. 3 (1992): 712–21.

Walsh, Michael. "N.C. Gov. Pat McCrory Defends HB2: I Can't Believe We're Talking about This." *Yahoo! News*, April 29, 2016; www.yahoo.com/news/nc-gov-pat-mccrory-defends-hb2-i-cant-believe-161442832.html.

Ward, Jane. *Respectably Queer: Diversity Culture in LGBT Activist Organizations.* Nashville: Vanderbilt University Press, 2008.

Warner, Michael. "Introduction: Fear of a Queer Planet." *Social Text* 29 (1991): 3–17.

———. *Fear of a Queer Planet: Queer Politics and Social Theory*. Minneapolis: University of Minnesota Press, 1993.

———. "Publics and Counterpublics." *Public Culture* 14, no. 1 (2002): 49–90.

———. *Publics and Counterpublics.* New York: Zone Books, 2005.

Williams, Patricia J. *The Alchemy of Race and Rights*. Cambridge: Harvard University Press, 1992.

Wolfson, Evan. "What's Next in the Fight for Gay Equality?" *The New York Times*, June 26, 2015; www.nytimes.com/2015/06/27/opinion/evan-wolfson-whats-next-in-the-fight-for-gay-equality.html.

Woods, Jordan Blair, Frank H. Galvan, Mohsen Bazargan, Jody L. Herman, and Ying-Tung Chen. "Latina Transgender Women's Interactions with Law Enforcement in Los Angeles County." *Policing* 7, no. 4 (2013): 379–91.

Zebrowitz, Leslie A., Benjamin White, and Kristin Wieneke. "Mere Exposure and Racial Prejudice: Exposure to Other-Race Faces Increases Liking For Strangers of That Race." *Social Cognition* 26, no. 3 (2008): 259–75.

Index